LITERARY PORTRAITS

LITERARY PORTRAITS

An Anthology of Modern American Prose and Poetry for Students of English

J. DONNIE SNYDER

THE UNIVERSITY OF TEXAS AT AUSTIN

HH Heinle & Heinle Publishers
Boston, Massachusetts 02116, U.S.A.

Library of Congress Cataloging-in-Publication Data

Snyder, J. Donnie.
    Literary portraits: an anthology of modern American prose and
poetry for students of English / J. Donnie Snyder.
        p. cm.

        1. College readers.   2. English language — Textbooks for foreign
speakers.   3. American literature — 20th century.   I. Title.
PE1122.S54 1989
428.6'4–dc19   88-25227
                                              CIP

Copyright © 1989 by Heinle & Heinle Publishers, a division of Wadsworth, Inc.

ISBN 0-8384-3334-0

Cover Painting: Edward Hopper, *Automat*. Des Moines Art Center, James D. Edmundson Fund.
Interior Design: Ros Herion Freese

Photo Credits: (p. xiv) Brown Brothers;   (p. 4) Alfred Stieglitz, *The Steerage* (1907). Photogra-
vure (artist's proof) from *Camera Work*, No. 3, 1911. 7¾ x 6½″. Collection, The
Museum of Modern Art, New York. Gift of Alfred Stieglitz;   (pp. 10, 52, 59)
Jacob A. Riis Collection, Museum of the City of New York;   (p. 12) Historical
Pictures Service, Chicago;   (p. 18) Frederick Sutter;   (pp. 20, 28, 84, 90, 102,
132, 172, 178, 186, 210, 216) Eric Liebowitz;   (pp. 26, 42, 110) Fern Logan;
(p. 51) South Dakota State Historical Society;   (p. 44) Barker Texas History
Center, University of Texas at Austin;   (pp. 60, 67, 76, 78, 83, 112, 124, 126,
134, 138) UPI/Bettmann Newsphotos;   (p. 68) Edward W. Souza, News and Pub-
lications Service, Stanford University;   (p. 92) Jill Robbins;   (p. 104) Carlin/
Frederick Lewis Stock Photos;   (pp. 140, 146) National Aeronautics and Space
Administration (NASA);   (pp. 148, 150, 177, 192, 212) Agatha Lorenzo;   (pp.
158, 188) Harold M. Lambert/Frederick Lewis Stock Photos;   (p. 160)
H. Armstrong Roberts;   (p. 165) New York University (NYU)/Jon Roemer
Photo;   (p. 166) Alejandro F. Pascual;   (p. 170) Andres E. Salomon;   (p. 194)
Frederick Lewis Stock Photos.

Grateful acknowledgment is given for the permission to use the following copyright material: (for page 116) William Carlos Williams: *Collected Poems Vol. I
1909–1939*. Copyright 1938 by New Directions Publishing Corporation. Reprinted
by permission of New Directions Publishing Corporation. (for page 183) "what
does little Ernest croon" is reprinted from NO THANKS by E.E. Cummings,
edited by George James Firmage, by permission of Liveright Publishing Corporation. Copyright 1935 by E.E. Cummings. Copyright © 1968 by Marion Morehouse
Cummings. Copyright © 1973, 1978 by the Trustees for the E.E. Cummings
Trust. Copyright © 1973, 1978 by George James Firmage. Additional permission
to reprint given by Grafton Books a Division of the Collins Publishing Group.

Printing: 2 3 4 5 6 7   Year: 1 2 3 4 5

Acknowledgments

It is gratifying to have the opportunity to acknowledge the wonderful people who helped me bring this textbook to completion.

Dr. John G. Bordie, Director of the Foreign Language Education Center at the University of Texas at Austin, gave counsel and encouragement. Also of UT-Austin, Dr. Carlos A. Solé, Professor of Spanish; Dr. James L. Kinneavy, Professor of English; and Charlotte Gilman, English as a Second Language Instructor, all shared their publishing expertise. Book author and ESL instructor Carol E. King, Esq., also should be mentioned here for her valuable publishing hints.

Susan Collins, my Austin–Collier Macmillan connection, ably and graciously served as liaison. And at Collier Macmillan headquarters, ESL Editor Mary Jane Peluso nurtured the project while her Assistant Editor Maggie Scarry and Editorial Assistant Eric Stragar conscientiously helped every step of the way. Production Supervisor Lisa Chuck ensured the excellence of the finished product.

Finally, my family lent immeasurable support. In particular, Anne Coty Snyder deserves the highest recognition for being my efficient and indefatigable editorial assistant.

Introduction

The Book

Literary Portraits: An Anthology of Modern American Prose and Poetry for Students of English contains twenty-four essays and three poems. It is geared toward students of ESL/EFL in English classes in the U.S. and abroad. *Literary Portraits* addresses the special academic needs of international students who require supplementary cultural and historical information to make the reading of American literature more comprehensible.

The Level

Literary Portraits is a literature textbook edited for high-intermediate and advanced ESL/EFL students and nonstudent readers. International students in colleges, universities, language institutes, and adult education programs both in the U.S. and abroad, as well as lay readers desiring to gain insight into American culture through literature, will find *Literary Portraits* to be a valuable source book.

Literary Portraits is a bona fide literature anthology; the reading selections are not simplified. It is assumed that high-intermediate and advanced ESL/EFL students have dictionary skills. Therefore, vocabulary that can be looked up in a standard English-language dictionary is not defined in this textbook. At the same time, idiomatic usage, historio-cultural references, and uncommon turns of phrases characteristic of a particular author or generation *are* clarified.

The Content

The selections contained in *Literary Portraits* address diverse issues, ranging from immigration to sports and from family structure to the Vietnam Conflict. Many of the topics are controversial, and all serve to provide glimpses of a multifaceted United States.

The authors are highly regarded in their respective fields: anthropology, art criticism, journalism, social and political commentary, and nonfiction. Some of the writers have received the coveted Pulitzer Prize, and several have earned other distinguished awards and honors for their literary achievements.

The Organization

Literary Portraits consists of three major parts: *Observing the Melting Pot*, *American Introspection*, and *Changing Roles and Perspectives*. Each of these parts includes an introductory poem and eight essays.

Every essay is preceded by three sections: *About the Author, Setting the Scene,* and *Pre-Reading Considerations. About the Author* conveys biographical data together with mention of other works by that writer. *Setting the Scene* introduces the cultural and historical context of the piece. *Pre-Reading Considerations* stimulates the readers to examine their own views concerning the major issues of the essay *before* they read it.

Footnotes and glosses accompany each reading selection. Short definitions of unusual usages and idiomatic words and phrases are glossed in the margin, with lengthier definitions and explanations of historio-cultural references appearing as footnotes.

There are three post-reading sections per essay: *Discussion Points, Composition Topics,* and *Research Ideas.* The questions of *Discussion Points* and the themes offered in *Composition Topics* are devised to encourage the readers to compare their home culture with that aspect of American culture portrayed in the essay. *Research Ideas* presents a list of topics related to the historio-cultural backdrop of the essay. This post-reading activity provides further opportunity for students to augment their understanding of the literature.

J. DONNIE SNYDER, PH.D
The University of Texas at Austin

Contents

PART I   Observing the Melting Pot

PART II   American Introspection

PART III   Changing Roles and Perspectives

PART I

Observing the Melting Pot

In "Theme for English B," poet Langston Hughes (1902–1967) expresses the ambiguity and diversity of American culture. Often referred to as "the melting pot," the population of the United States has its origin in all corners of the globe. Members of communities in Asia, Africa, Europe, and North and South America have settled in the United States, and each ethnic group has left its imprint on the greater social fabric. It is imperative to note here the vital mark made by the indigenous Native Americans. Further, it is equally important to mention that, unlike the other groups, the majority of black Americans arrived in America per force of the slave trade. Together, the distinct ethnic populations have experienced a reciprocal relationship to one another and to the overall American culture: giving and receiving.

1

Theme for English B

LANGSTON HUGHES

The instructor said,

> Go home and write
> a page tonight.
> And let that page come out of you—
> Then, it will be true.

I wonder if it's that simple?
I am twenty-two, colored, born in Winston-Salem.[1]
I went to school there, then Durham,[1] then here
to this college on the hill above Harlem.[2]
I am the only colored student in my class.
The steps from the hill lead down into Harlem,
through a park, then I cross St. Nicholas,
Eighth Avenue, Seventh, and I come to the Y,[3]
the Harlem Branch Y, where I take the elevator
up to my room, sit down, and write this page:

It's not easy to know what is true for you or me
at twenty-two, my age. But I guess I'm what
I feel and see and hear, Harlem, I hear you:
hear you, hear me—we two—you, me, talk on this page.
(I hear New York, too.) Me—who?

Well, I like to eat, sleep, drink, and be in love.
I like to work, read, learn, and understand life.
I like a pipe for a Christmas present,
or records—Bessie,[4] bop,[5] or Bach.[6]
I guess being colored doesn't make me *not* like
the same things others folks like who are other races.
So will my page be colored that I write?

[1] Winston-Salem and Durham: cities in North Carolina
[2] Harlem: section of New York City populated mainly by Blacks and Hispanics
[3] Y: short for "Young Men's Christian Association," a recreational club and residence
[4] Bessie: Smith (1894–1937), black American female blues singer
[5] bop: short for "bebop," rapid, highly accented jazz music
[6] Bach: Johann Sebastian (1685–1750), German organist and composer

Being me, it will not be white.
But it will be
a part of you, instructor,
You are white—
yet a part of me, as I am a part of you.
That's American.
Sometimes perhaps you don't want to be a part of me.
Nor do I often want to be a part of you.
But we are, that's true!
As I learn from you,
I guess you learn from me—
although you're older—and white—
and somewhat more free.

This is my page for English B.

CHAPTER 1

◆ At Ellis Island

BY IRVING HOWE

About the Author:
IRVING HOWE
(1920–   )

Irving Howe was born in New York City. He established a distinguished career as author, biographer, literary critic, editor, and social historian. He has taught at Brandeis University (Massachusetts), Stanford University (California), and at City University of New York, as Distinguished Professor of English. Howe is the recipient of numerous fellowships and awards. The following is a partial listing of his published works: *William Faulkner: A Critical Study* (1952), *A Treasury of Yiddish Stories* (with Eliezer Greenberg, 1954), *Politics and the Novel: A World More Attractive* (book of essays, 1957), *The Decline of the New* (1969), *World of Our Fathers* (winner of the National Book Award, 1976), and *Essential Works of Socialism* (as editor, 1976).

Setting the Scene

From the end of the nineteenth century until the mid-1940s, immigrants who arrived to the United States through New York City passed through Ellis Island in New York Harbor. Ellis Island became a U.S. historic site in 1965, and has recently undergone extensive physical improvements. In the following essay, excerpted from Howe's book *World of Our Fathers*, the writer portrays the experiences shared by millions whose first contact with America was Ellis Island.

Pre-Reading Considerations

1. Can you imagine a situation in your homeland which would cause you to emigrate?
2. What kind of emotional identification do you share with an immigrant who has been uprooted from a familiar land and is subjected to physical examination in an unfamiliar place?

(photo, opposite page) Alfred Stieglitz, *The Steerage* (1911).

At Ellis Island
IRVING HOWE

1   "The day of the emigrants' arrival in New York was the nearest earthly likeness to the final Day of Judgment,[1] when we have to prove our fitness to enter Heaven." So remarked one of those admirable journalists who in the early 1900's exposed themselves to the experience of the immigrants and came to share many of their feelings. No previous difficulties roused such overflowing anxiety, sometimes self-destructive panic, as the anticipated **test** of Ellis Island. Nervous chatter, foolish rumors spread through each cluster of immigrants:

strenuous physical and mental experience

"There is Ellis Island!" shouted an immigrant who had already been in the United States and knew of its alien laws. The name acted like magic. Faces grew taut, eyes narrowed. There, in those red buildings, fate awaited them. Were they ready to enter? Or were they to be sent back?
"Only God knows," shouted an elderly man, his withered hand gripping the railing.

2   Numbered and lettered before debarking, in groups corresponding to entries on the ship's manifest, the immigrants are herded onto the Customs Wharf. "Quick! Run! Hurry!" shout officials in half a dozen languages.
3   On Ellis Island they pile into the massive hall that occupies the entire width of the building. They break into dozens of lines, divided by metal railings, where they file past the first doctor. Men whose breathing is heavy, women trying to hide a limp or deformity behind a large bundle — these are marked with chalk, for later inspection. Children over the age of two must walk by themselves, since it turns out that not all can. (A veteran inspector recalls: "Whenever a case aroused suspicion, the alien was set aside in a cage apart from the rest . . . and his coat lapel or shirt marked with colored chalk, the color indicating why he had been isolated.") One out of five or six needs further medical checking — H chalked for heart, K for hernia, Sc for scalp, X for mental defects.
4   An interpreter asks each immigrant a question or two: can he respond with reasonable alertness? Is he dull-witted? A question

---

[1] Day of Judgment: according to various theologies, the day of God's judgment of humanity at the end of the world

also to each child: make sure he's not deaf or dumb. A check for **TB**, regarded as "the Jewish disease." *short for tuberculosis*

5   Then a sharp turn to the right, where the second doctor waits, a specialist in "contagious and loathsome diseases." Leprosy? Venereal disease? Fauvus, "a contagious disease of the skin, especially of the scalp, due to a parasitic fungus, marked by the formation of yellow flattened scabs and baldness"?

6   Then to the third doctor, often feared the most. He

> stands directly in the path of the immigrant, holding a little stick in his hand. By a quick movement and the force of his own compelling gaze, he catches the eyes of his subject and holds them.[2] You will see the immigrant stop short, lift his head with a quick jerk, and open his eyes very wide. The inspector reaches with a swift movement, catches the eyelash with his thumb and finger, turns it back, and peers under it. If all is well, the immigrant is passed on . . . Most of those detained by the physician are Jews.

7   The eye examination hurts a little. It terrifies the children. Nurses wait with towels and basins filled with disinfectant. They watch for trachoma, cause of more than half the medical detentions. It is a torment hard to understand, this first taste of America, with its poking of flesh and prying into private parts[3] and mysterious chalking of clothes.

8   Again into lines, this time according to nationality. They are led to stalls at which multilingual inspectors ask about character, anarchism, polygamy, insanity, crime, money, relatives, work. You have a job waiting? Who paid your passage? Anyone meeting you? Can you read and write? Ever in prison? Where's your money?

9   For Jewish immigrants, especially during the years before agencies like the Hebrew Immigrant Aid Society (HIAS) could give them advice, these questions pose a dilemma: to be honest or to lie? Is it good to have money or not? Can you bribe these fellows, as back home, or is it a mistake to try? Some are so accustomed to bend and evade and slip a ruble into a waiting hand[4] that they get themselves into trouble with needless lies. "Our Jews," writes a Yiddish paper,

> **love to** get tangled up with dishonest answers, so that the officials have no choice but to send them to the detention area. A Jew who had money in his pocket decided to lie and said he didn't have a penny. . . . A woman with four children and *often unintentionally*

---

[2] catches . . . them: gets and holds the attention of the person
[3] private parts: parts of the body not exposed in public
[4] slip a ruble into a waiting hand: in the U.S.S.R., the accepted custom of bribing an official with Soviet currency in exchange for permission to emigrate

pregnant with a fifth, said her husband had been in America
fourteen years. . . . The HIAS man learned that her husband
had recently arrived, but she thought fourteen years would make
a better impression. The officials are sympathetic. They know
the Jewish immigrants get "confused" and tell them to sit down
and "remember." Then they let them in.

Especially bewildering is the idea that if you say you have a job
waiting for you in the United States, you are liable to deportation
—because an 1885 law prohibits the importation of contract labor.
But doesn't it "look better" to say a job is waiting for you? No,
the HIAS man patiently explains, it doesn't. Still, how can you
be sure *he* knows what he's talking about? Just because he wears
a little cap with those four letters embroidered on it?

10   Except when the flow of immigrants was simply beyond the
staff's capacity to handle it, the average person passed through
Ellis Island in about a day. Ferries ran twenty-four hours a day
between the island and both the Battery[5] and points in New Jersey.
As for the unfortunates detained for medical or other reasons, they
usually had to stay at Ellis Island for one or two weeks. Boards of
special inquiry, as many as four at a time, would sit in permanent
session, taking up cases where questions had been raised as to the
admissibility of an immigrant, and it was here, in the legal infight-
ing and appeals to sentiment, that HIAS proved especially valuable.

11   The number of those detained at the island or sent back to
Europe during a given period of time varied according to the
immigration laws then in effect . . . and, more important, according to the strictness with which they were enforced. It is a sad
irony, though familiar to students of democratic politics, that under
relatively lax administrations at Ellis Island, which sometimes al-
lowed rough handling of immigrants and even **closed an eye to**   *pretended not to see*
corruption, immigrants had a better chance of getting past the
inspectors than when the commissioner was a **public-spirited Yan-**   *loyal American*
kee intent upon literal adherence to the law.   *citizen*

12   Two strands of opinion concerning Ellis Island have come down
to us, among both historians and the immigrant masses themselves:
first, that the newcomers were needlessly subjected to bad treatment, and second, that most of the men who worked there were
scrupulous and fair, though often overwhelmed by the magnitude
of their task.

13   The standard defense of Ellis Island is offered by an influential
historian of immigration, Henry Pratt Fairchild:

[5] the Battery: an area of New York City that was the location of the entry point for immigrants
before the well-known Ellis Island center was opened

During the year 1907 five thousand was fixed as the maximum number of immigrants who could be examined at Ellis Island in one day; yet during the spring of that year more than fifteen thousand immigrants arrived at the port of New York in a single day.

As to the physical handling of the immigrants, this is [caused] by the need for haste. . . . The conditions of the voyage are not calculated to land the immigrant in an alert and clear-headed state. The bustle, confusion, rush and size of Ellis Island **complete the work**, and leave the average alien in a state of stupor. *add to the misery of the hard conditions of the voyage*
. . . He is in no condition to understand a carefully-worded explanation of what he must do, or why he must do it, even if the inspector had the time to give it. The one suggestion which is immediately comprehensible to him is a pull or a push; if this is not administered with actual violence, there is no unkindness in it.

14   Reasonable as it may seem, this analysis meshed Yankee elitism with a defense of the bureaucratic mind. Immigrants *were* disoriented by the time they reached Ellis Island, but they remained human beings with all the sensibilities of human beings; the problem of numbers *was* a real one, yet it was always better when interpreters offered a word of explanation than when they resorted to "a pull or a push." Against the view expressed by Fairchild, we must weigh the massive testimony of the immigrants themselves, the equally large body of material gathered by congressional investigations, and such admissions, all the more **telling** because casual *revealing, clear* in intent, as that of Commissioner Corsi:[6] "Our immigration officials have not always been as humane as they might have been." The Ellis Island staff was often badly overworked, and day after day it had to put up with an atmosphere of fearful anxiety which required a certain deadening of response, if only **by way of** self- *for* defense. But it is also true that many of the people who worked there were rather simple fellows who lacked the imagination to respect cultural styles radically different from their own.

15   One interpreter who possessed that imagination richly was a young Italo-American named Fiorello La Guardia,[7] later to become an insurgent mayor of New York. "I never managed during the years I worked there to become callous to the mental anguish, the disappointment and the despair I witnessed almost daily. . . . At best the work was an ordeal." For those who cared to see, and those able to feel, there could finally be no other verdict.

[6] Commissioner Corsi: Edward Corsi (1896–1965), New York politician and chief officer of the Department of Immigration for New York, from 1931 to 1933
[7] Fiorello La Guardia: (1882–1947), American politician

Discussion Points

1. What did Ellis Island signify to the immigrants?
2. How did Ellis Island officials subdivide the new arrivals?
3. Describe the medical inspection the immigrants underwent. Which diseases were considered grave enough to require isolation of the victims?
4. Why did the HIAS representative advise many against telling the immigration officials about the promise of a job?
5. According to Howe, what two observations about the handling of newcomers at Ellis Island are now thought to be fair historical conclusions?
6. Interpret Fiorello La Guardia's words: "At best the work was an ordeal."
7. Based on this essay, what do you believe Howe's impression of the turn-of-the-century Ellis Island is?

Composition Topics

Prepare a two-page composition on one of the following topics:

1. Compare and contrast the lines and classifications of separation experienced by immigrants at Ellis Island to a process to which you have been subjected, for example, visa application, college course registration, and so forth. Include an account of your emotional reaction to these official procedures.
2. Pretend that you are a new arrival to the U.S. who is being processed at Ellis Island. Depict the inspection stages you and

your family have to endure before being allowed to enter the country legally. Describe your emotional responses as well.

3. Argue for or against the need for immigration procedures such as those depicted in this essay.

4. Compare and contrast the Ellis Island immigration screening to that used in your country. Mention any controversy that might surround this issue there.

Research Ideas

To better comprehend the underlying history of Howe's essay, write a two-page report on at least one of these themes:

1. American Immigration Legislation
2. Early Twentieth-Century Immigration into the United States
3. Ellis Island
4. Henry Pratt Fairchild
5. Health Screening of Immigrants into the United States

CHAPTER **2**

◆ *Ántonia*

BY WILLA CATHER

**About the
Author:**
WILLA CATHER
(1873–1947)

Willa Sibert Cather was born in Virginia and grew up in Nebraska among immigrant farmers. Her University of Nebraska degree led to an initial career as a magazine editor in New York City. Thereafter, she became a poet, a journalist, a novelist, and an English teacher during her admirable working life. Owing to her upbringing, many of Cather's novels deal with pioneer settlers. Among her publications are the following: *O Pioneers!* (1913), *One of Ours* (recipient of the Pulitzer Prize,[1] 1922), *The Professor's House* (1925), and *Death Comes to the Archbishop* (1927). "Ántonia" derives from the author's 1918 novel *My Ántonia*.

**Setting the
Scene**

The state of Nebraska, childhood home to Willa Cather, was populated by immigrant pioneers from Europe: Bohemians, Danes, English, Germans, Irish, Swedes, and others. Many of these newcomers established separate colonies, within which they could function comfortably in their respective native languages. Nearly all were extremely poor; they had come to this country for economic reasons. Their main objective in life was to support themselves, and most did this by farming. Gradually, these diverse ethnic groups emerged from their isolation to integrate into the mainstream society. They began to take part in the already established American cultural and political scenes. Of course, by now all have blended into "the melting pot," but there are still traces of their distinct ethnicity, which enhances the ever-expanding cultural fabric of the United States.

**Pre-Reading
Considerations**

1. Imagine that you are a new arrival to an area in which there are several established immigrant groups (one of which is yours), as well as a community of American-born settlers. Would you be inclined to reside with those who share your language and culture? Or would you instead opt to assimilate directly into the nonimmigrant population?
2. As a new immigrant head of a household, what would your three highest priorities be? Explain your choices.

---

[1] Pulitzer Prize: one of various annual prizes (here, in literature) established in 1918 by the will of Joseph Pulitzer, an American publisher

Ántonia

WILLA CATHER

1   On Sunday morning Otto Fuchs was to drive us over to make the acquaintance of our new Bohemian neighbours. We were taking them some provisions, as they had come to live on a wild place where there was no garden or chicken-house, and very little **broken land**. Fuchs brought up a sack of potatoes and a piece of *cultivated land* cured pork from the cellar, and grandmother packed some loaves of Saturday's bread, a jar of butter, and several pumpkin pies in the straw of the wagon-box. We clambered up to the front seat and jolted off past the little pond and along the road that climbed to the big cornfield.

2   I could hardly wait to see what lay beyond that cornfield; but there was only red grass like ours, and nothing else, though from the high wagon-seat one could look off a long way. The road ran about like a wild thing, avoiding the deep draws, crossing them where they were wide and shallow. And all along it, wherever it looped or ran, the sunflowers grew; some of them were as big as little trees, with great rough leaves and many branches which bore dozens of blossoms. They made a gold ribbon across the prairie. Occasionally one of the horses would tear off with his teeth a plant full of blossoms, and walk along munching it, the flowers nodding in time to his bites as he ate down toward them.

3   The Bohemian family, grandmother told me as we drove along, had bought the homestead of a fellow countryman, Peter Krajiek, and had paid him more than it was worth. Their agreement with him was made before they left the **old country**, through a cousin *in Europe* of his, who was also a relative of Mrs. Shimerda. The Shimerdas were the first Bohemian family to come to this part of the country. Krajiek was their only interpreter, and could tell them anything he chose. They could not speak enough English to ask for advice, or even to **make** their most pressing wants **known**. One son, Fuchs *reveal* said, was well-grown, and strong enough to work the land; but the father was old and frail and knew nothing about farming. He was a weaver by trade, had been a skilled workman on tapestries and upholstery materials. He had brought his fiddle with him, which wouldn't be of much use here, though he used to **pick up** *earn a little* **money** by it at home. *money*

4   'If they're nice people, I hate to think of them spending the winter

in that **cave** of Krajiek's,' said grandmother. 'It's no better than a **badger hole**; no proper **dugout** at all. And I hear he's made them pay twenty dollars for his old cookstove that ain't worth ten.'

references to a crude and inadequate home

5   'Yes'm,' said Otto; 'and he's sold 'em his oxen and his two bony old horses for the price of good work-teams. I'd have interfered about the horses — the old man can understand some German — if I'd **'a'** thought it would do any good. But Bohemians has a natural distrust of Austrians.'

short for have

6   Grandmother looked interested. 'Now, why is that, Otto?'

7   Fuchs wrinkled his brow and nose. 'Well, ma'am, it's politics. It would take me a long while to explain.'

8   The land was growing rougher; I was told that we were approaching Squaw Creek, which cut up the west half of the Shimerdas' place and made the land of little value for farming. Soon we could see the broken, grassy clay cliffs which indicated the windings of the stream, and the glittering tops of the cottonwoods and ash trees that grew down in the ravine. Some of the cottonwoods had already **turned,** and the yellow leaves and shining white bark made them look like the gold and silver trees in fairy tales.

changed color

9   As we approached the Shimerdas' dwelling, I could still see nothing but rough red hillocks, and draws with shelving banks and long roots hanging out where the earth had crumbled away. Presently, against one of those banks, I saw a sort of shed; thatched with the same wine-coloured grass that grew everywhere. Near it tilted a shattered windmill frame, that had no wheel. We drove up to this skeleton to tie our horses, and then I saw a door and window sunk deep in the drawbank. The door stood open, and a woman and a girl of fourteen ran out and looked up at us hopefully. A little girl trailed along behind them. The woman had on her head the same embroidered shawl with silk fringes that she wore when she had alighted from the train at Black Hawk. She was not old, but she was certainly not young. Her face was alert and lively, with a sharp chin and shrewd little eyes. She shook grandmother's hand energetically.

10   'Very glad, very glad!' she ejaculated. Immediately she pointed to the **bank** out of which she had emerged and said, 'House no good, house no good!'

rising ground forming a side of a hollowed-out house

11   Grandmother nodded consolingly. 'You get fixed up comfortable after while, Mrs. Shimerda; make good house.'

12   My grandmother always spoke in a very loud tone to foreigners, as if they were deaf. She made Mrs. Shimerda understand the friendly intention of our visit, and the Bohemian woman handled the loaves of bread and even smelled them, and examined the pies with lively curiosity, exclaiming, 'Much good, much thank!' — and again she wrung grandmother's hand.

13   The oldest son, Ambrož — they called it Ambrosch — came out

of the cave and stood beside his mother. He was nineteen years
old, short and broad-backed, with a close-cropped, flat head, and
a wide, flat face. His hazel eyes were little and shrewd, like his
mother's, but more sly and suspicious; they fairly snapped at the
food. The family had been living on corncakes and sorghum
molasses for three days.

14   The little girl was pretty, but Án-tonia—they accented the
name thus, strongly, when they spoke to her—was still prettier.
I remembered what the conductor had said about her eyes. They
were big and warm and full of light, like the sun shining on brown
pools in the wood. Her skin was brown, too, and in her cheeks
she had a glow of rich, dark colour. Her brown hair was curly
and wild-looking. The little sister, whom they called Yulka (Julka),
was fair, and seemed mild and obedient. While I stood awkwardly
confronting the two girls, Krajiek came up from the barn to see
what was going on. With him was another Shimerda son. Even
from a distance one could see that there was something strange
about this boy. As he approached us, he began to make uncouth
noises, and held up his hands to show us his fingers, which were
webbed to the first knuckle, like a duck's foot. When he saw me
draw back, he began to crow delightedly, 'Hoo, hoo-hoo, hoo-hoo!'
like a rooster. His mother scowled and said sternly, 'Marek!' then
spoke rapidly to Krajiek in Bohemian.

15   'She wants me to tell you he won't hurt nobody, Mrs. Burden.
He was born like that. The others are smart. Ambrosch, he make
good farmer.' He struck Ambrosch on the back and the boy smiled
knowingly.

16   At that moment the father came out of the hole in the bank.
He wore no hat, and his thick, iron-grey hair was brushed straight
back from his forehead. It was so long that it brushed out behind
his ears, and made him look like the old portraits I remembered
in Virginia. He was tall and slender, and his thin shoulders stooped.
He looked at us understandingly, then took grandmother's hand
and bent over it. I noticed how white and well-shaped his own
hands were. They looked calm, somehow, and skilled. His eyes
were melancholy, and were set back deep under his brow. His
face was ruggedly formed, but it looked like ashes—like something
from which all the warmth and light had died out. Everything
about this old man **was in keeping with** his dignified manner. He   *conformed to*
was neatly dressed. Under his coat he wore a knitted grey vest,
and, instead of a collar, a silk scarf of a dark bronze-green, carefully
crossed and held together by a red coral pin. While Krajiek was
translating for Mr. Shimerda, Ántonia came up to me and held
out her hand coaxingly. In a moment we were running up the
steel drawside together, Yulka trotting after us.

17   When we reached the level and could see the gold tree-tops,
I pointed toward them, and Ántonia laughed and squeezed my

hand as if to tell me how glad she was I had come. We raced off toward Squaw Creek and did not stop until the ground itself stopped—fell away before us so abruptly that the next step would have been out into the tree-tops. We stood panting on the edge of the ravine, looking down at the trees and bushes that grew below us. The wind was so strong that I had to hold my hat on, and the girls' skirts were blown out before them. Ántonia seemed to like it; she held her little sister by the hand and chattered away in that language which seemed to me spoken so much more rapidly than mine. She looked at me, her eyes fairly blazing with things she could not say.

18   'Name? What name?' she asked, touching me on the shoulder. I told her my name, and she repeated it after me and made Yulka say it. She pointed into the gold cottonwood tree behind whose top we stood and said again, 'What name?'

19   We sat down and made a nest in the long red grass. Yulka curled up like a baby rabbit and played with a grasshopper. Ántonia pointed up to the sky and questioned me with her glance. I gave her the word, but she was not satisfied and pointed to my eyes. I told her, and she repeated the word, making it sound like 'ice.' She pointed up to the sky, then to my eyes, then back to the sky, with movements so quick and impulsive that she distracted me, and I had no idea what she wanted. She got up on her knees and wrung her hands. She pointed to her own eyes and shook her head, then to mine and to the sky, nodding violently.

20   'Oh,' I exclaimed, 'blue, blue sky.'

21   She clapped her hands and murmured, 'Blue sky, blue eyes,' as if it amused her. While we snuggled down there out of the wind, she learned a score of words. She was quick, and very eager. We were so deep in the grass that we could see nothing but the blue sky over us and the gold tree in front of us. It was wonderfully pleasant. After Ántonia had said the new words over and over, she wanted to give me a little **chased** silver ring she wore on her *designed by hammering and ornamenting* middle finger. When she coaxed and insisted, I repulsed her quite sternly. I didn't want her ring, and I felt there was something reckless and extravagant about her wishing to give it away to a boy she had never seen before. No wonder Krajiek **got the better of** *was able to fool* these people, if this was how they behaved.

22   While we were disputing about the ring, I heard a mournful voice calling, 'Án-tonia, Án-tonia!' She sprang up like a hare. '**Tatinek**! **Tatinek**!' she shouted, and we ran to meet the old man *(Cz.) Daddy* who was coming toward us. Ántonia reached him first, took his hand and kissed it. When I came up, he touched my shoulder and looked searchingly down into my face for several seconds. I became somewhat embarrassed, for I was used to being **taken for** *underappreciated* **granted** by my elders.

23   We went with Mr. Shimerda back to the dugout, where

grandmother was waiting for me. Before I got into the wagon, he took a book out of his pocket, opened it, and showed me a page with two alphabets, one English and the other Bohemian. He placed this book in my grandmother's hands, looked at her entreatingly, and said, with an earnestness which I shall never forget, 'Te-e-ach, te-e-ach my Án-tonia!'

Discussion Points

1. Explain Peter Krajiek's relationship to the Shimerdas. Also comment on his role in the sale of the homestead.
2. What was the purpose of Otto Fuchs' Sunday morning visit to the Shimerdas?
3. Describe Mr. Shimerda's physical condition and his occupational ability. How did he adapt to his new farming environment?
4. Characterize the homestead sale by Peter Krajiek to the Shimerdas.
5. Why didn't Otto Fuchs intervene in the sales transaction between Krajiek and the new family from Bohemia?
6. Name and describe the members of the Shimerda family.
7. Describe Ántonia's personality.
8. What was Mrs. Shimerda's reaction to the kindly Sunday morning visit?
9. Comment on Mr. Shimerda's hopes regarding the English language.

Composition Topics

Write a composition of at least a page on one of the following topics:

1. If you were a neighbor of a newly arrived immigrant family, what approach would you take toward these newcomers?
2. Combine the information contained in the essay with your personal experience to foresee how the Shimerdas eventually adapted to their new home.
3. Recall an experience you have had that is similar to the "blue sky, blue eyes" story of "Ántonia."
4. Interpret Peter Krajiek's treatment of the Shimerdas. Compare the relationship with one personally familiar to you in which one person partly takes advantage of another.

Research Ideas

What follows is a list of topics that you might consider researching. They relate directly to the cultural and historical issues that are contained in "Ántonia."

1. Bohemian Immigration to the U.S.
2. Immigrant Farming in the Midwest
3. Immigrant Trades in the Midwest
4. Nebraska in the Late Nineteenth and Early Twentieth Centuries

C H A P T E R **3**

◆ *Autobiographical Notes*

BY JAMES BALDWIN

About the Author:
JAMES BALDWIN (1924–1987)

Between the ages of fourteen and seventeen, James Baldwin was a preacher in the Harlem section of New York City, his birthplace. At seventeen, he changed his profession, from the ministry (his father's work) to writing. Baldwin wrote mainly about the relationship between Whites and Blacks in the U.S. To his writing credit are numerous stories, essays, and novels, both fiction and nonfiction. "Autobiographical Notes" is the introductory piece to *Notes of a Native Son* (1955). Among his many other works are *Go Tell It on the Mountain* (1953), *Another Country* (1961), *The Fire Next Time* (1963), *Tell Me How Long the Train's Been Gone* (1968), *The Devil Finds Work* (1976), and *Just Above My Head* (1979).

Setting the Scene

The Harlem of the 1920s, the decade in which Baldwin was born, was an area in transition — part of New York City that turned from a residential section into a slum. Discrimination in housing was a fact of life, and it was not uncommon to see signs reading "for respectable colored families only." Blacks were moving into Harlem in great numbers, migrating from southern rural communities. Wages for Blacks were quite low relative to those earned by Whites. The average black Harlemite in the 1920s held an unskilled, low-paying position — sometimes regardless of higher qualifications. This is the environment in which Baldwin spent his early years.

Pre-Reading Considerations

1. Can you imagine what it would be like being subjected to job and housing discrimination?
2. When you write, do you feel that you represent a certain segment of the population? Or do you speak for everyone?
3. Do your parents intend for you to enter a career that you do not prefer?
4. Has your view of your native country changed since you have lived abroad?

Autobiographical Notes

JAMES BALDWIN

1   I was born in Harlem thirty-one years ago. I began plotting novels at about the time I learned to read. The story of my childhood is the usual bleak fantasy, and we can dismiss it with the restrained observation that I certainly would not consider living it again. In those days my mother was given to the exasperating and mysterious habit of having babies. As they were born, I took them over with one hand and held a book with the other. The children probably suffered, though they have since been kind enough to deny it, and in this way I read *Uncle Tom's Cabin*[1] and *A Tale of Two Cities*[2] over and over and over again; in this way, in fact, I read just about everything I could get my hands on — except the Bible, probably because it was the only book I was discouraged to read. I must also confess that I wrote — a great deal — and my first professional triumph, in any case, the first effort of mine to be seen in print, occurred at the age of twelve or thereabouts, when a short story I had written about the Spanish revolution won some sort of prize in an extremely short-lived church newspaper. I remember the story was censored by the lady editor, though I don't remember why, and I was outraged.

2   Also wrote plays, and songs, for one of which I received a letter of congratulations from Mayor La Guardia,[3] and poetry, about which the less said, the better. My mother was delighted by all these goings-on, but my father wasn't; he wanted me to be a preacher. When I was fourteen I became a preacher, and when I was seventeen I stopped. Very shortly thereafter I left home. For God knows how long I struggled with the world of commerce and industry — I guess they would say they struggled with *me* — and when I was about twenty-one I had enough done of a novel to get a Saxton Fellowship. When I was twenty-two the fellowship was over, the novel turned out to be unsalable, and I started waiting on tables in a Village[4] restaurant and writing book reviews — mostly, as it turned out, about the Negro problem, concerning which the color of my skin made me automatically an expert. Did another book, in company with photographer Theodore Pelatowski, about the

[1] *Uncle Tom's Cabin*: by Harriet Beecher Stowe; published in 1852
[2] *A Tale of Two Cities*: by Charles Dickens; published in 1859
[3] Mayor La Guardia: Fiorello Henry (1882–1947), American politician
[4] Village: Greenwich Village, a district in New York City with unique shops and restaurants; known for artists, writers, and musicians

store-front churches[5] in Harlem. This book met exactly the same
fate as my first—fellowship, but no sale. (It was a Rosenwald
Fellowship.) By the time I was twenty-four I had decided to stop
reviewing books about the Negro problem—which, by this time,
was only slightly less horrible in print than in life—and I packed
my bags and went to France, where I finished, God knows how,
Go Tell It on the Mountain.

3   Any writer, I suppose, feels that the world into which he was
born is nothing less than a conspiracy against the cultivation of
his talent—which attitude certainly has a great deal to support
it. On the other hand, it is only because the world looks on his
talent with such a frightening indifference that the artist is compelled to make his talent important. So that any writer, looking
back over even so short a span of time as I am here forced to
assess, finds that the things which hurt him and the things which
helped him cannot be divorced from each other; he could be
helped in a certain way only because he was hurt in a certain
way; and his help is simply to be enabled to move from one
conundrum to the next—one is tempted to say that he moves
from one disaster to the next. When one begins looking for influences one finds **them by the score.** I haven't thought much about
my own, not enough anyway; I **hazard** that the King James Bible,
the rhetoric of the store-front church, something ironic and violent
and perpetually understated in Negro speech—and something of
Dickens' love for bravura—have something to do with me today;
but I wouldn't stake my life on it.[6] Likewise innumerable people
have helped me in ways; but finally, I suppose, the most difficult
(and most rewarding) thing in my life has been the fact that I
was born a Negro and was forced, therefore, to effect some kind
of truce with this reality. (Truce, by the way, is the best one can
hope for.)

4   One of the difficulties about being a Negro writer (and this is
not special pleading, since I don't mean to suggest that he has it
worse than anybody else) is that the Negro problem is written
about so widely. The bookshelves **groan under the weight of**
information and everyone therefore considers himself informed.
And this information, furthermore, operates usually (generally,
popularly) to reinforce traditional attitudes. Of traditional attitudes
there are only two—For or Against—and I, personally, find it
difficult to say which attitude has caused me the most pain. I am
speaking as a writer; from a social point of view I am perfectly
aware that the change from ill-will to good-will, however moti-
vated, however expressed, is better than no change at all.

5   But it is part of the business of the writer—as I see it—to

---

[5] store-front churches: churches housed in the back of stores
[6] stake my life on it: go so far as to say I would offer my life if this were not so

examine attitudes, to go beneath the surface, **to tap the source**.
From this point of view the Negro problem is nearly inaccessible.
It is not only written about so widely; it is written about so badly.
It is quite possible to say that the price a Negro pays for becoming
articulate is to find himself, at length, with nothing to be articulate
about. ("You taught me language," says Caliban to Prospero,[7] "and
my profit on't is I know how to curse.") Consider: the tremendous
social activity that this problem generates imposes on whites and
Negroes alike the necessity of looking forward, of working to bring
about a better day. This is fine, it keeps the waters troubled;[8] it
is all, indeed, that has made possible the Negro's progress.
Nevertheless, social affairs are not generally speaking the writer's
prime concern, whether they ought to be or not; it is absolutely
necessary that he establish between himself and these affairs a
distance which will allow, at least, for clarity, so that before he
can look forward in any meaningful sense, he must first be allowed
to take a long look back. In the context of the Negro problem
neither whites nor blacks, for excellent reasons of their own, have
the faintest desire to look back; but I think that the past is all
that makes the present coherent, and further, that the past will
remain horrible for exactly as long as we refuse to assess it honestly.

to examine the root or origin

6   I know, in any case, that the most crucial time in my own
development came when I was forced to recognize that I was a
kind of bastard of the West; when I followed the line of my past
I did not find myself in Europe but in Africa. And this meant
that in some subtle way, in a really profound way, I brought to
Shakespeare, Bach, Rembrandt, to the stones of Paris, to the
cathedral at Chartres,[9] and to the Empire State Building,[10] a
special attitude. These were not really my creations, they did not
contain my history; I might search in them **in vain** forever for any
reflection of myself. I was an interloper; this was not my heritage.
At the same time I had no other heritage which I could possibly
hope to use—I had certainly been unfitted for the jungle or the
tribe. I would have to appropriate these white centuries, I would
have to make them mine—I would have to accept my special
attitude, my special place in this scheme—otherwise I would have
no place in *any* scheme. What was the most difficult was the fact
that I was forced to admit something I had always hidden from
myself, which the American Negro has had to hide from himself
as the price of his public progress; that I hated and feared white
people. This did not mean that I loved black people; on the

without success

[7] Caliban to Prospero: characters in Shakespeare's *The Tempest*. Caliban is Prospero's crude
   slave.
[8] it keeps the waters troubled: It keeps the bad, unfair conditions at the surface, known.
[9] Shakespeare . . . Chartres: references to high points in European cultural history
[10] Empire State Building: a skyscraper located in New York City

contrary, I despised them, possibly because they failed to produce Rembrandt. In effect, I hated and feared the world. And this meant, not only that I thus gave the world an altogether murderous power over me, but also that in such a self-destroying (limbo I could never hope to write. *paradise*

7   One writes out of one thing only—one's own experience. Everything depends on how relentlessly one forces from this experience the last drop, sweet or bitter, it can possibly give. This is the only real concern of the artist, to recreate out of the disorder of life that order which is art. The difficulty then, for me, of being a Negro writer was the fact that I was, in effect, prohibited from examining my own experience too closely by the tremendous demands and the very real dangers of my social situation.

8   I don't think the dilemma outlined above is uncommon. I do think, since writers work in the disastrously explicit medium of language, that it goes a little way towards explaining why, out of the enormous resources of Negro speech and life, and despite the example of Negro music, prose written by Negroes has been generally speaking so pallid and so harsh. I have not written about being a Negro at such length because I expect that to be my only subject, but only because it was **the gate I had to unlock** before I could hope to write about anything else. I don't think that the Negro problem in America can be even discussed coherently without bearing in mind its context; its context being the history, traditions, customs, the moral assumptions and preoccupations of the country; in short, the general **social fabric.** Appearances to the contrary, no one in America escapes its effects and everyone in America bears some responsibility for it. I believe this the more firmly because it is the overwhelming tendency to speak of this problem as though it were a thing apart. But in the work of Faulkner,[11] in the general attitude and certain specific passages in Robert Penn Warren,[12] and, most significantly, **in the advent of** Ralph Ellison,[13] one sees the beginnings—at least—of a more genuinely penetrating search. Mr. Ellison, by the way, is the first Negro novelist I have ever read to utilize in language, and brilliantly, some of the ambiguity and irony of Negro life.

that which I had to do first

customs and attitudes

with the appearance of works by

9   About my interests: I don't know if I have any, unless the morbid desire to own a sixteen-millimeter camera and make experimental movies can be so classified. Otherwise, I love to eat and drink—it's my melancholy conviction that I've scarcely ever had enough to eat (this is because it's *impossible* to eat enough if you're worried about the next meal)—and I love to argue with people

---

[11] Faulkner: William Cuthbert (1897–1962), American novelist
[12] Robert Penn Warren: (1905–), American author and educator
[13] Ralph Ellison: (1914–)

who do not disagree with me too profoundly, and I love to laugh. I do *not* like bohemia,[14] or bohemians, I do not like people whose principal aim is pleasure, and I do not like people who are *earnest* about anything. I don't like people who like me because I'm a Negro; neither do I like people who find in the same **accident** grounds for contempt. I love America more than any other country in the world, and, exactly for this reason, I insist on the right to criticize her perpetually. I think all theories are suspect, that the finest principles may have to be modified, or may even be pulverized by the demands of life, and that one must find, therefore, one's own moral center and move through the world hoping that this center will guide one aright. I consider that I have many responsibilities, but none greater than this: to last, as Hemingway says, and get my work done.

circumstance (of being born black)

10   I want to be an honest man and a good writer.

---

[14] bohemia: residency of avant-garde artists, writers, and poets (bohemians), predominantly in Greenwich Village, New York City

Discussion Points

1. Describe Baldwin's youth. Include mention of his parents' influence on his life.
2. At age 24, Baldwin changed his life style. Characterize this change and explain his reasons for it.
3. In Baldwin's opinion, what major difficulty does the black writer have?
4. Explain why the author considered himself an "interloper" in American society.
5. How did Baldwin view the challenge of writing?
6. What were the writer's interests outside his career?
7. What did Baldwin feel his responsibilities as a writer were?

**Composition
Topics**

*Select one of the following themes on which you will compose a two-
page paper:*

1. Baldwin relates how his parents shaped his attitudes and career
   goals. He also tells how he later broke away from this earlier
   direction. Depict the influences on your childhood, and indicate
   how you have either followed or broken with these early patterns.
2. Express your views as to what a writer's responsibilities to society
   should be. How does Baldwin's opinion on this subject compare
   with yours?
3. Think of a well-known minority writer of your country who sees
   himself/herself as an "interloper" in the mainstream culture.
   What achievements has this figure accomplished?

**Research
Ideas**

*In order to more fully appreciate the cultural and historical
references in "Autobiographical Notes," prepare a research report on
one of these topics:*

1. James Baldwin
2. Black Writers in Twentieth-Century American Literature
3. Harlem: 1920–1950
4. Race Relations in the U.S.: 1920–1950

CHAPTER 4

◆ *Halfway to Dick and Jane:*
A Puerto Rican Pilgrimage

BY JACK AGUEROS

**About the
Author:**
JACK AGUEROS
(1934–   )

Jack Agueros was born in New York City of parents who had just recently arrived there from Puerto Rico. The author was raised in Spanish Harlem, a part of New York City, and attended Brooklyn College in that city. Agueros worked in administrative positions for the City of New York before writing this essay, his first published work.

**Setting the
Scene**

In 1917, the United States enacted The Jones Act, which granted U.S. citizenship to Puerto Ricans. Not until the 1930s, however, did the Puerto Ricans begin to migrate to the U.S. in increased numbers. During that decade, they settled predominantly in the area of the Brooklyn Navy Yard (in N.Y.C.), thereafter gradually relocating in a different portion of the city, East Harlem. The Puerto Ricans left their island in search of economic opportunity. Their goal was to earn enough money to return to Puerto Rico, but what typically happened was that the social and economic conditions that greeted them tended to lock them into permanent residence in New York. Agueros portrays this migration pattern graphically and personally in his essay.

**Pre-Reading
Considerations**

1. If you felt forced to leave your homeland to seek higher earnings, would you set out alone or would you have your family accompany you?
2. If you were the head of a family facing economic depression, do you think you would accept government assistance (welfare)?
3. Have you ever felt peer pressure to use drugs?

Halfway to Dick and Jane: A Puerto Rican Pilgrimage
JACK AGUEROS

1   I was born in Harlem[1] in 1934. We lived on 111th Street off
Fifth Avenue. It was a block of mainly three-story buildings — with
brick fronts, or brownstone, or limestone imitations of brownstone.
Our apartment was a three-room first-floor walk-up.[2] It faced north
and had three windows on the street, none in back. There was a
master bedroom,[3] a living room, a kitchen-dining room, a foyer
with a short hall, and a bathroom. In the kitchen there was an
air shaft to evacuate cooking odors and grease — we converted it
to a chimney for Santa Claus.[4]

2   The kitchen was dominated by a large Victorian[5] china closet,
and the built-in wall shelves were lined with oilcloth, trimmed
with ruffle, both decorated by brilliant and miniature fruits.
Prominent on a wall of the kitchen was a large reproduction of a
still life, a harvest table full of produce, framed and under glass.   *a painting of stationary objects*
From it I learned to identify apples, pumpkins, bananas, pears,
grapes, melons, and "peaches without worms." A joke between
my mother and me. (A peach we had bought in the city market,
under the New Haven's elevated tracks, **bore**, like the trains above,   *contained worms*
passengers.)

3   On one shelf of the kitchen, over the stove, there was a lineup
of ceramic canisters that carried words like "nutmeg," "ginger,"
and "basil." I did not know what those words meant and I don't
know if my mother did either. "Spices," she would say, and that
was that. They were of a yellow color that was not unlike the
yellow of the stove. The kitchen was itself painted yellow, I think,
very pale. But I am sure of one thing, it was not "Mickey Moused."
"Mickey Mousing"[6] was a technique used by house painters to
decorate the areas of the walls that were contained by wood
molding. Outside the molding they might paint a solid green.
Inside the wood mold, the same solid green. Then with a twisted-up
rag dipped in a lighter green they would trace random patterns.

[1] Harlem: a section of New York City populated mainly by Blacks and Hispanics
[2] walk-up: apartment (or office) in a building that has no elevator
[3] master bedroom: the larger or largest bedroom of a home, usually reserved for the husband
and wife
[4] Santa Claus: jolly grandfatherlike, gift-bearing figure symbolic of Christmas
[5] Victorian: attitudes and designs characteristic of the times of Queen Victoria of England
[6] "Mickey Moused/Mousing": named after the Walt Disney-created animated movie character,
Mickey Mouse

4   We never used wallpaper or rugs. Our floors were covered with linoleum in every room. My father painted the apartment every year before Christmas, and in addition, he did all the maintenance, doing his own plastering and plumbing. **No sooner** would we move into an apartment **than** my father would repair holes or cracks, and if there were bulges in the plaster, he would break them open and redo the area—sometimes a whole wall. He would immediately modify the bathrooms to add a shower with separate valves, and usually as a routine matter, he cleaned out all the elbow traps,[7]and changed all the washers on faucets. This was true of the other families in the buildings where I lived. **Not a December came without** a painting of the apartment.

As soon as

Every December included

5   We had Louis XIV furniture[8] in the living room, reflected in the curved glass door and curved glass sides of the china closet. On the walls of the living room hung two **prints** that I loved. I would spend hours playing games with my mother based on the pictures, making up stories, etc. One day at Brooklyn College, a slide projector **slammed**, and I awoke after having dozed off during a dull lecture to see Van Gogh's "The Gleaners" on the screen. I almost cried. Another time I came across the other print in a book. A scene of Venice by Canaletto.

copies of paintings

malfunctioned

6   The important pieces of the living room, for me, were a **Detrola** radio with magic-eye tuning[9] and the nightingale, Keero. The nightingale and the radio **went back before my recollection**. The bird could not stop singing, and people listened on the sidewalk below and came upstairs offering to buy Keero.

a brand name

were there before my first memories of them

7   The Detrola, shaped like a Gothic arch with inlaid woodwork, was a great source of entertainment for the family. I memorized all the hit songs sung by Libertad Lamarque[10] and Carlos Gardel.[11] Sundays I listened to the Canary Hour presented by Hartz Mountain Seed Company. Puppy, a white Spitz, was my constant companion. Puppy slept at the foot of my bed from the first day he came to our house till the day he died, when I was eleven or twelve and he was seven or eight.

8   I am an only child. My parents and I always talked about my becoming a doctor. The law and politics were not highly regarded in my house. Lawyers, my mother would explain, had to defend people whether they were guilty or not, while politicians, my

[7] elbow traps: water pipe sections that catch debris in the plumbing system; in the shape of an elbow
[8] Louis XIV furniture: of the style of the times of Louis XIV of France
[9] magic eye tuning: advanced mechanism for stabilizing the station selected
[10] Libertad Lamarque: (1909–) Argentine singer, dancer, and film star. She helped popularize the tango dance form.
[11] Carlos Gardel: (1887–1935) a famous Argentine singer, who popularized the tango, a Latin American dance; also appeared in motion pictures

father would say, were all crooks. A doctor helped everybody, rich and poor, black and white. If I became a doctor, I could study hay fever[12] and find a cure for it, my godmother would say. Also, I could take care of my parents when they were old. I liked the idea of helping, and for nineteen years my sole ambition was to study medicine.

9   My house had books, not many, but my parents encouraged me to read. As I became a good reader they bought books for me and never refused me money for their purchase. My father once built a bookcase for me. It was an important moment, for I had always believed that my father was not too happy about my being a **bookworm**. The atmosphere at home was always warm. We seemed to be a popular family. We entertained frequently, with two **standing** parties a year—at Christmas and for my birthday. Parties were always large. My father would dismantle the beds and move all the furniture so that the full two rooms could be used for dancing. My mother would **cook up a storm**, particularly at Christmas. *Pasteles, lechon asado, arroz con gandules,* and a lot of *coquito* to drink (meat-stuffed plantain, roast pork, rice with pigeon peas, and coconut nog). My father always brought in a band. They played without compensation and were guests at the party. They ate and drank and danced while a **victrola covered the intermissions**. One year my father brought home a whole pig and hung it in the foyer doorway. He and my mother prepared it by rubbing it down with oil, oregano, and garlic. After preparation, the pig was taken down and carried over to a local bakery where it was cooked and returned home. Parties always went on till daybreak, and in addition to the band, there were always volunteers to sing and declaim poetry.

10   My mother kept an immaculate household. Bedspreads (chenille seemed to be very **in**) and lace curtains, washed at home like everything else, were hung up on huge racks with rows of tight nails. The racks were assembled in the living room, and the moisture from the wet bedspreads would fill the apartment. **In a sense**, that seems to be the lasting image of that period of my life. The house was clean. The neighbors were clean. The streets, with few cars, were clean. The buildings were clean and uncluttered with people on the stoops. The park was clean. The visitors to my house were clean, and the relationships that my family had with other Puerto Rican families, and the Italian families that my father had met through baseball and my mother through the garment center, were clean. Second Avenue was clean and most of the apartment windows had awnings. There was always music, there seemed to be no rain, and snow did not become slush.

studious person

traditional

prepare a wonderful assortment of foods

record player substituted during the band's rest periods

popular

In one way

[12] hay fever: an allergy marked by sneezing, coughing, and watery, red eyes

School was fun, we wrote essays about how grand America was, we put up hunchbacked cats at Halloween,[13] we believed Santa Claus visited everyone. I believed everyone was Catholic.[14] I grew up with dogs, nightingales, my godmother's guitar, rocking chair, cat, guppies, my father's occasional roosters, kept in a cage on the fire escape. Laundry delivered and collected by horse and wagon, fruits and vegetables sold the same way, windowsill refrigeration in winter, iceman and box in summer. The police my friends, likewise the teachers.

11   In short, the first seven or so years of my life were not too great a variation on Dick and Jane,[15] the school book figures who, if my memory serves me correctly, were blond Anglo-Saxons, not immigrants, not migrants like the Puerto Ricans, and not the children of either immigrants or migrants.

12   My family moved in 1941 to Lexington Avenue[16] into a larger apartment where I could have my own room. It was a light, sunny, railroad flat on the top floor of a well-kept building. I transferred to a new school, and whereas before my classmates had been mostly black, the new school had few blacks. The classes were made up of Italians, Irish, Jews, and **a sprinkling of** Puerto Ricans. *only a few* My block was populated by Jews, Italians, and Puerto Ricans.

13   And then a whole series of different events began. I went to junior high school. We played in the backyard, where we tore down fences to build fires to cook stolen potatoes. We tore up whole hedges, because the green tender limbs would not burn when they were peeled, and thus made perfect skewers for our stolen "**mickies**."[17] We played tag[18] in the abandoned buildings, *potatoes* tearing the plaster off the walls, tearing the wire lath off the wooden slats, tearing the wooden slats themselves, good for fires, for kites, for sword fighting. We ran up and down the fire escapes playing tag and over and across many rooftops. The **war** ended *World War II* and the heavy Puerto Rican migration began. The Irish and Jews disappeared from the neighborhood. The Italians tried to **consolidate** *group together* east of Third Avenue.

14   What caused the clean and open world to end? Many things. Into an ancient neighborhood came pouring four to five times more people than it had been designed to hold. Men who came running at the promise of jobs were jobless as the war ended.

---

[13] Halloween: October 31 holiday marked by festivities and tricks and symbolized by hunchbacked cats, witches, and pumpkins made into Jack-O-Lanterns.

[14] Catholic: the religion of the majority of Puerto Ricans

[15] Dick and Jane: boy and girl storybook characters found in traditional elementary school reading books in the U.S.

[16] Lexington Avenue: a main street in New York City

[17] "mickies": slang for potatoes; derived from the "Mc" beginning of many Irish surnames. The diet of Irish and Irish Americans typically includes white (also called Irish) potatoes.

[18] tag: children's running game in which players are pursued and tagged (touched) if caught

They were confused. They could not see the economic forces that ruled their lives as they drank beer on the corners, reassuring themselves of good times to come while they were **hell-bent** toward alcoholism. The sudden surge in numbers caused new resentments, and prejudice was intensified. Some were forced to live in cellars, and were then characterized as cave dwellers. Kids came who were confused by the new surroundings; their Puerto Ricanness[19] forced us against a mirror asking,[20] "If they are Puerto Ricans, what are we?" and thus they confused us. In our confusion we were sometimes pathetically reaching out, sometimes pathologically striking out. Gangs. Drugs. Wine. Smoking. Girls. Dances and slow-drag music.[21] Mambo. Spics, Spooks, and Wops.[22] Territories, brother gangs, and war councils establishing rules for right of way on blocks and avenues and for seating in the local theater. Pegged pants[23] and zip guns.[24] Slang.

progressing very fast

15 Dick and Jane were dead, man. Education collapsed. Every classroom had ten kids who spoke no English. Black, Italian, Puerto Rican relations in the classroom were good, but we all knew we couldn't visit one another's neighborhoods. Sometimes we could not move too freely within our own blocks. On **109th**, from the lamp post west, the Latin Aces, and from the lamp post east, the Senecas, the "club" I belonged to. The kids who spoke no English became known as Marine Tigers, picked up from a popular Spanish song. (The *Marine Tiger* and the *Marine Shark* were two ships that sailed from San Juan to New York and brought over many, many migrants from the island.)

Street

16 The neighborhood had its boundaries. Third Avenue and east, Italian. Fifth Avenue and west, black. South, there was a hill on 103rd Street known locally as Cooney's Hill. When you got to the top of the hill, something strange happened: America began, because from the hill south was where the "Americans" lived. Dick and Jane were not dead; they were alive and well in a better neighborhood.

17 When, as a group of Puerto Rican kids, we decided to go swimming to Jefferson Park Pool, we knew we risked a fight and a beating from the Italians. And when we went to La Milagrosa Church in Harlem, we knew we risked a fight and a beating from the blacks. But when we went over Cooney's Hill, we risked dirty looks, disapproving looks, and questions from the police like,

[19] Puerto Ricanness: strongly identifying with their Puerto Rican heritage
[20] forced us . . . asking: caused us to reexamine our identity
[21] slow-drag music: slow dance music
[22] Spics, Spooks and Wops: derogatory slang for Hispanics, Blacks, and Italian Americans, respectively
[23] pegged pants: wide at the top and narrow at the bottom
[24] zip guns: crudely homemade single-shot pistols

"What are you doing in this neighborhood?" and "Why don't you kids go back where you belong?"

18   Where we belonged! Man, I had written compositions about America. Didn't I belong on the Central Park tennis courts, even if I didn't know how to play? Couldn't I watch Dick play? Weren't these policemen working for me too?

19   Junior high school was a **waste**. I can say with 90 per cent accuracy that I learned nothing. The woodshop was used to manufacture stocks for "home-mades" after Macy's[25] stopped selling zipguns. We went from classroom to classroom answering "**here**" and trying to be "good." The math class was generally permitted to go to the gym after roll call. English was still a good class. Partly because of a damn good, tough teacher named Miss Beck, and partly because of the grade-number system (7-1 the smartest seventh grade and 7-12, the dumbest). Books were left in school, there was little or no homework, and the whole thing seemed to be a **holding operation** until high school. **Somehow or other**, I passed the entrance exam to Brooklyn Technical High School. But I couldn't **cut the mustard**, either academically or with the "American" kids. After one semester, I came back to **PS** 83, waited a semester, and went on to Benjamin Franklin High School.

waste of time

response to attendance check; signifies being present

temporary stop/ Somehow

succeed

public school

20   I still wanted to study medicine and excelled in biology. English was always an interesting subject, and I still enjoyed writing compositions and reading. In the neighborhood it was becoming a problem being categorized as a bookworm and as one who used "Sunday words," or "big words." I **dug** school, but I wanted to be one of the boys more. I think the boys respected my intelligence, despite their **ribbing**. Besides which, I belonged to a club with a number of members interested in going to college, and so I wasn't **so far out**.

liked

ridiculing

that different

21   My introduction to marijuana was in junior high school in 1948. A kid named Dixie from 124th Street brought a pack of **joints** to school and taught about twelve guys to smoke. He told us we could buy joints at a quarter each or five for a dollar. Bombers, or thicker cigarettes, were thirty-five cents each or three for a dollar. There were a lot of experimenters, but not too many buyers. Actually, among the boys there was a strong taboo on drugs, and the Spanish word "*motto*" was a term of disparagement. Many clubs would kick out members who were known to use drugs. Heroin was easily available, and in those days packaged in capsules or "caps" which sold for fifty cents each. Method of use was inhalation through the nose, or "sniffing," or "snorting."

marijuana cigarettes

(Sp.) slang term for drug addict

22   I still remember vividly the first kid I ever saw who was mainlining.[26] Prior to this encounter, I had known of "skin-popping,"

[25] Macy's: famous department store and one of the largest in the world, located in New York City
[26] mainlining: injecting the drugs directly into the veins

or subcutaneous injection, but not of mainlining. Most of the sniffers were afraid of skin-popping because they knew of the danger of addiction. They seemed to think that you could not become addicted by sniffing.

23   I went over to 108th Street and Madison where we played softball on an empty lot. This kid came over who was maybe sixteen or seventeen and asked us if we wanted to buy **Horse**. He started telling us about **shooting up** and showed me his arms. He had tracks, big black marks on the inside of his arm from the inner joint of the elbow down to his wrist and then over onto the back of his hand. I was stunned. Then he said, "That's nothing, man. I ain't **hooked**, and I ain't no **junky**. I can stop anytime I want to." I believe that he believed what he was saying. Invariably the kids talked about their drug experiences and would say **over and over**, "I ain't hooked. I can stop anytime."

heroin
injecting drugs

addicted /
drug addict
repeatedly

24   But they didn't stop; and the drug traffic grew greater and more open. Kids were smoking on the corners and on the stoops. Deals were made on the street, and you knew fifteen places within a block radius where you could buy anything you wanted. Cocaine never seemed to **catch on** although it was readily available. In the beginning, the kids seemed to be able to get the money for stuff easily. As the number of shooters grew and the prices went up, the kids got more desperate and apartment robbing became a real problem.

become popular

25   More of the boys began to leave school. We didn't use the term drop out; rather, a guy would say one day, after forty-three **truancies**, "I'm quitting school." And so he would. It was an irony, for what was really happening was that after many years of being rejected, ignored, and shuffled around by the school, the kid wanted to quit. Only you can't quit something you were never a part of, nor can you drop out if you were never in.

unexcused absences
from school

26   Some of the kids lied about their age and joined the army. Most just **hung around**. Not drifting to drugs or crime or to work either. They used to talk about going back at night and getting the diploma. I believe that they did not believe they could get their diplomas. They knew that the schools had abandoned them a long time ago—that to get the diploma meant starting all over again and that was impossible. Besides, day or night, it was the same school, the same staff, the same shit. But what do you say when you are powerless to get what you want, and what do you say when the other side has all the **cards** and writes all the rules? You say, "Tennis is for **fags**," and "School is for fags."

did nothing,
loitered

power
homosexuals

27   My mother leads me by the hand and carries a plain brown shopping bag. We enter an immense airplane hangar. Structural steel crisscrosses on the ceiling and walls; large round and square rivets look like buttons or bubbles of air trapped in the girders.

There are long metallic counters with people bustling behind them. It smells of **C.N. disinfectant**. Many people stand on many lines up to these counters; there are many conversations going on simultaneously. The huge space plays tricks with voices and a very eerie combination of sounds results. A white cabbage is rolled down a counter at us. We retaliate by throwing down stamps.

abbr. of chlorinated naphthalene *disinfectant*

28   For years I thought that sequence happened in a dream. The rolling cabbage rolled in my head, and little unrelated incidents seemed to bring it to the surface of my mind. I could not understand why I remembered a once-dreamt dream so vividly. I was sixteen when I picked up and read Freud's *The Interpretation of Dreams.* One part I understood immediately and well, sex and symbolism. In no time, I had hung my shingle;[27] Streetcorner Analyst. My friends would tell me their dreams and with the most outrageous sexual explanations we laughed whole evenings away. But the rolling cabbage could not be stopped and neither quack analysis nor serious thought could **explain it away**. One day I asked my mother if she knew anything about it.

rationalize it

29   "That was home relief, 1937 or 1938. You were no more than four years old then. Your father had been working at a restaurant and I had a job downtown. I used to take you every morning to Dona Eduvije who cared for you all day. She loved you very much, and she was very clean and neat, but I used to cry on my way to work, wishing I could stay home with my son and bring him up like a proper mother would. But I guess I was fated to be a **workhorse**. When I was pregnant, I would get on the crowded subway and go to work. I would get on a crowded elevator up. Then down. Then back on the subway. Every day I was afraid that the crowd would hurt me, that I would lose my baby. But I had to work. I worked for the WPA[28] right into my ninth month."

hard-working person

30   My mother was telling it "like it was," and I sat stupefied, for I could not believe that what she said applied to the time I thought of as open and clean. I had been existing all my life like a small plant in a bell jar, my parents defining my awareness. There were things all around me I could not see.

31   "When you were born we had been living as boarders. It was hard to find an apartment, even in Harlem. You saw signs that said 'No Renting to Colored or Spanish.' That meant Puerto Ricans. We used to say, 'This is supposed to be such a great country?' But with a new baby we were determined not to be boarders and we took an apartment on 111th Street. Soon after we moved, I lost my job because my factory closed down. Your father was

[27] had hung my shingle; Streetcorner Analyst: had established my "profession" as an amateur psychoanalyst

[28] WPA: Works Progress Administration, a program set up during the F. D. Roosevelt presidency to put unemployed persons to work

making seven or eight dollars a week in a terrible job in a carpet
factory. They used to clean rugs, and your father's hands were
always in strong chemicals. You know how funny some of his
fingernails are? It was from that factory. He came home one night
and he was looking at his fingers, and he started saying that he
didn't come to this country to lose his hands. He wanted to hold
a bat and play ball and he wanted to work—but he didn't want
to lose his hands. So he quit the job and went to a restaurant for
less pay. With me out of work, a new apartment and therefore
higher rent, we couldn't manage. You father was furious when I
mentioned home relief. He said he would rather starve than **go
on relief.** But I went and filled out the papers and answered all
the questions and **swallowed my pride** when they treated me like
an intruder. I used to say to them, 'Find me a job—get my husband
a better job—we don't want home relief.' But we had to take it.
And all that mess with the stamps in exchange for food. And
they used to have weekly 'specials' sort of—but a lot of things
were useless—because they were American food. I don't remember
if we went once a week or once every two weeks. You were so
small I don't know how you remember that place and the long
lines. It didn't last long because your father had everybody trying
to find him a better job and finally somebody did. Pretty soon I
went into the WPA and thank God, we never had to deal with
those people again. I don't know how you remember that place,
but I wish you didn't. I wish I could forget that home relief thing
myself. It was the worst time for your father and me. He still
hates it.

*receive financial
assistance from the
government /
ignored my pride
and embarrassment*

32   (He still hates it and so do many people. The expression, "I'd
rather starve than go on welfare" is common in the Puerto Rican
community. This characteristic pride is well chronicled throughout
Spanish literature. For example, one episode of *Lazarillo de Tormes*,
the sixteenth-century picaresque novel, tells of a squire who struts
around all day with his shiny sword and pressed cape. At night
the squire takes food from the boy, Lazarillo—who has begged or
stolen it—explaining that it is not proper for a squire to beg or
steal or even to work! Without Lazarillo to feed him, the squire
would probably starve.)

33   "You don't know how hard it was being married to your father
then. He was young and very strong and very active and he wanted
to work. **Welfare** deeply disturbed him, and I was afraid that he
would actually get very violent if an investigator came to the
house. They had a terrible way with people, like throwing that
cabbage, that was the way they gave you everything, the way we
used to throw the kitchen slop to the pigs in Puerto Rico. **Some
giving!** Your father was, is, *muy macho,* and I used to worry if
anybody says anything or gives him that why-do-**you-people**-come-
here-to-ruin-things look he'll be in jail for thirty years. He almost

*Governmental
assistance*

*sarcastic way of
saying "not very
generous"/ (Sp.) very
proudly masculine /
Puerto Ricans*

got arrested once when you were just a baby. We went to a hospital clinic—I don't remember now if it was Sydenham or Harlem Hospital—you had a swelling around your throat—and the doctor told me, 'Put on cold compresses.' I said I did that and it didn't help. The doctor said, 'Then put hot compresses.' Your father **blew up**. In his **broken English**, he asked the doctor to do that to his mother and then invited him to transfer over to the stable on 104th Street. 'You do better with horses—maybe they don't care what kind of compresses they get.'

became very angry / English spoken with a foreign accent and errors in grammar

34   "One morning your father tells me, 'I got a new job. I start driving a truck delivering soft drinks.' That night I ask him about the job—he says, 'I quit—a bunch of Mafia[29]—I went to the first four places on my list and each storeowner said, "I didn't order any soda." So I got the idea real fast. The Mafia was going to leave soda in each place and then make the guys buy from them only. As soon as I figured it out, I took the truck back, left it parked where I got it, and didn't even say good-bye.' The restaurant took him back. They liked him. The chef used to give him eggs and meats; it was very important to us. Your father never could **keep still** (still can't), so he was loved wherever he worked. I feel sorry for people on welfare—forget about the cabbage—I never should have taken you there."

stay quiet

35   My father and I are walking through East Harlem, south down Lexington from 112th toward 110th, in 1952. Saturday in late spring, I am eighteen years old, sun brilliant on the streets, people running back and forth on household errands. My father is telling me a story about how back in nineteen thirty something, we were very poor and Con Ed[30] light meters were in every apartment. "The Puerto Ricans, maybe everybody else, would hook up a shunt wire around the meter, specially in the evening when the use was heavy—that way you didn't pay for all the electric you used. We called it '*pillo*' (thief)."

36   We arrive at 110th Street and all the cart vendors are there peddling plantains, avocados, yams, various subtropical roots. I make a casual remark about how foolish it all seemed, and my father catches that I am **looking down on them**. "Are they stealing?" he asks. "Are they selling people colored water? Aren't they working honestly? Are they any different from a bank president? Aren't they **hung** like you and me? They are *machos*, and to be respected. Don't let college go to your head. You think a Ph.D. is automatically better than a peddler? Remember where you come

regarding them as inferior

made, created

---

[29] Mafia: a secret criminal society originating in Sicily, Italy
[30] Con Ed: short for *Consolidated Edison* Electric Company, named after Thomas Alva Edison (1847–1931), American inventor (including the light bulb)

from—poor people. I mopped floors for people and I wasn't ashamed, but I never let them look down on me. Don't you look down on anybody."

37　We walk for a way in silence, I am mortified, but he is not angry. "One day I decide to play a joke on your mother. I come home a little early and knock. When she says 'Who?' I say '**Edison man.**' Well, there is this long silence and then a scream. I open the door and run in. Your mother's on a chair, in tears, her right arm black from **pinky** to elbow. She ran to take the *pillo* out, but in her nervousness she got a very slight shock, the black from the spark. She never has forgiven me. After that, I always thought through my jokes."

worker for the electric company

little (fifth) finger

38　We walk some more and he says, "I'll tell you another story. This one **on me**. I was twenty-five years old and was married to your mother. I took her down to Puerto Rico to meet Papa and Mama. We were sitting in the living room, and I remember it like it happened this morning. The room had rattan furniture very popular in that time. Papa had climbed in rank back to captain and had a new house. The living room had double doors which opened onto a large **balcón**. At the other end of the room you could see the dining table with a beautiful white handmade needlework cloth. We were sitting and talking and I took out a cigarette. I was smoking **Chesterfields** then. No sooner had I lit up than Papa got up, came over, and smacked me in the face. 'You haven't received my permission to smoke,' he said. Can you imagine how I felt?" So my father dealt with his love for me through lateral actions: building bookcases, and through tales of how he got his wounds, he anointed mine.

with me as the object of the joke

(Sp.) balcony

cigarette brand

39　What is a migration? What does it happen to? Why are the Eskimos still dark after living in that snow all these centuries? Why don't they have a word for snow? [31] What things are around me with such high saturation that I have not named them? What is a migration? If you rob my purse, are you really a fool? Can a poor boy really be president? In America? Of anything? If he is not white? Should one man's achievement fulfill one million people? Will you let us come near your new machine: after all, there is no more ditch digging? What is a migration? What does it happen to?

40　The most closely watched migrants of this world are birds. Birds migrate because they get bored singing in the same place to the same people. And they see that the environment gets hostile. Men move for the same reasons. When a Puerto Rican comes to

---

[31] word for snow: The Eskimo language has many words for different kinds of snow but no single word for *snow*.

America, he comes looking for a job. He takes the cold as one of a negative series of **givens**. The **mad hustle**, the filthy city, filthy air, filthy housing, sardine transportation[32] are in the series. He knows life will be tough and dangerous. But he thinks he can **make a buck**. And in his mind, there is only one tableau: himself retired, owner of his home in Puerto Rico, chickens cackling in the back yard.

unavoidable conditions / very fast pace

earn money

41 It startles me still, though it has been five years since my parents went back to the island. I never believed them. My father, driving around New York for the Housing Authority,[33] knowing more streets in more boroughs than I do, and my mother, curious in her later years about museums and theaters, and reading my books as fast as I would put them down, then giving me cryptic reviews. Salinger is really silly (*Catcher in the Rye*), but entertaining. That evil man deserved to die (*Moby Dick*). He's **too much** (Dostoevski in *Crime and Punishment*). I read this when I was a little girl in school (*Hamlet* and *Macbeth*). It's too sad for me (*Cry, the Beloved Country*).

wonderful, extraordinary

42 My father, intrigued by the thought of passing the foreman's exam, sitting down with a couple of arithmetic books, and teaching himself at age fifty-five to do work problems and mixture problems and fractions and decimals, and going into the civil service exam[34] and scoring a seventy-four and waiting up one night for me to show me three poems he had written. These two cosmopolites, gladiators without skills or language, battling hostile environments and prejudiced people and systems, had **graduated** from Harlem to the Bronx, had risen into America's dream-cherished lower middle class, and then **put it down** for Puerto Rico after thirty plus years.

elevated themselves socio-economically

abandoned it

43 What is a migration, when is it not just a long visit?

44 I was born in Harlem, and I live downtown. And I am a migrant, for if a migration is anything, it is a state of mind. I have known those Eskimos who lived in America twenty and thirty years and never voted, never attended a community meeting, never filed a complaint against a landlord, never informed the police when they were robbed or swindled, or when their daughters were molested. Never appeared at the State or City Commission on Human Rights, never reported a business fraud, never, in other words, saw the snow.

45 And I am very much a migrant because I am still not quite at home in America. Always there are hills; on the other side — people inclined to throwing cabbages. I cannot "earn and **return**" — there is no position for me in my father's tableau.

go back to Puerto Rico

[32] sardine transportation: tightly crowded conditions in public transportation
[33] Housing Authority: official agency in charge of housing
[34] civil service exam: job admission or promotion test given by the city

46   However, I approach the future with optimism. Fewer Puerto
Ricans like Eskimos, a larger number of leaders like myself trained
in the university, tempered in the ghetto, and with a vision of
America moving from its unexecuted policy to a society open and
clean, accessible to anyone.

47   Dick and Jane? They, too, were **tripped** by society, and in our   *cheated*
several ways, we are all still migrating.

Discussion Points

1. Describe the author's memories of the Fifth Avenue apartment. What features stood out?
2. How did Agueros's father help maintain their apartment?
3. What career plans did the author's parents have for their son? Why was this their choice?
4. Was Agueros a "bookworm"? Explain your answer.
5. Who are Dick and Jane? How does the writer relate his childhood experiences to theirs?
6. Discuss the changes that took place after the Agueros family moved to Lexington Avenue?
7. Characterize the residents of the Lexington Avenue neighborhood. Did the various ethnic groups there live in harmony? Explain.

8. What was junior high like for the author?
9. Relate the role of drugs in Agueros's environment.
10. Interpret Agueros's cabbage dream. What was its origin?
11. Explain the author's father's attitude toward welfare.
12. Relate the practical joke that Agueros's father played on his mother.
13. Why did Puerto Ricans migrate to New York City during the 1930s?
14. Interpret the last paragraph of the essay.

Composition Topics

Compose a one-page paper on one of the topics that follow:

1. Trace the author's parents' attitudes toward U.S. culture. Then express your understanding of their decision to return to their native Puerto Rico after a thirty-year absence.
2. Outline the major causes of the deterioration of Agueros's childhood environment. Include an analysis of how his education was affected by these factors.
3. Agueros refers to Dick and Jane, two popular storybook characters appearing in primary grade school readers. Consider one or two well-known characters seen in your school reading books. Do they reflect the mainstream culture accurately?
4. During your precollege days, did you have to change neighborhoods? Describe any environmental and/or cultural differences between the two communities. In addition, name any differences you noted between the two schools.
5. In his work, Agueros refers to ethnic divisiveness in one of the neighborhoods he lived in. Compare and contrast these multiethnic relationships with those in your community.

Research Ideas

To augment your knowledge of the cultural and historical background of "Halfway to Dick and Jane: A Puerto Rican Pilgrimage," write a background report on one of the following subject areas:

1. Drug Culture in the U.S.
2. Ethnic Neighborhoods in New York City
3. Puerto Rican Culture in the U.S.
4. Puerto Rican Migration to the U.S.
5. Spanish Harlem
6. Welfare Assistance
7. Works Progress Administration

CHAPTER 5

◆ *The Way to Rainy Mountain*

BY N. SCOTT MOMADAY

About the Author:

N. SCOTT MOMADAY

(1934–   )

Natachee Scott Momaday was born in Oklahoma to Native American parents. His Kiowa-Cherokee heritage is the theme of much of his literature. He is a professor of English, as well as a writer and a poet. His 1969 novel *House Made of Dawn* earned the coveted Pulitzer Prize.[1] Additional works by this author include *Angle of Geese* (1973), *The Gourd Dancer* (1976), and *The Names* (a memoir, 1976). The essay that follows introduces his 1969 collection of Kiowa legends, also named *The Way to Rainy Mountain*.

Setting the Scene

The Southern Great Plains, including Western Oklahoma, Northwestern Texas, and Eastern New Mexico, was home to the Kiowas for about two hundred years. This territory, featuring prairies, plains, and mountains, was mostly unconducive to farming and inhospitable to travelers. The unpredictable acts of Nature, such as severe electrical storms and tornadoes, further deterred pioneering settlers from making permanent stops in this region. By contrast, the Kiowas' appreciation for Nature, coupled with their fatalistic philosophy (characterized by an acceptance of natural occurrences), led them to remain in this territory. For the most part, until the construction of railroads in the nineteenth century, the Kiowas inhabited the Southern Great Plains unshared.

Pre-Reading Considerations

1. In the time your grandparents were growing up, how was life different from that of your childhood years?
2. Did your grandparents adhere to certain traditions that are no longer carried out by your generation?
3. Do you have a favorite grandparent who is now aged? What is your emotional attachment to him or her?

---

[1] Pulitzer Prize: one of various annual prizes (here, in literature) established in 1918 by the will of Joseph Pulitzer, an American publisher

The Way to Rainy Mountain

N. SCOTT MOMADAY

1   A single knoll rises out of the plain in Oklahoma, north and
west of the Wichita range. For my people, the Kiowas, it is an
old landmark, and they gave it the name Rainy Mountain. The
hardest weather in the world is there. Winter brings blizzards, hot
tornadic winds arise in the spring, and in summer the prairie is
an anvil's edge. The grass turns brittle and brown, and it cracks
beneath your feet. There are green belts along the rivers and
creeks, linear groves of hickory and pecan, willow and witch hazel.
At a distance in July or August the steaming foliage seems almost
to writhe in fire. Great green and yellow grasshoppers are everywhere in the tall grass, popping up like corn to sting the flesh,
and tortoises crawl about on the red earth, going nowhere in the
plenty of time. Loneliness is an aspect of the land. All things in
the plain are isolate; there is no confusion of objects in the eye,
but *one* hill or *one* tree or *one* man. To look upon that landscape
in the early morning, with the sun at your back, is to lose the
sense of proportion. Your imagination comes to life, and this, you
think, is where Creation[1] was begun.

2   I returned to Rainy Mountain in July. My grandmother had
died in the spring, and I wanted to be at her grave. She had lived
to be very old and at last infirm. Her only living daughter was
with her when she died, and I was told that in death her face
was that of a child.

3   I like to think of her as a child. When she was born, the
Kiowas were living the last great moment of their history. For
more than a hundred years they had controlled the open range
from the Smoky Hill River to the **Red**, from the headwaters of   *Red River*
the **Canadian** to the fork of the **Arkansas** and **Cimarron**. In   *rivers*
alliance with the Comanches, they had ruled the whole of the
Southern Plains. War was their sacred business, and they were
the finest horsemen the world has ever known. But warfare for
the Kiowas was pre-eminently a matter of disposition rather than
of survival, and they never understood the grim, unrelenting
advance of the U.S. Cavalry.[2] When at last, divided and ill
provisioned, they were driven onto the Staked Plains in the cold
of autumn, they fell into panic. In Palo Duro Canyon they
abandoned their crucial stores to pillage and had nothing then

---

[1] Creation: religious or philosophical reference to the act of bringing into existence from nothing
the universe and the things in it
[2] U.S. Cavalry: a division of the U.S. Army that is mounted on horseback

---

From N. Scott Momaday, "The Way to Rainy Mountain," from *Fields of Writing* (New York: St.
Martin's Press, 1984), pp. 653–57. Reprinted by permission of The University of New Mexico Press.

but their lives. In order to save themselves, they surrendered to the soldiers at Fort Sill and were imprisoned in the old stone corral that now stands as a military museum. My grandmother **was spared** the humiliation of those high gray walls by eight or ten years, but she must have known from birth the affliction of defeat, the dark brooding of old warriors.

did not have to experience

4   Her name was Aho, and she belonged to the last culture to evolve in North America. Her forebears came down from the high country in western Montana nearly three centuries ago. They were a mountain people, a mysterious tribe of hunters whose language has never been classified in any major group. In the late seventeenth century they began a long migration to the south and east. It was a journey toward the **dawn**, and it led to a golden age.[3] Along the way the Kiowas were befriended by the Crows,[4] who gave them the culture and religion of the Plains. They acquired horses, and their ancient nomadic spirit was suddenly free of the ground. They acquired Tai-me, the sacred sun-dance doll, from that moment the object and symbol of their worship, and so shared in the divinity of the sun. Not least, they acquired the sense of destiny, therefore courage and pride. When they entered upon the Southern Plains they had been transformed. No longer were they slaves to the simple necessity of survival; they were a lordly and dangerous society of fighters and thieves, hunters and priests of the sun. According to their origin myth, they entered the world through a hollow log. From one point of view, their migration was the **fruit** of an old prophecy, for indeed they emerged from a sunless world.

poetic reference to the beginning

predicted result

5   Though my grandmother lived out her long life in the shadow of Rainy Mountain, the immense landscape of the continental interior lay like memory in her blood. She could tell of the Crows, whom she had never seen, and of the Black Hills, where she had never been. I wanted to see in reality what she had seen more perfectly in **the mind's eye**, and drove fifteen hundred miles to begin my pilgrimage.

the imagination

6   A dark mist lay over the Black Hills, and the land was like iron. At the top of a ridge I caught sight of Devil's Tower upthrust against the gray sky as if in the birth of time the core of the earth had broken through its crust and the motion of the world was begun. There are things in nature that engender an awful quiet in the heart of man; Devil's Tower is one of them. Two centuries ago, because of their need to explain it, the Kiowas made a legend at the base of the rock. My grandmother said:

7   "Eight children were there at play, seven sisters and their brother. Suddenly the boy was struck dumb; he trembled and began to run upon his hands and feet. His fingers became claws,

---

[3] golden age: period of great cultural achievement
[4] Crows: a Native American tribe

and his body was covered with fur. There was a bear where the boy had been. The sisters were terrified; they ran, and the bear after them. They came to the stump of a great tree, and the tree spoke to them. It bade them climb upon it, and as they did so, it began to rise into the air. The bear came to kill them, but they were just beyond its reach. It reared against the tree and scored the bark all around with its claws. The seven sisters were borne into the sky, and they became the stars of the Big Dipper."[5] From that moment, and so long as the legend lives, the Kiowas have kinsmen in the night sky. Whatever they were in the mountains, they could be no more. However tenuous their well-being, however much they had suffered and would suffer again, they had found a way out of the wilderness.

8   My grandmother had a reverence for the sun, a holy regard that now is **all but** gone out of mankind. There was a wariness   *almost all*
in her, and an ancient awe. She was a Christian in her later years, but she had come a long way about,[6] and she never forgot her birthright. As a child she had been to the sun dances; she had taken part in that annual rite, and by it she had learned the restoration of her people in the presence of Tai-me. She was about seven when the last Kiowa sun dance was held in 1887 on the Washita River above Rainy Mountain Creek. The buffalo were gone. In order to consummate the ancient sacrifice — to impale the head of a buffalo bull upon the Tai-me tree — a delegation of old men journeyed into Texas, there to beg and barter for an animal from the Goodnight herd.[7] She was ten when the Kiowas came together for the last time as a living sun-dance culture. They could find no buffalo; they had to hang an old hide from the sacred tree. Before the dance could begin, a company of soldiers rode out from Fort Sill under orders to disperse the tribe. Forbidden without cause the essential act of their faith, having seen the wild herds slaughtered and left to rot upon the ground, the Kiowas backed away forever from the tree. That was July 20, 1890, at the great bend of the Washita. My grandmother was there. Without bitterness, and for as long as she lived, she bore a vision of deicide.

9   Now that I can have her only in memory, I see my grandmother in the several postures that were peculiar to her: standing at the wood stove on a winter morning and turning meat in a great iron skillet; sitting at the south window, bent above her beadwork, and afterwards, when her vision failed, looking down for a long

---

[5] Big Dipper: stellar group

[6] but she had come a long way about: but she had lived most of her life as a traditional Kiowa (non-Christian)

[7] Goodnight herd: cattle transferred through areas of Texas, New Mexico, Colorado, and as far north as Wyoming. Charles Goodnight (1836–1929) was the main cattleman and trailblazer in this territory.

time into the fold of her hands; going out upon a cane, very slowly as she did when the weight of age came upon her; praying. I remember her most often at prayer. She made long, rambling prayers out of suffering and hope, having seen many things. I was never sure that I had the right to hear, so exclusive were they of all mere custom and company.[8] The last time I saw her she prayed standing by the side of her bed at night, naked to the waist, the light of a kerosene lamp moving upon her dark skin. Her long black hair, always drawn and braided in the day, lay upon her shoulders and against her breasts like a shawl. I do not speak Kiowa, and I never understood her prayers, but there was something inherently sad in the sound, some merest hesitation upon the syllables of sorrow. She began in a high and descending pitch, exhausting her breath to silence; then again and again — and always the same intensity of effort, of something that is, and is not, like urgency in the human voice. Transported so in the dancing light among the shadows of her room, she seemed beyond the reach of time. But that was illusion; I think I knew then that I should not see her again.

10   Houses are like sentinels in the plain, old keepers of the weather watch. There, in a very little while, wood takes on the appearance of great age. All colors wear soon away in the wind and rain, and then the wood is burned gray and the grain appears and the nails turn red with rust. The window panes are black and opaque; you imagine there is nothing within, and indeed there are many ghosts, bones given up to the land. They stand here and there against the sky, and you approach them for a longer time than you expect. They belong in the distance; it is their domain.

11   Once there was a lot of sound in my grandmother's house, a lot of coming and going, feasting and talk. The summers there were full of excitement and reunion. The Kiowas are a summer people; they abide the cold and keep to themselves, but when the season **turns** and the land becomes warm and vital they cannot *changes* hold still; an old love of going **returns upon** them. The aged *returns to* visitors who came to my grandmother's house when I was a child were made of lean and **leather**, and they bore themselves upright. *references to aged,* They wore great black hats and bright ample shirts that shook in *sun-dried skin* the wind. They rubbed fat upon their hair and wound their braids with strips of colored cloth. Some of them painted their faces and carried the scars of old and cherished enmities. They were an old council of warlords, come to remind and be reminded of who they were. Their wives and daughters served them well. The women might indulge themselves; gossip was **at once** the mark and *both* compensation of their servitude. They made loud and elaborate talk among themselves, full of jest and gesture, fright and false alarm. They went abroad in fringed and flowered shawls, bright

---

[8] so exclusive . . . company: because they were so personalized and private

beadwork and German silver. They were at home in the kitchen, and they prepared meals that were banquets.

12   There were frequent prayer meetings, and nocturnal feasts. When I was a child I played with my cousins outside, where the lamplight fell upon the ground and the singing of the old people rose up around us and carried away into the darkness. There were a lot of good things to eat, a lot of laughter and surprise. And afterwards, when the quiet returned, I lay down with my grandmother and could hear the frogs away by the river and feel the motion of the air.

13   Now there is a funereal silence in the rooms, the endless wake of some final word. The walls have closed in upon my grandmother's house. When I returned to it in mourning, I saw for the first time in my life how small it was. It was late at night, and there was a white moon, nearly full. I sat for a long time on the stone steps by the kitchen door. From there I could see out across the land; I could see the long row of trees by the creek, the low light upon the rolling plains, and the stars of the Big Dipper. Once I looked at the moon and **caught sight of** a strange thing. A cricket had   *saw* perched upon the handrail, only a few inches away. My line of vision was such that the creature filled the moon like a fossil. It had gone there, I thought, to live and die, for there, **of all places**,   *ironically* was its small definition made whole and eternal. A warm wind rose up and purled like the longing within me.

14   The next morning, I awoke at dawn and went out on the dirt road to Rainy Mountain. It was already hot, and the grasshoppers began to fill the air. Still, it was early in the morning, and birds sang out of the shadows. The long yellow grass on the mountain shone in the bright light, and a **scissortail** hied above the land.   *bird* There, where it ought to be, at the end of a long and legendary way, was my grandmother's grave. She had at last **succeeded to**   *reached* that holy ground. Here and there on the dark stones were ancestral names. Looking back once, I saw the mountain and came away.

Discussion Points

1. Describe Rainy Mountain and tell what kind of mood it inspires.
2. When the author's grandmother was a child, what was the Kiowas' place in U.S. history?
3. What is the significance of Tai-me?
4. Relate the Kiowas' legendary explanation of the Big Dipper stars.
5. Describe one ancient Kiowa ritual.
6. How does Momaday remember his grandmother?
7. What part did prayers play in Aho's life-style?
8. Portray the role of women in Kiowa society.
9. Does Momaday consider his grandmother's resting place appropriate? Explain your answer.

Composition Topics

Select one of the following subjects for a one-page composition:

1. Compare the significance of Rainy Mountain to a similar natural landmark known to you. Include any legendary information that might be applicable.
2. Consider the relationship you have had with a grandparent. Compare this with the closeness portrayed between the author and his grandmother.
3. Nature plays an important role in Native American culture and life-style. Write about the relevance of Nature to your native culture.
4. In Kiowa society, women are assigned to a certain fixed role. Express your views about traditional female duties among the Kiowas, and compare them to role assignment in your culture.

Research Ideas

What follows is a list of research topics included here to assist you in understanding Momaday's essay. Choose one of them on which to prepare a two-page report:

1. Crow Indians
2. Kiowa Indians
3. The Role of Nature in Native American Culture
4. Plains Indians

CHAPTER 6

◆ *For Two Cents Plain*

BY HARRY GOLDEN

About the Author:
HARRY
GOLDEN
(1902–1981)

Harry Golden gained fame as a newspaper editor, a biographer, and an essayist. Born in Austro-Hungary, Golden arrived in the U.S. as a child and was raised on New York City's Lower East Side, home to many immigrant families at the beginning of the twentieth century. Later, Golden made his home in Charlotte, North Carolina, where he edited *The Carolina Israelite* newspaper. The humorous essays he wrote for his newspaper were collected in three volumes: *Only in America* (1958, made into a play in 1959), *For 2¢ Plain* (1958), and *Enjoy! Enjoy!* (1960).

Setting the Scene

At the end of the nineteenth century and beginning of the twentieth, the Lower East Side of Manhattan, a section of New York City, was home to many different immigrant groups. The Goldhursts[1] were Jewish people living in this community. All the Lower East Side residents lived in very crowded conditions in tenement apartment buildings and were very poor. They were commonly employed in back-breaking jobs, such as peddling and factory work. Work, education, religion, and adapting to their new American environment occupied their daily lives. Many features of their new surroundings contrasted measurably with their native culture. In particular, the younger members of the immigrant families were confronted with great temptations to abandon old habits and adopt new ones. In the following essay, Golden depicts these temptations as he portrays the changing life-style of the "eating-days" rabbinical students, who were trying to carry on the traditional Jewish Orthodox patterns while being attracted to the new and different way of life around them.

Pre-Reading Considerations

1. Have you ever been torn between surrendering to peer pressure in a new environment and following a religious or cultural tradition?

2. If you made a new friend who was from a different culture, would you encourage him or her to adhere to his or her past ways (if different from yours), or would you try to persuade him or her to adapt quickly to the new culture?

[1] Goldhursts: The author's family name was Goldhurst, which he later changed to Golden; many immigrants and first-generation Americans modified their names to make them sound and look more American — they did this in order to assimilate into American society more easily because some prejudice against immigrants did exist.

For Two Cents Plain

HARRY GOLDEN

1   The rabbinical students in Europe and in America had a regular schedule of "eating days." Mondays he ate with family A; Tuesdays with B; and so forth. On the Lower East Side this system still lingered to some extent, but it usually involved a young boy who had immigrated without a family. His fellow-townsmen set up his seven eating days. Usually this was a very religious boy who would not take a chance to eat "out" or could not yet afford to buy his meals. Some of the hosts on these eating days used the fellow to **check up on** the melamed (Hebrew teacher). The melamed came *evaluate* at half past three and taught the children for a half-hour — for a twenty-five-cent fee. Learning the prayers was entirely **by rote.** *memorized* There was no explanation or translation of the Hebrew into English or Yiddish. Once in a while the mother would ask the eating-days fellow to come a half-hour earlier. The boy came with his usual appetite, but soon learned the reason for the early appointment. The mother wanted him to test the children to see if the melamed was doing all right. The boy always gave the melamed a **clean** *good rating* **bill of health**.

2   Sometimes the eating-days boy ate too much and in poor households this was quite a problem. But in most homes the mother **saw to it** that he kept **packing it away**, and in addition *made sure / eating* always had something wrapped up for him to take back to his *fully* room — for later. Many households had these strangers at their tables, but only the very religious boys remained, those who expected to continue their religious studies.

3   The others were soon gone. America was too great and too wonderful; there were too many things to see and do, and even a hot dog at a pushcart was an adventure, **to say nothing of** the *without even* wonderful Max's Busy Bee.[1] *considering*

4   The streets were crowded with vendors with all sorts of delightful and exotic tidbits and nasherei (delicacies).

5   Across the border (the Bowery)[2] was the Italian hot-dog man. The hot plate (a coal fire) was mounted on his pushcart, and behind the stove was a barrel of lemonade to which he added chunks of ice every few hours. The hot dog, roll, mustard, and relish was three cents; the drink, two cents; and it was all a memorable experience.

6   A few years ago I saw a fellow with a similar cart near the

[1] Max's Busy Bee: a store
[2] the Bowery: a section of N.Y.C. populated by homeless people and derelicts

Battery[3] on Lower Broadway and I **made a mad dash for** him. The whole operation was now fifteen cents, but it wasn't anywhere near as wonderful as it was when I was twelve years old.

went very quickly toward

7   In the late fall and winter came the fellow with the haiseh arbus (hot chick-peas). He started to **make his rounds** a few minutes before noon as the children were leaving the schools for lunch. You sat in the classroom and everything was quiet and dignified, and all of a sudden you heard those loud blasts — "Haiseh arbus," "Haiseh, haiseh" (hot, hot) — and you knew it was time to go. Sometimes he was a little early and the teacher had to close the window. The price was one penny for a portion which the man served in a rolled-up piece of newspaper, like the English working people buy their fish and chips. There were also fellows with roasted sweet potatoes; two cents each, and three cents for an extra large one. These people used a galvanized tin contraption on wheels which looked exactly like a bedroom dresser with three drawers. In the bottom drawer were the potatoes he was roasting, while in the upper drawers were the two different sizes ready to serve. On the bottom of everything, of course, was the coal-burning fire. He had a small bag of coal attached to the front of the stove and every once in a while he shook up the fire.

go from selling point to selling point

8   My uncle Berger once operated one of those sweet-potato pushcarts with the stove on the bottom, and years later he always said that he began life in America as an engineer. He boasted of this after he had made a million dollars operating the Hotel Normandie on Broadway and 38th Street[4] during World War I.

9   An interesting fellow was the peddler with a red fez, a "Turk," who sold an exotic sweet drink. He carried a huge bronze water container strapped to his back. This beautiful container had a long curved spout which came over his left shoulder. Attached to his belt, in front, was a small pail of warm water to rinse his two glasses. The drink was one penny. You held the glass, and he leaned toward you as the liquid came forth.

10   Nuts were very popular. There were pushcarts loaded down with "polly seeds." I have forgotten the authentic name for this nut but the East Side literally **bathed in the stuff**. "Polly seed" because it was the favorite food of parrots — "Polly want a cracker?"[5]

had a lot of it

11   Indian nuts, little round brown nuts. The father of one of the kids on the block sold Indian nuts, **of all things**. On his pushcart he had a huge glass bowl the size of an army soup vat, and it was filled with Indian nuts. I had daydreams of taking my shoes off

surprisingly

[3] the Battery: an area of N.Y.C. that was the location of the entry point for immigrants before the well-known Ellis Island immigration center was established; also known for its entertainment places; on the harbor

[4] Broadway and 38th Street: a higher-class section of N.Y.C.

[5] "Polly want a cracker?": popular question asked of a trained parrot, a pet often named Polly

and jumping up and down in that vat of Indian nuts, like the French girls make champagne.

12   This was the era when people walked a great deal. Shoeshine **parlors** were all over the place. On Sunday mornings you went out to get a shine and did not mind waiting in line for it either. "We are going for a walk next Saturday night." Sounds silly today, but it was an event, and make no mistake. And on every corner there were pushcarts selling fruit in season. Apples, pears, peaches, and above all, grapes. A common sight was a boy and girl eating grapes. They boy held the stem aloft as each of them pulled at the bunch and walked along the street. The grapes were sold by weight per bunch; the other fruits were sold individually, of course. And "in season" there was the man or the woman with "hot corn." I did not hear the term "corn-on-the-cob" till quite a few years later. We knew it only as "hot corn." The vendor had boiled the **ears** at home and usually carried the huge vat to a convenient street corner, or he put the vat on a baby carriage and wheeled it around the neighborhood. A lot of women were in this hot-corn business. The hot corn was a nickel, and there was plenty of bargaining. "Throw it back, give me that one, the one over there." We kids waited around until the lady was all sold out, except the ones which had been thrown back, and often we paid no more than a penny. There are two moments when it is best to buy from a peddler, a "first" and the **"close-out."**

shops or stands

of corn

final sale of the day

13   Confections of all sorts were sold, many of them famous in the Orient and eastern Europe. Fellows sold candy known as "rah-hott," which sounds Turkish or Arabic. It was beautiful to look at and there were two or three different tastes with each bite. Halvah, of course, was the real big seller, and the memory of this has lingered to this day. No delicatessen store today is without halvah, although I shall not **do** them **the injustice of comparing** the East Side halvah and the stuff they sell today. But at least you are getting a whiff of it, which is worth anything you pay. I had a Gentile friend here who had been courting a widow for years without any success and I gave him a box of chocolate-covered halvah to take to her, and the next time I saw the guy he was dancing in the streets of Charlotte. We used to eat it between slices of rye bread, "a halvah **sonavich,**" and it was out of this world. There was another candy called "buckser" (St. John's bread), imported from Palestine. It had a long, hard, curved shell and inside a very black seed with an interesting taste which is hard to describe.

compare unfairly

sandwich (Yiddish-American dialect)

14   There were pushcarts loaded down with barrels of dill pickles and pickled tomatoes, which we called "sour tomatoes." Working people, men and women on the way home from needle factories,[6]

---

[6] needle factories: garment-sewing factories

stopped off to buy a sour tomato as a sort of appetizer for their evening meal, or perhaps to **take the edge off the appetite**. These tidbits sold for two or three cents each, and you served yourself. You put your hand into the vinegar barrel and pulled one out. Years later a relative of mine asked me to accompany him to a lawyer's office "to talk for him." I met him on the old East Side and we decided to walk out of the district and into Lower Broadway.

blunt the appetite

15   Suddenly I noticed that he was no longer at my side. I looked back and there he was biting into one sour tomato and holding a fresh one in the other hand, all ready to go. I had become a **fancy guy** by then and he was afraid he would embarrass me, but **my mouth was watering**, Broadway and all.

successful, well-dressed man/it was appetizing to me

16   And then there were the permanent vendors — the soda-water stands. On nearly every corner a soda-water stand. These were the size and shape of the average newsstand you see in most of the big cities today. There was a soda fountain behind a narrow counter, and a rack for factory-made American candy, which was becoming increasingly popular, especially the Hershey bar.[7] The fellow also sold cigarettes. No woman was ever seen smoking a cigarette in those days. The brands were Mecca, Hassan, Helmar, Sweet Caporal (which are still sold), Egyptian Deities, Moguls, Schinasi, Fifth Avenue, and Afternoons.

17   My father smoked Afternoons. Half the cigarette was a hard mouthpiece, or what the **advertising boys** today call a filter. I bought many a box of Afternoons and they were seven cents for ten cigarettes. I also bought whiskey. There was no inhibition about it and no sense of guilt. We had no drunks down there, and a kid could buy a bottle of whiskey for his father the same as he could buy a loaf of bread. I read the label many times on the way home, "Pennsylvania Rye Whiskey; we guarantee that this whiskey has been **aged in the wood** twenty years before bottling; signed, Park and Tilford." Cost, $1.80 for an imperial quart.[8] No fancy "fifth-shmifth"[9] business.

professionals (usually men then) in the advertising business

stored in wooden kegs (barrels)

18   The fellow with the stand had a small marble counter on which he served his drinks and made change for candy and cigarettes. Along the counter were jars of preserves — cherry, raspberry, mulberry — for his mixed drinks. He also had a machine to make **malted milks.** How the immigrants **took to** the malted milk!

milk shakes with malt / developed a liking for

19   Like the other folks, my mother pronounced it "ah molta." But, of course, the big seller was seltzer (carbonated water), either plain or with syrup. A small glass of seltzer cost a penny — "Give me a small plain." That meant no syrup. And for the large glass you

---

[7] Hershey bar: trade name of a chocolate candy bar
[8] imperial quart: 12 percent more than the American quart
[9] fifth-shmifth: one-fifth of an American gallon (Yiddish-American dialectal rhyming word play)

said, "Give me for two cents plain." For an extra penny he ladled
out a spoonful of one of his syrups and mixed it with the seltzer.
Here, too, there was plenty of bargaining. A fellow said, "Give
me for two cents plain," and as the man was filling the glass with
seltzer the customer said, casuallike, "Put a little on the top." This
meant syrup, of course, and yet it did not mean the extra penny.
You did not say, "Give me a raspberry soda." It was all in the
way you said it, nonchalantly and in a sort of deprecating tone,
"Put a little on the top." It meant that you were saving the fellow
the trouble of even stirring the glass. Well, the man had already
filled the glass with seltzer and what could he do with it unless
you paid for it? So he "put a little on the top" but not the next
time if he could help it. Often he would take the two cents first
and give you a glass of plain. "I know my customers," he'd say.
The man who had the stand on our corner was an elderly gent,
"Benny," and once when I was playing around his counter, one
of his jars fell down and the syrup got all over me. Every time I
came near Benny's stand after that he took extra precautions; "Go
way hard luck," he always said to me. Benny wore a coat he had   *away bad luck*
brought from Europe and it reached down to his ankles. He would
take a handful of that coat, feel it a while, and tell you whether
it was going to rain the next day. People came from blocks around
to get a weather forecast from Benny and his coat. He rarely missed.

20   And so you can hardly blame the young boy, the eating-days
boy, when he quit the table of those home-cooked meals and went
down into this world of pleasures and joys.

**Discussion
Points**

1. Explain what tempted many of the rabbinical "eating-days" boys from continuing their religious studies.
2. What does Golden mean by "America was too great and too wonderful"?
3. When Golden was an adult, why was his relative afraid of embarrassing Golden on their walk on Lower Broadway?
4. What was Golden's reaction to his old neighborhood?
5. Describe the author's attitude toward the old days he portrays in this essay.

Composition Topics

Compose a two-page paper on one of the following themes:

1. Golden notes that women did not used to smoke in public. Detail a custom or habit that used to be either male-only or female-only in your society. Refer to any controversy that surrounded the transition.
2. Describe the temptations of a new cultural environment to young newcomers in your home country. Compare and contrast these with the ones featured in "For Two Cents Plain."
3. With your own impressions of the United States, elaborate on the author's reference that "America was too great and too wonderful."

Research Ideas

In order to grasp more fully the essence of "For Two Cents Plain," select one of these subject areas on which to prepare a background report:

1. Harry Golden
2. Jewish Immigration to the U.S.: Early Twentieth Century
3. Orthodox Jewish Dietary Laws
4. Rabbinical Studies

CHAPTER 7

◆ *Jackie Robinson: Each Game*
Was a Crusade

BY MARK HARRIS

About the Author:
MARK HARRIS
(1922–)

Born in New York, Mark Harris has been a professor of English for many years. He has combined his special interest in social history with his particular enthusiasm for baseball to produce outstanding pieces for magazines and prize-winning longer works. Publications by Harris include *The Southpaw* (1953), *Bang the Drum Slowly* (1956, and made into a movie in the 1970s), *Mark the Glove Boy, or The Last Days of Richard Nixon* (1964), *Killing Everybody* (1973), *Best Father Ever Invented* (an autobiography, 1976), *Short Work of It* (collection of articles, 1979), and *Lying in Bed* (1984).

Setting the Scene

Organized American baseball originated in 1869, just four years after the end of the bitter Civil War.[1] The absence of black players in big-league baseball became a tradition. Toward the end of the nineteenth century, only rarely had a black player entered this professional sports scene, but the strong racism that prevailed made such an appearance short-lived. By the 1920s, black players were resigned to this socioeconomic barrier; consequently, they began exhibiting their athletic skills in their own Negro leagues. One such player was Jack Roosevelt Robinson, shortstop for the Kansas City (Kansas) Monarchs.

Pre-Reading Considerations

1. Have you ever experienced discrimination in either the work world or a social context?
2. Do you have a friend who, despite high qualifications, has been denied opportunity on account of social bias?

---

[1] Civil War: (1861–1865) conflict between the North and the South (U.S.) over the issue of slavery

Jackie Robinson: Each Game Was a Crusade
MARK HARRIS

1   Sometimes on summer television when I watch a black fellow come to bat during somebody's Game of the Day or Night or Week, I wonder how much he knows about a recent fellow named Jackie Robinson.

2   Who was Jackie Robinson? I wondered if my students at the University of Pittsburgh knew, so I asked them to scribble me a little answer to the question, "What does the name 'Jackie Robinson' mean to you?" For fun, try it on your own resident student. My students were born, on the average, in 1957. Some of their answers were these. "A very beautiful blonde woman I met in my dental office." "Jackie Robinson—female or male, related possible to Mrs. Robinson in the movie 'The Graduate' & in the song 'Mrs. Robinson' by Simon & Garfunkel.[1] Or is it a baseball player? A musician? I'm guessing."

3   Yes, baseball player, **getting warm**. Who was Jackie Robinson? "I thought of a boxer," one student wrote. Another: "He might be a baseball player or a numbers runner."[2] My one black student wrote: "Jackie Robinson is a baseball player. This is a real person, in fact, he played on a baseball team. Not sure what the team was." *approaching the correct answer*

4   The most nearly correct answer was this: "All I know (think) is he's the first black man to play major-league[3] baseball—broke the color barrier."[4]

5   **Take nothing for granted.** Hey, you, batter, twirling that stick, spitting that nifty spit (never TV's most appetizing moment), what does the name "Jackie Robinson" mean to you? *Do not assume anything.*

6   In ancient 1947,[5] Robinson, male, a baseball player, a real person, became the first black man to play big-league baseball, and a lonesome figure he was. In 1947 we had sixteen major-league baseball teams, and every player on every team was white and **that was that**. Except for Robinson, who played first base for the (then) Brooklyn Dodgers[6] of the National League. *there was no exception to this*

---

[1] Simon & Garfunkel: Paul Simon (1942–   ) and Art Garfunkel (1942–   ), pop and folk-singing duo of the 1960s and 1970s; now they perform individually.

[2] numbers runner: person acting for bettors on the numbers game (lottery based on published numbers); illegal at that time

[3] major-league: the most important baseball organization of teams

[4] broke the color barrier: was the first of the traditionally excluded race to be accepted by the predominating racial group

[5] ancient 1947: sarcastic reference to the contemporary student's perspective of history

[6] the (then) Brooklyn Dodgers: This team moved its permanent base to Los Angeles in 1958, when its name was changed to the Los Angeles Dodgers.

---

7   If some people had **had their way** he would have been not   *had the power to*
only the first but the last. The fact that those people did not have   *impose their*
their way is due in large part to Robinson's interior fortitude. But   *preference*
he could also hit and run and field with superior skill at several
positions. He had played in four sports at UCLA.[7] He soon became
not only an outstanding player but the spiritual leader of his own
group (the Dodgers) and a dreaded opponent of all the other
groups (the other teams of the National League), whose spirits he
often destroyed with his daring and his surprises.

8   Robinson had been specially selected by Branch Rickey for the
pioneer work he did. Rickey, the Dodger's president, was one of
baseball's shrewdest innovators. He had invented the minor-league
"farm system" by which big-league organizations developed and
nurtured talented young players. Now he was to embark upon a
second major innovation: the introduction of black players into
organized baseball. The first black player would need to be an
extraordinary human being. He would suffer anguish and abuse
throughout the cities of the league. The shock of Robinson's
presence would not be **cushioned** in a day.   *soothed, relieved*

9   In 1946, when Robinson was signed to a contract by the
Brooklyn organization, a sportswriter in St. Louis assured me that
neither Robinson nor any other Negro (that was the proper word
then)[8] would ever play baseball against the Cardinals. But after
an extremely productive season in Montreal, which was (then) in
the International League, Robinson *did* play baseball — for the
Dodgers, against the Cardinals, who at first refused to **take the**   *get into position to*
field. When **at length** the St. Louis players obeyed the order of   *begin the game /*
(then) National League president Ford Frick to play or be punished,   *finally*
baseball and America had arrived at a new moment.

10   In his first game for Montreal, Robinson hit one home run and
three singles, stole two bases, scored four runs. It was only the
beginning. He was to be remembered finally, however, not for
statistics alone but for incalculable moments when he won baseball
games in ways that never enter the box score. He played several
positions afield, and he was several persons at the bat; he could
hit long balls and he could bunt. He could hit to left or right.
He could run very fast and stop very short. He could feint, and
he could feint feinting.

11   He took long, careless leads off base, forcing opposition pitchers
into foolish errors. Since he was not only powerful but frequently
enraged, he often inflicted injury upon other players in skirmishes
along the base paths. His power was sustained by a mission not
only personal but historic. Every game, every event, was in the
interest of Robinson, of the Dodgers, and of Robinson's

[7] UCLA: the University of California at Los Angeles
[8] that was the proper word then: Negro was the accepted term until the mid 1950s; thereafter,
  Black was the correct term (Afro-American was also popular in the 1970s).

equalitarian interpretation of the United States Constitution.[9]
During **warm-up** for an exhibition game in New Orleans he once *pregame practice*
took time to condemn the black fans when they cheered because
a new section of grandstand was opened to them: in Robinson's
view, their expanded location was not a gift but a *right*.

12 He pursued every moment to its absolute end. Possibly nothing
can describe him better than his almost unwitnessed action on
that famous day, Oct. 3, 1951, when the New York Giants defeated
the Dodgers in the final play-off game[10] following a pennant race[11]
that had been breathlessly contested for weeks. It was the ninth
inning. The Dodgers were leading by two runs, but the Giants
had two men on base, and Bobby Thomson was at the bat.
Thomson soon stroked a home run more electrifying, more
memorable than almost any home run ever struck.

13 On the field the Giants leaped and tumbled with inexpressible
joy. The Dodgers ran dejected and ruined to their privacy.
Thousands upon thousands of fans screamed with ecstacy, other
thousands upon thousands wept—and Jackie Robinson followed
Bobby Thomson with his eyes to be sure that Thomson touched
every base.[12] He never stopped playing.

14 What if the Robinson experiment had failed? Nobody will ever
know whether the thing that succeeded was good old-fashioned
liberal tradition[13] in its most happy manifestation, or whether the
thing that succeeded was old-fashioned **dollar pragmatism**. Rob- *profit motive*
inson was a winner, and Brooklyn loved a winner, even if he was
black. One winner **drew** a second, and so forth, and their names *led to*
were Campanella, Black, Newcombe, Gilliam,[14] and they were
black, and they all played for Brooklyn during the decade 1947–
1956, when the Dodgers won six pennants.

15 In the American League the Cleveland Indians with a black
outfielder named Larry Doby won the pennant in 1948. Doby was
the first black *American* League player at a time when I could
count on my fingers all the black players. As time passed, my
fingers were unable to keep up.[15]

16 It began with Robinson, Brooklyn, 1947—and radio. In those
days—my diary always tells it this way—"I listened to the ball
game." In 1950 I more and more "watched the ball game," and
anyone could see that the hitter's head or the pitcher's head was

[9] United States Constitution: legal framework established in 1787 to govern the U.S.A.
[10] play-off game: final game to determine the pennant winner in their league
[11] pennant race: competition to win the pennant, a flag symbolizing league championship, the prerequisite to entering the World Series competition
[12] touched every base: while running around the baseball diamond, made sure to contact every one of the four bases
[13] liberal tradition: standing for the protection of individual and civil liberties
[14] Roy Campanella (1921–), Joe Black (1924–), Don Newcombe (1926–) and Jim Gilliam (1928–1978)
[15] my fingers were unable to keep up: the number of black players increased

the size of the screen itself, and sometimes black. It was color television.

17   Thus the generation of my students, born in 1957 and propped at an early age in front of the **tube** for the Game of the Day or Night or Year, must have believed from infancy that baseball players had always come in two colors. One never imagined that any such person existed who could be described as "the first black player" any more than anyone could name the first white player. The players came with the game, like artificial turf, the World Series[16] at night, the umpires whose names one never knew, the announcers heard but seldom seen, and the instrument of television itself, even as Adam and Eve[17] had seen it on **Opening Day.** *television set*

first day

18   The appearance of Robinson and the consciousness he raised among athletes quickened thinking and hastened expectations upon many topics **apart from** race. He broke more than the color barrier. Robinson meant not only to play the game equally with all Americans but to sleep equally in hotels, and he rallied other black players, often to their discomfort, for they sometimes said to him, "Jackie, we like it here, don't rock the boat."[18] But he had already rocked it **climbing in**, and the spirit of reform was contagious. White players joined black players to demand unprecedented rights through union organization and other forms of professional representation. *besides*

entering Major League baseball

19   Their ultimate achievement was freedom from the "reserve clause" in players' contracts. In the past, this clause gave the baseball organization or "club" exclusive rights to the players' services. Simply stated, a player was deprived of the opportunity to seek another employer, and therefore he was effectively denied the opportunity to bargain for his own wage. Players now won the right to be "free agents," to own themselves. The odd resemblance of the "reserve clause" to features of black slavery was remote in quality but similar in outline.

20   So complete, so thorough have been the ultimate effects of this chapter of social evolution that we have difficulty today in distinguishing differences of attitude, if any, between the white and black players. From the distant grandstand skin colors merge, nor does anything we see on television **betray** the ideal of interracial peace. *contradict*

21   Robinson made his impact upon literature, too, for when he **stirred** controversy the game attracted renewed interest among educated classes who could now view the game as both frivolous and meaningful. We have had more serious literature about baseball *caused*

---

[16] World Series: the season-end culminating competition between the two major leagues' respective winning teams

[17] Adam and Eve: according to some theologies, the first two humans created by God

[18] don't rock the boat: Don't go against tradition because it might cause unpleasant reactions.

during the last thirty years than ever before. For myself, Robinson's advent in 1947 inspired my renewed interest in the game. I soon began the first of my baseball novels (*The Southpaw*, 1953), whose heroes include a black second baseman modeled on Robinson and bearing his number 42.

left-handed pitcher

22   After his playing career ended, Robinson might have become the game's first black manager, but he had never been a truly lovable company man.[19] The **front office** rejected him. He entered other business, and he **made gestures toward** politics, but his timing failed, as it never had in baseball; he supported Nixon in 1960, when Kennedy won; and he supported Rockefeller for the 1964 Republican nomination, when Goldwater won.

decision-making administrators / tried to enter

23   Family tragedy struck. In 1971 one of his sons, at 24, was killed in an automobile mishap at the end of a long, winning fight against heroin and unspeakable memories of battle in Vietnam.

24   Robinson's own health failed swiftly thereafter. Red Smith[20] wrote: "At 53 Jackie Robinson was sick of body, white of hair. He had survived one heart attack, he had diabetes and high blood pressure and he was going blind."

25   A good deal of my own perception of Robinson's character and historic uniqueness I gleaned from Roger Kahn's wonderful book, *The Boys of Summer*. When Robinson died, October 24, 1972, Kahn was quoted in the papers. Someone asked him what Jackie Robinson had done for his race. Kahn, a white man, beautifully replied, "His race was humanity, and he did a great deal for us."

Discussion Points

1. Explain the purpose of Harris's classroom question about Jackie Robinson. Interpret the results.
2. How does the author analyze Robinson's success in combating negative social pressure?
3. Who was Branch Rickey and what were his contributions to baseball?
4. Discuss Robinson's historic and personal mission.
5. Define Robinson's "equalitarian" interpretation of the U.S. Constitution.
6. Explain Robinson's negative reaction to the cheering black spectators at the New Orleans exhibition game warm-up.
7. Differentiate between the contrasting motives of "old-fashioned liberal tradition" and "old-fashioned dollar pragmatism."
8. What does Harris mean in paragraph 15 when he writes, "my fingers were unable to keep up"?
9. In what areas did Robinson intend to break the color barrier?
10. Define the "reserve clause" in sports contracts. How does Harris equate this player-team relationship with slavery?

[19] company man: a worker loyal to his/her employer
[20] Red Smith: Walter Wellesley Smith (1905–1982), *The New York Times* newspaper sportswriter

11. Discuss Robinson's political timing.
12. Interpret Roger Kahn's quoted reaction to a question about Jackie Robinson's contributions.

Composition Topics

Choose one of the following topics on which to compose a two-page paper:

1. From your country's sports history, consider a prominent figure who, like Jackie Robinson, broke a social or political barrier in order to further his or her career. Elaborate upon the hardships and achievements experienced by this individual.

2. Jackie Robinson overcame many obstacles in his lifetime, and yet it was his son's untimely death which contributed to his own premature demise. How have personal tragedy and resulting grief played a devastating role in the life of someone you know? Depict both the tragic event and its impact on the person you have in mind.

3. Visualize yourself as a university professor fifteen years from now. What questions about events or public figures — not necessarily in the sports world — would you ask your students? Would you expect them to be knowledgeable about these references? Fully explain your choices and the responses of your future students.

Research Ideas

In order to gain more knowledge about the subject matter in "Jackie Robinson: Each Game Was a Crusade," prepare a two-page research paper on one of these topics:

1. Blacks in Baseball
2. New York Dodgers
3. Race Relations in American Sports
4. Branch Rickey
5. Jackie Robinson

CHAPTER 8

◆ *Anglo vs. Chicano: Why?*

BY ARTHUR L. CAMPA

About the Author:
ARTHUR L. CAMPA (1905–1978)

Arthur Leon Campa was born in Mexico to missionary parents. In the United States, he distinguished himself as a public school and university teacher, a writer and a diplomat. Campa taught modern languages at the University of Denver (Colorado). He also served as cultural attaché in several U.S. embassies in Latin America. Hispanic folklore was a subject of great interest to Campa, and the following works by him reflect that interest: *Hispanic Culture in the Southwest* (1979), *Sayings and Riddles in New Mexico* (1982), *Spanish Religious Folktheatre in the Southwest* (Second Series, 1982), and *Treasure of the Sangre De Cristos: Tales and Traditions of the Spanish Southwest* (1984).

Setting the Scene

The Americas were explored and settled by representatives from various European nations, and the author of this essay delves into the cultural backgrounds and differences of two of them: the English and the Spaniards. Dating from the 1960s, "Anglos" (narrowly, those descending from England, but popularly meaning all non-Hispanic Whites) and "Chicanos" (Mexican Americans) have been the terms used to designate the two predominant groups living in the southwestern part of the U.S. By using "vs." in his essay title, Campa sets up a contrastive relationship between the two populations. In this piece, the writer details many of the perspectives that differentiate Chicanos from Anglos.

Pre-Reading Considerations

1. What is your definition of individualism? How is individualism manifested in your society?
2. Which is more valued in your culture — being or doing?
3. Is materialism highly regarded in your country?

Anglo vs. Chicano: Why?

ARTHUR L. CAMPA

1   The cultural differences between Hispanic and Anglo-American people have been dwelt upon by so many writers that we should all be well informed about the values of both. But audiences are usually of the same **persuasion** as the speakers, and those who consult published works are for the most part specialists looking for affirmation of what they believe. So, let us consider the same subject, exploring briefly some of the basic cultural differences that cause conflict in the Southwest, where Hispanic and Anglo-American cultures meet.

opinion or background

2   Cultural differences are implicit in the conceptual content of the languages of these two civilizations, and their value systems **stem from** a long series of historical circumstances. Therefore, it may be well to consider some of the English and Spanish cultural configurations before these Europeans set foot on American soil. English culture was basically insular, geographically and ideologically; was more integrated **on the whole**, except for some strong theological differences; and was particularly zealous of its racial purity. Spanish culture was peninsular, a geographical circumstance that made it a catch-all of Mediterranean, central European and north African peoples. The composite nature of the population produced a marked regionalism that prevented close integration, except for religion, and led to a strong sense of individualism. These differences were reflected in the colonizing enterprise of the two cultures. The English isolated themselves from the Indians physically and culturally; the Spanish, who had strong notions about *pureza de sangre* [purity of blood] among the nobility, were not collectively averse to adding one more strain to their **racial cocktail**. Cortés[1] led the way by siring the first *mestizo*[2] in North America, and the rest of the **conquistadores followed suit**. The ultimate products of these two orientations meet **today** in the Southwest.

derive from

overall

racial composition

(Sp.) conquerors/ followed his example / in present times

3   Anglo-American culture was absolutist at the onset; that is, all the dominant values were considered identical for all, regardless of time and place. Such values as justice, charity, honesty were considered the superior social order for all men and were later embodied in the American Constitution.[3] The Spaniard brought with him a relativistic viewpoint and saw fewer moral implications

---

[1] Cortés: Hernán (Hernando), 1485–1547; Spanish conqueror of Mexico
[2] *mestizo* (Sp.): a person of mixed Spanish and Native American ancestry (Native American is synonymous with American Indian here.)
[3] American Constitution: legal framework established in 1787 to govern the U.S.A.

---

in man's actions. Values were looked upon as the result of social and economic conditions.

4 The motives that brought Spaniards and Englishmen to America also differed. The former came on an enterprise of discovery, searching for a new route to India initially, and later for new lands to conquer, the fountain of youth,[4] minerals, the Seven Cities of Cíbola[5] and, in the case of the missionaries, new souls to win for the Kingdom of Heaven.[6] The English came to escape religious persecution, and once having found a haven, they settled down to cultivate the soil and establish their homes. Since the Spaniards were not seeking a refuge or running away from anything, they continued their explorations and circled the globe 25 years after the discovery of the New World.

5 This peripatetic tendency of the Spaniard may be accounted for in part by the fact that he was the product of an equestrian culture. Men on foot do not venture far into the unknown. It was almost a century after the landing on Plymouth Rock[7] that Governor Alexander Spotswood of Virginia crossed the Blue Ridge Mountains,[8] and it was not until the nineteenth century that the Anglo-Americans began to move west of the **Mississippi**. *a U.S. river*

6 The Spaniard's equestrian role meant that he was not close to the soil, as was the Anglo-American pioneer, who tilled the land and built the greatest agricultural industry in history. The Spaniard cultivated the land only when he had Indians available to do it for him. The uses to which the horse was put also varied. The Spanish horse was essentially a mount, while the more robust English horse was used in cultivating the soil. It is therefore not surprising that the viewpoints of these two cultures should differ when we consider that the pioneer is looking at the world at the level of his eyes while the *caballero* [horseman] is looking beyond and down at the rest of the world.

7 One of the most commonly quoted, and often misinterpreted, characteristics of Hispanic peoples is the deeply ingrained individualism in all walks of life. Hispanic individualism is a revolt against the incursion of collectivity, strongly asserted when it is felt that the ego is being **fenced in**. This attitude leads to a deficiency in *suppressed* those social qualities based on collective standards, an attitude that Hispanos do not consider negative because it manifests a

---

[4] the fountain of youth: legendary body of water said to restore one's youth; located in Bimini of the Bahama Islands

[5] the Seven Cities of Cíbola: According to legend, these were located in the southwestern part of the U.S. and said to be rich in gold; they were the expected destination of numerous expeditions.

[6] Kingdom of Heaven: Biblical reference to the dwelling place of God and of the blessed dead

[7] Plymouth Rock: where the early settlers (Pilgrims) are said to have landed on the Massachusetts coast

[8] Blue Ridge Mountains: part of the Appalachian Mountains that extend from Pennsylvania to Georgia

measure of resistance to standardization in order to achieve a
measure of individual freedom. Naturally, such an attitude has no
reglas fijas [fixed rules].

8   Anglo-Americans who achieve **a measure of** success and security
through institutional guidance not only **do not mind** a few fixed
rules but demand them. The lack of a concerted plan of action,
whether in business or in politics, appears unreasonable to Anglo-
Americans. They have a sense of individualism, but they achieve
it through action and self-determination. Spanish individualism is
based on feeling, on something that is the result not of rules and
collective standards but of a person's momentary, emotional
reaction. And it **is subject to** change when the mood changes.
In contrast to Spanish emotional individualism, the Anglo-American strives for objectivity when choosing a course of action or
making a decision.

some

*do not resent or
dislike*

may

9   The Southwestern Hispanos voiced strong objections to the lack
of courtesy of the Anglo-Americans when they first met them in
the early days of the Santa Fe trade. The same accusation is **leveled
at** the *Americanos* today in many quarters of the Hispanic world.
Some of this results from their different conceptions of polite
behavior. Here too one can say that the Spanish have no *reglas
fijas* because for them courtesy is simply an expression of the way
one person feels towards another. To some they extend the hand,
to some they bow and for the more *íntimos* there is the well-
known **abrazo**. The concepts of "good or bad" or "right and wrong"
in polite behavior are moral considerations of an absolutist culture.

directed toward

*(Sp.) very close
friends, relatives /
(Sp.) hug*

10   Another cultural contrast appears in the way both cultures share
part of their material substance with others. The pragmatic Anglo-
American contributes regularly to such institutions as the Red
Cross, the United Fund[9] and a myriad of associations. He also
establishes **foundations** and quite often leaves **millions** to such
institutions. The Hispano prefers to give his contribution directly
to the recipient so that he can see the person he is helping.

*philanthropic
organizations /
of dollars*

11   A century of association has inevitably acculturated both
Hispanos and Anglo-Americans **to some extent**, but there still
persist a number of culture traits that neither group has relinquished
altogether. Nothing is more disquieting to an Anglo-American
who believes that time is money than the time perspective of
Hispanos. They usually refer to this attitude as the "*mañana*
psychology." Actually, it is more of a "today psychology," because
Hispanos cultivate the present to the exclusion of the future;
because the latter has not arrived yet, it is not a reality. They are
reluctant to relinquish the present, so they hold on to it until it
becomes the past. To an Hispano, nine is nine until it is ten, so
when he arrives at nine-thirty, he jubilantly exclaims: "*¡Justo!*"
[right on time]. This may be why the clock is slowed down to a

somewhat

(Sp.) tomorrow

---

[9] Red Cross, United Fund: charities

walk[10] in Spanish while in English it runs. In the United States, our future-oriented civilization plans our lives so far in advance that the present loses its meaning. January magazine issues [including **ID's**] are out in December; 1973 cars have been out since October; cemetery plots and even funeral arrangements are bought on the installment plan.[11] To a person engrossed in living today the very idea of planning his funeral sounds like **the tolling of the bells**.

issue dates

signals of death

12   It is a natural corollary that a person who is present oriented should be compensated by being good at improvising. An Anglo-American is told in advance to prepare for an "impromptu speech," but an Hispano usually can improvise a speech because *"Nosotros lo improvisamos todo"* [we improvise everything].

13   Another source of cultural conflict arises from the difference between *being* and *doing*. Even when trying to be individualistic, the Anglo-American achieves it by what he does. **Today's** young generation decided to be themselves, to get away from standardization, so they let their hair grow, wore ragged clothes and even went barefoot in order to be different from the Establishment.[12] As a result they all **ended up doing** the same things and created another stereotype. The freedom **enjoyed by** the individuality of *being* makes it unnecessary for Hispanos to strive to be different.

of the 1960s

finally did
experienced in

14   In 1963 a team of psychologists from the University of Guadalajara in Mexico and the University of Michigan compared 74 upper-middle-class students from each university. Individualism and personalism were found to be central values for the Mexican students. This was explained by saying that a Mexican's value as a person lies in his *being* rather than, as is the case of the Anglo-American, in concrete accomplishments. Efficiency and accomplishments are derived characteristics that do not affect worthiness in the Mexican, whereas in the American it is equated with success, a value of highest priority in the American culture. Hispanic people disassociate themselves from material things or from actions that may impugn a person's sense of being, but the Anglo-American shows great concern for material things and assumes responsibility for his actions. This is expressed in the language of each culture. In Spanish one says *"Se me cayó la taza"* [the cup fell away from me] instead of "I dropped the cup."

15   In English, one speaks of money, cash and all related transactions with frankness because material things of this high order do not trouble Anglo-Americans. In Spanish such materialistic concepts are circumvented by referring to cash as *efectivo* [effective]

[10] the clock is slowed down to a walk: This is the linguistic commentary on the Spanish expression that is equivalent to the English "the clock *runs*" (not walks).

[11] installment plan: procedure of paying a small amount of the price at specified intervals until the item is completely paid off (instead of paying the total price at the time of purchase)

[12] the Establishment: reference to the government and the customs and traditions that are practiced at a particular time in history

and when buying or selling as something *al contado* [counted out], and when without it by saying *No tengo fondos* [I have no funds]. This disassociation from material things is what produces *sobriedad* [sobriety] in the Spaniard according to Miguel de Unamuno,[13] but in the Southwest the disassociation from materialism leads to *dejadez* [lassitude] and *desprendimiento* [disinterestedness]. A man may lose his life defending his honor but is unconcerned about the lack of material things. *Desprendimiento* causes a man to spend his last cent on a friend, which when added to lack of concern for the future may mean that tomorrow he will eat beans as a result of today's binge.

16   The implicit differences in words that appear to be identical in meaning are astonishing. Versatile is a compliment in English and an insult in Spanish. An Hispano student who is told to apologize cannot do it, because the word doesn't exist in Spanish. *Apología* means words in praise of a person. The Anglo-American either apologizes, which is form of retraction abhorrent in Spanish, or compromises, another concept foreign to Hispanic culture. *Compromiso* means a date, not a compromise. In colonial Mexico City, two **hidalgos** once entered a narrow street from opposite *(Sp.) noblemen, gentlemen* sides, and when they could not go around, they sat in their coaches for three days until the viceroy ordered them to back out. All this because they could not **work out** a compromise. *agree upon*

17   It was that way then and to some extent now. Many of today's conflicts in the Southwest have their roots in polarized cultural differences, which need not be irreconcilable when approached with mutual respect and understanding.

Discussion Points

1. How did Spain's and England's geographical settings influence their respective views on race relations? Explain how they manifested this difference in the New World.
2. Compare the explore-and-conquer motivations of the English and the Spaniards.
3. Discuss the role of the horse in English and Spanish societies. Explain how this distinction affected their respective settlement patterns.
4. Describe the methods Chicanos and Anglos use in giving charity. Supply reasons for these differences.
5. Define individualism according to the Hispano and Anglo cultures. Give examples to illustrate both viewpoints.
6. Campa refers to the contrast between doing and being. Define and exemplify both in the context of this essay.

---

[13] Miguel de Unamuno: (1864–1936), Spanish philosopher and writer

7. Materialism and financial matters are considered differently by the Anglo and the Chicano. Explain these distinctions and compare your own philosophy about materialism to theirs.
8. What is the so-called "*mañana* psychology"? Is this term an accurate one? Clarify your answer.
9. How do Chicanos and Anglos relate to time? Interpret how their disparate views affect relationships between them.
10. The author devotes the closing portion of his essay to psycholinguistic references (how language reflects the psychology of its speakers). Cite two such vocabulary items of this section and interpret how they represent culture.

Composition Topics

Select one of the following themes on which to write a two-page paper:

1. At the opening of this selection, the author asserts that persons prefer to listen to speakers whose opinions they share. Consider the speeches you have recently attended voluntarily, and assess how your views compare with those of the speakers.
2. The essay explains how Spain's and England's geographical positions have historically influenced their respective outlooks. Relate your country's physical setting to its cultural and/or political perspectives.
3. Chicano and Anglo concepts of individualism differ. Provide your personal definition of individualism, and compare it to theirs. Illustrate your definition with anecdotal examples.
4. Campa writes of the contrast between being and doing. Begin your composition by depicting the Anglo and Chicano perspectives as the author regards them. Then present your own notions of this dichotomy.
5. Time perspective is one of the points of contrast brought out by Campa. Describe the relationship of the Anglo and the Chicano to time. Mention whether your concept of time agrees with either of these.

Research Ideas

To provide you with a greater appreciation for the cultural and historical themes that underlie "Anglo vs. Chicano: Why?" prepare a two-page report on one of the following related research subjects:

1. Chicano Culture
2. English Exploration of the New World
3. English Settlements in the United States
4. Hispanic Settlements in the United States
5. Individualism
6. Materialism
7. Spanish Exploration in the New World
8. Time Perspective

PART II

American Introspection

"Non Stop" by Anne Waldman (1945–   ) sets the tone for Part II: overall emphasis on the negative things in life, with specific aim at the American political scene. Waldman alludes to her own physical malaise as she perceives the destructive forces around her: Fascism, air and noise pollution, and "cat doo doo." Despite the pessimism she portrays in her poem, Waldman does reveal her optimistic side—she gets up, brushes her teeth, and washes before facing the new day . . . and she returns to the media coverage of that year's election. Like "Non Stop," the eight essays of Part II are critical of society, yet express hope for an improved future.

Non Stop
ANNE WALDMAN

Today is a terrible day for the nation
                          I don't feel like getting up
                                          this morning
I'm a grouch
                I have a headache
                                    I hate the world
                                                  Fascism
              air pollution   cat doo doo[1]
                                      noise
        But I get up anyway to stretch
                                brush teeth
                              wash
                  turn on TV faces   turn on radio voices
                          get election returns[2] horrors

[1] feces
[2] voting results

CHAPTER 9

◆ *Children of Vietnam*

BY SHANA ALEXANDER

About the Author:
SHANA
ALEXANDER
(1925–   )

During her celebrated career, Shana Alexander has been a lecturer, an editor, a journalist, an author, and a radio and television commentator. For her journalistic writings, she has received several professional awards. In addition to countless magazine articles and media essays, Alexander has authored the following: *The Feminine Eye* (1970), *Talking Woman* (1976), *Anyone's Daughter* (1979), *Nutcracker: Money, Madness, Murder, A Family Album* (1986), and *The Pizza Connection: Lawyers, Money, Drugs, Mafia* (1988).

Setting the Scene

In the 1950s, the United States found itself involved in a civil conflict being waged in Vietnam, a nation in Southeast Asia. At that time, only our military advisers were sent to assist the South Vietnamese in their strategy against their northern adversaries. But by 1964, American combat troops were also assigned to that war-torn country. The battling continued until early 1973, when peace was negotiated. In the years that American military personnel were stationed in Vietnam, inevitable socializing with the local civilian population took place. A regrettable consequence of this fraternization was the birth of illegitimate children fathered by U.S. soldiers. Shana Alexander addresses the plight of these Amerasian children in "Children of Vietnam."

An historical footnote to this essay was the release of sixty-five of those Amerasians on December 31, 1987, under Vietnam's Orderly Departure Program. They were to undergo English language and American culture training in the Philippines for about one year before entering the U.S. At that time, it was reported that an estimated twelve thousand additional part-Americans still remained in Vietnam.

Pre-Reading Considerations

1. What is your knowledge of the conduct of soldiers abroad during wartime?
2. Do you believe that the father of an illegitimate child has a responsibility toward that child? Moral? Financial?

Children of Vietnam
SHANA ALEXANDER

1   The American prisoners of war continue coming home. Each night on TV they recapture the national imagination: a parade of lean, grinning men seized up in wild family embraces. These repeating images of rejoicing and reunion have immense symbolic **weight**. They help appease the insatiable appetite all Americans feel just now to somehow come together as a nation once again. *significance*

2   Yet in the midst of great national rejoicing, agony over amnesty tears us apart. Some of us demand "justice" in the name of Vietnam's thousands of injured and dead; others urge forgiveness and reconciliation. Parent is set against parent, son against son. Some cannot forget, some cannot forgive, and all our sensibilities are rubbed raw.

3   We all make mistakes, says the President[1] magisterially. But we must be made to pay for those mistakes. Evenhandedness is perceived in the White House as next-to-Godliness;[2] mercy is a sign of weakness.

4   Vice-President Agnew[3] blames the **hue and cry** over amnesty on the antiwar people's need for "a new issue to shout about." The Vice-President accuses the news media of magnifying this shouting disproportionately. But to blame the media for the amnesty uproar makes no more sense than did the ancient practice of killing the messenger who brought the bad news to the King. It is not the media but our own **sandpapered** sensibilities to morality and justice that make the amnesty issue feel so raw. If anything, the media have attempted to soothe these sensibilities. *public protest*   *exposed, raw*

5   The other day, CBS[4] canceled the telecast of *Sticks and Bones*, a fine, bitter play by David Rabe about the homecoming of a blinded Vietnam veteran, **on the ground that** Rabe's subject matter might be too "abrasive" just now. It is this playwright's talent first to make you smile at Middle America's[5] family foibles, and then to **ram** that smile down your throat, and I wish that *Sticks and Bones*, which a year ago won a top prize on Broadway,[6] could receive the broad national audience it deserves. Good drama *should* **sandpaper** the mind. Still, the network is right that the nation's attention is "emotionally dominated" just now by the images of returning **POW's** and others who have suffered the ravages of war. *because*   *force*   *gnaw at*   *prisoners of war*

[1] President: Richard Milhous Nixon (1913–), U.S. president from 1969–74
[2] next-to-Godliness: nearly as virtuous as Godliness (being a firm believer in God)
[3] Agnew: Spiro (1918–), vice president from 1969-73
[4] CBS: Columbia Broadcasting System television network
[5] Middle America: average middle class citizens
[6] Broadway: theatre district in New York City; name of a street in this area

6   In thinking about amnesty, it helps somewhat to remember the meaning of the word: not to forgive, but to forget. It is a plea not for absolution but for amnesia. My dictionary calls it "an act of oblivion . . . reconcilement and passing over that which is passed."

7   I'm not sure whether 100 per cent forgiveness is any more possible to achieve than 100 per cent forgetfulness, but still one must try. The difficulty is that at the same time one **longs for** *strongly desires* universal healing and forgetting, it is impossible to deny the bewildered rage and impotent anguish of those other Americans who grope the ashes of war seeking some "fairness" and "justice" at long last.

8   While I agree that it may have taken as much or more courage to resist this war on moral grounds as it did to fight in it, I also agree that to now invite home the tens of thousands of men who have fled the country or gone **underground** seems to mock those *into hiding* thousands of others who sacrificed all their freedom and even their lives. Finally, as a practical matter, even supposing all the **draft** *evaders of military* **dodgers** and deserters could be **rounded up**, how could we possibly *service / located,* **sort out** the idealists from the opportunists, the brave from the *apprehended /* cowardly? *separate*

9   It helps, too, in thinking about amnesty, to weigh another responsibility, another sad legacy of war. While we struggle to forget, or to forgive our older children for what they did or failed to do, we might turn our attention to the other children whose only crime is to have been born. These others are the children fathered by American soldiers in Vietnam. Are there 15,000 or 100,000 of them? Nobody seems to know. Some relief officials[7] appear to inflate the figures to inflame world sympathy. **Whatever** *Regardless of the* **their numbers**, these children, too, are assuredly prisoners of war, *exact statistic* as well as its casualties and accidents. But these prisoners will never come home. They have no homes to come to.

10   **Journalistic old hands** in Vietnam warn newcomers away. They *Experienced* call it "the unwritable story." A British journalist reports: "Even *journalists* a 'relatively good' orphanage is chaotic, filthy, **stuffed with** children *overpopulated with* so **starved of** adult contact that the moment you step inside the *lacking* courtyard your whole lower body and legs are covered with small, exploring hands."

11   Soldiers always leave children behind, in every army. The occupation of Germany and Japan produced thousands of such children, the Korean War thousands more. Yet our government has never devised any legislation to provide for them. Rather we appear to **go to some pains** to deny that these children are our responsi- *try hard* bility.

12   The French, too, fought a bad war in Vietnam, but in the end they made some injustices of that war just. They allowed the

---

[7] relief officials: those in charge of relief assistance programs

illegitimate children of their soldiers to be brought to France to be educated, fed, clothed, and raised. The spawnings of the French Army were recognized, cared for, and given citizenship. U.S. policy toward such children, by contrast, appears to be one of **benign neglect** *unmalicious inattention* at best. They received less than one-tenth of 1 per cent of the relief funds sent to Vietnam. Thousands of them have been abandoned, left in city slums, **herded into** primitive, unfunded *collected and placed like animals in* ophanages, used as servants, or just left to die. Less than 5 per cent are adopted, due to the intricacies of Vietnamese law and to political, religious, and racial bigotries. In Southeast Asia, black is not considered beautiful at all.[8]

13   Pearl Buck,[9] who died last week, left most of her estate to the **foundation** for American-Asian children which she had herself *agency supported by donated funds* established long ago. The novelist was raised in China by missionary parents, spoke Chinese before she did English. To the end of her life, she sometimes dreamed in Chinese. Because she was the product of two cultures, and felt somewhat an outsider, a curiosity, in each, Pearl Buck once referred to herself as "mentally bifocal" — a quality more people should cultivate in themselves. She said she was drawn to the plight of these children not primarily by maternal feelings, but by some acute sensitivity to "disorder" which compelled her to try to **set it right**.   *do good, rectify*

14   While we struggle to repair the disorder at home, most Americans surely would welcome some gesture of fatherhood and responsibility to the part-American children of Vietnam.

Discussion Points

1. Explain the White House view of the policies of mercy and even-handedness during the Vietnam War years.
2. Define amnesty and discuss the controversy surrounding it.
3. Interpret Vice-President Agnew's comments regarding the media's coverage of antiwar cries for amnesty.
4. Why did a national television network cancel "Sticks and Bones"?
5. Why do you think that the author waited until midway through her essay before introducing her central concern: the part-American children abandoned by their fathers?
6. How does the French government handle its soldiers' abandoned illegitimate children? Is there a comparable American provision for this legacy of war?
7. How did novelist Pearl Buck help provide for disadvantaged Amerasian children?
8. According to the essayist, what action would the majority of Americans prefer be taken to ease the plight of the part-American children forsaken in Vietnam?

---

[8] black is not considered beautiful at all: This is an allusion to the "Black is beautiful" slogan that was popularized in the 1970s to instill pride in Black Americans.
[9] Pearl Buck: (1892–1973) American novelist

Composition Topics

Select one of these topics on which to prepare a two-page composition:

1. Present your point of view concerning the role of the media in covering a war. Give examples to illustrate your stand.
2. Write a composition indicating the pro and con sides of amnesty.
3. If you were the head of a television network, would you censor a controversial program on account of its potential effect on the audience? Explain why or why not, and give one contemporary programming example.
4. Assume that you were empowered to formulate a national policy affecting children fathered and abandoned by American soldiers in a foreign country. What would that policy be? Include a philosophical rationale for your plan.
5. Consider a philanthropic person of your country. Describe his or her charitable deeds and compare them with those of Pearl Buck.

Research Ideas

To better understand the cultural and historical underpinnings of "Children of Vietnam," select one of the following subjects on which to develop a short research paper:

1. Spiro Agnew's Part in the Vietnam War
2. Amnesty
3. Pearl Buck
4. Censorship in Television Programming
5. Richard Nixon's Role in the Vietnam War
6. Vietnamese Americans Under the Orderly Departure Program

CHAPTER **10**

◆ *Sold at Fine Stores Everywhere, Naturellement*

BY MYRNA KNEPLER

About the Author:
MYRNA KNEPLER (1934–)

Myrna Knepler is a university linguistics professor. Together with her husband, Henry Knepler, she has produced two highly respected textbooks: *Let's Talk About It* (1982) and *Crossing Cultures* (1983). She is currently writing a college English grammar guide.

Setting the Scene

Linguistic and cultural exchanges are universal, and in the United States, there is much evidence of this borrowing. In particular, there has always been a fascination in this country for the sounds and sights of the French language. Over the years, French vocabulary has filtered into American product advertising (especially perfume!). But the borrowing is not one-way. On the streets of Paris, one can observe signs heralding City Rock Cafe and Cactus Charly; some advertising Aerobics classes; and others selling Sweatshirts avec (with) American University Insignia. In her essay, Knepler comments on this reciprocal linguistic borrowing.

Pre-Reading Considerations

1. Are you aware of language borrowing that takes place between French and English?
2. What is your definition of "franglais"?
3. Is a product more appealing to you if it is advertised with French phrases?

Sold at Fine Stores Everywhere, Naturellement
MYRNA KNEPLER

1   Why is it that a high priced condominium is advertised in American newspapers as a *de luxe* apartment while French magazines try to sell their more affluent readers *appartements de grand standing?* Madison Avenue,[1] when constructing ads for high priced non-necessary items, may use French phrases to suggest to readers that they are identified as super-sophisticated, subtly sexy, and privy to the secrets of **old world** charm and tradition. In recent years French *European* magazines aimed at an increasingly affluent public have made equally canny use of borrowed English words to sell their wares.

2   The advertising pages of the *New Yorker*[2] and the more elegant fashion and home decorating magazines often depend on blatant flattery of the reader's sense of exclusiveness. **Time and time again** *Repeatedly* the reader is told "only *you* are elegant, sophisticated, discriminating and rich enough to use this product." Of course the "you" must encompass a large enough group to insure adequate sales. Foreign words, particularly prestigious French words, may be used to reinforce this selling message.

3   French magazines often use English words in their advertising to suggest to potential consumers a slightly different but equally flattering self-image. The reader is pictured as someone **in touch with** new *familiar with* ideas from home and abroad who has not forgotten the traditional French arts of living, but is modern enough to approach them in a completely up-to-date and casual manner.

4   Of course, each language has borrowed words from the other which have, **over the course of time**, been completely assimilated. *gradually* It is not these that the advertiser exploits but rather words that are foreign enough to evoke appealing images of an exotic culture. When the French reader is urged to try "Schweppes, le 'drink' des gens raffinés" or an American consumer is told that a certain manufacturer has "the *savoir faire* to design *la crème de la crème* of luxurious *(Fr.) knowledge of* silky knits," the foreign words do not say anything that could not *social behavior /* be as easily said by native ones. What they do convey is something *(Fr.) the best* else. They invite the reader to share in the prestige of the foreign

[1] Madison Avenue: in New York City, the street (district including Madison Avenue) known for its advertising agencies
[2] New Yorker: a magazine

language and the power of the images associated with that language's country of origin.

5   In each country a knowledge of the other's language is an important sign of cultivation. Today, English is the language studied by an overwhelming majority of French students, and the ability to speak it well is increasingly valued as a symbol of prestige as well as a marketable skill.[3] Despite the decrease in foreign language study in the United States, French has maintained its reputation as a language people ought to know. Adding a few obvious foreign words from the prestige language not only increases the prestige of the product itself but also flatters the reader by reminding him that he has enough linguistic talent to understand what is being said. As in the "only-*you*-are-elegant,-sophisticated,-discrimating-and-rich enough" appeal, the advertiser must be careful not to exclude too many potential customers, and the foreign expressions are usually transparent cognates or easily understood words. A French reader may be urged to buy cigarettes by being told that "partout dans le monde c'est YES á Benson and Hedges" while the *New Yorker* reader can consider a vacation on "an island [off the coast of South Carolina] where change hasn't meant commercialism, and tranquility still comes ***au naturelle.***"   *(Fr.) in its natural state*

6   Even monolinguals are not excluded from this flattery. The word can be given in the foreign language and then translated; the reader **is** still **in on** the secret; "'goût' is the French word for taste and Christofle[4] is the universal word for taste in vases."   *can share*

7   The prestige of a foreign term and its possible ambiguity for the reader may serve to disguise a negative fact about the product. A necklace of Perle de Mer advertised in an American magazine is not composed of real pearls made by nature in the seas but of simulated pearls produced by a large American manufacturer. **By the same token**, when a French advertisement for a packaged tour[5] offers "aller et retour en classe coach" the prestige of the English word *coach* disguises the fact that it is the less luxurious form of airline transportation that is being offered.   *Similarly*

8   But the most important function of borrowed words in advertising is to project an image of their country of origin in order to create for the reader the illusion that the product, and by implication its user, will share in the good things suggested by that image. French names like *Grand Prix, Coupe De Ville,* and *Monte Carlo* attached to American car models help the advertiser to **get across** the message that the car is luxurious, sophisticated, and elegantly **appointed** and   *communicate decorated*

---

[3] marketable skill: a skill that enables a person to be better qualified for a job
[4] Christofle: French manufacturer of silver-plated flatware at this time; established in 1830
[5] packaged tour: preplanned traveling arrangements

that driving such an automobile reflects positively on the taste of its potential owner. In almost all cases French names are reserved for the more expensive models while American words are favored for small meat-and-potatoes cars[6] like *Charger, Maverick, Pinto,* and *Bronco.* Similarly, the French reader **is likely to encounter** a large number of American terms in ads for appliances, radio and television equipment, cameras, and "gadgets de luxe," since the manufacturer benefits by associating American mechanical skill with his products. An advertisement for French-made hi-fi equipment appearing in a French magazine spoke of the product's "push-pull ultra linéaire, 6 haut-parleurs, 2 elliptiques et 4 tweeters . . . montés sur baffle."

will probably find

9   Images, which are used again and again, are often based on myths of the other country's culture. Words like *tomahawk* and *trading posts* are used in French advertisements to evoke images of a western-movie America[7] of naturalness, freedom, and adventure in order to sell products like "Chemise de 'cow girl,'" "bottes Far West," and vests in the style of "Arizona Bill," irrespective of the real West that is or was. The name *Monte Carlo* attached to an American-made car **trades on** the American consumer's image of a **once-exclusive** vacation spot, now available as part of low-cost travel packages. Thus the name *Monte Carlo* can convey to an automobile a prestige that the real trip to Monte Carlo has long since lost.

was chosen to appeal to / was exclusive in the past

10   Those images that are not completely mythic are usually gross stereotypes of the other country's culture. Few Americans would recognize the image of American life presented in French advertising—a new world filled with eternally youthful, glamourously casual, up-to-date men and women devoted to consuming the products of their advanced technology. Similarly, few French men and women would recognize the nation of elegant and knowing consumers of food, wine, and sophisticated sex pictured in American ads.

11   The image of France as a nation of lovers, bold yet unusually subtle in their relations with the opposite sex, is often **called upon** to sell perfume and cosmetics, sometimes of French origin but packaged and advertised specifically for the American market. An ad which appeared several years ago in the *New Yorker* showed a bottle of perfume labeled "voulez-vous" implanted next to a closeup of a sexy and elegant woman, her face shadowed by a male hand lighting her cigarette. The text: "The spark that starts the fire. Voulez-vous a new perfume." *Audace, Robe d'un Soir,* and *Je Reviens* are other perfumes advertised in American magazines with pictures and **copy** that reinforce the sexual suggestiveness of the prominently featured French name on the label.

used

wording

---

[6] meat-and-potatoes cars: affordable, middle-class cars designed for practical, daily use
[7] western-movie America: that aspect of the U.S. portrayed in "westerns," movies set in the West or Southwest and featuring the cowboy life-style

12   It may be surprising for Americans to learn that English names are given to perfumes sold in France to enhance their romantic image. *My Love, Partner,* and *Shocking* are some examples. Advertisements for French-made men's cosmetics in French magazines may refer to products such as *l'after-shave* and *le pre-shave.* Givenchy's *Gentleman* is advertised to Frenchmen as an eau de toilette for the man who dares to appear at business lunches in a turtleneck sweater and has the courage to treat love in a casual manner.

13   The recent **swelling** of the list of Americanisms used in French   *growth, increase* advertising and in French speech has pained many Frenchmen and has even caused the government to take action. For a number of years the leader in this "war against anglicisms" has been René Etiemble, a professor at the Sorbonne.[8] Etiemble, through magazine articles, radio and television appearances and his widely read book, *Parlez-vous franglais?*[9] struggles vehemently against what he most often refers to as an "invasion" of American terms. He **does little to** disguise   *does not try to* his strong anti-American sentiments. American words are rejected as agents of a vulgar American culture and both are seen as threats to the French way of life. According to Etiemble "[the] heritage of words [is the] heritage of ideas: with *le twist*[10] and *la ségrégation, la civilisation cocolcoolique,*[11] the American manner of not living will disturb and contaminate all that remains of your cuisine, wines, love and free thought." It would be difficult to find a stronger believer in the power of words than Etiemble.

14   In response to the concerns of Etiemble and others, a series of committees composed of **highly placed** French scientists and language   *reputable,* experts were charged with the task of finding Gallic equivalents for   *distinguished* such popular terms as *le meeting, le marketing, le management,* and *le know-how.* The recommended replacements are: *la réunion, la commercialisation, la direction,* and of course, *le savoir faire.* The replacements do not seem to have **taken root.**   *become accepted*

15   At the end of 1975 a more radical step was taken. The French National Assembly passed a law banning the use of all foreign words in advertising in those cases in which a native alternative has been officially suggested, and instituting a fine against violators.

16   Both Etiemble and the government purists rely strongly on the "logical" argument that most loan words are not needed because there already exists a native equivalent with exactly the same meaning. Yet a look at the advertising pages of French and American magazines will show that borrowed words are used again and again

---

[8] Sorbonne: Paris university

[9] *franglais:* mixture of French and English

[10] *le twist:* the twist; a popular dance in the 1960s

[11] *la civilisation cocolcoolique:* French equivalent of "the Pepsi generation," but the literal translation is closer to "the Coca Cola civilization"

when there are obvious native equivalents. Certainly the English words "c'est YES á Benson and Hedges" and "Le 'drink' des gens raffinés" could be translated without loss of literal meaning—but they are not.

17 It is precisely because of the connotations associated with the culture of its country of origin, not its denotations, that advertisers find the borrowed word attractive.

Discussion Points

1. In general, when do American advertisers use French words to promote their products?
2. Name several French terms that even NON-students of French might recognize.
3. Why is the French language frequently used to advertise perfume?
4. Relate the controversy that rages in France with respect to the adoption of English terms.
5. Interpret the difference between connotation and denotation, and explain this distinction in advertising.
6. Do you feel that American consumers are truly influenced by the appearance of French words in advertisements?

Composition Topics

Write a one-page theme on any of these topics:

1. Comment on the psychological reasons for including foreign vocabulary in product advertising. Give examples of those commonly borrowed and used in your country's advertising.

2. If you were assigned to promote the sale of an expensive item in your country, which English words and phrases would you utilize? Specify the product and explain your choices.
3. Detail the linguistic borrowing that appears in your native language. Include an interpretation of why this borrowing occurs.

Research Ideas

In order to better appreciate the basic issues of Knepler's essay, prepare a two-page paper on one of the following topics:

1. English in Foreign Advertising
2. Franglais
3. Language Borrowing in U.S. Advertising

CHAPTER 11

◆ Rituals at McDonald's

BY CONRAD P. KOTTAK

About the Author:
CONRAD P. KOTTAK
(1942–   )

Conrad Phillip Kottak is an anthropologist and has written textbooks in his field. Research has taken him to Madagascar, Brazil, and many regions of the United States. Currently a professor of anthropology at the University of Michigan at Ann Arbor, Kottak is editor of *Research in American Culture*. Two recent works by this author are *Researching American Culture: A Guide for Student Anthropologists* (1982) and *Madagascar: Society and History* (as editor, 1986).

Setting the Scene

Since World War II,[1] as more women have assumed jobs outside the home, eating out has become a part of the American family's life-style. With one hour as the average time allowed for lunch, if a worker does not bring food from home (commonly called a "brown bag lunch"), a fast-food restaurant becomes the worker's choice. As a result of this expanding trend, many fast-food restaurant chains have developed, and the competition among them is keen. McDonald's is one of the world's most renowned chains—it is the one with the huge golden arch as its symbol. The cuisine common to many of these fast-food places is hamburgers, french fries, chicken, milkshakes, and carbonated drinks. In more recent times, still other chains have been founded, which provide regional and ethnic specialties, such as Oriental egg rolls, Mexican tacos, and American-style Italian pizza. In "Rituals at McDonald's," Kottak analyzes the McDonald's phenomenon in detail.

Pre-Reading Considerations

1. If you had two full hours for lunch, would you choose to eat in a regular dining place or in a fast-food restaurant?
2. What would you consider to be the advantages and disadvantages of eating in a fast-food restaurant?

---

[1] World War II: ended in 1945

Rituals at McDonald's

CONRAD P. KOTTAK

1   The world is blessed each day, on the average, with the opening of a new McDonald's restaurant. They now number more than 4,000 and dot not only the United States but also such countries as Mexico, Japan, Australia, England, France, Germany, and Sweden. The expansion of this international web of franchises and company-owned outlets has been fast and efficient; a little more than twenty years ago McDonald's was limited to a single restaurant in San Bernardino, California. Now, the number of McDonald's outlets has far **outstripped** the total number of fast-food chains   *exceeded* operative in the United States thirty years ago.

2   McDonald's sales reached $1.3 billion in 1972, propelling it past Kentucky Fried chicken as the world's largest fast-food chain. It has kept this position ever since. Annual sales now exceed $3 billion. McDonald's is the nation's leading buyer of processed potatoes[1] and fish. Three hundred thousand cattle die each year as McDonald's customers **down** another three billion burgers. A   *eat* 1974 advertising budget of $60 million easily made the chain one of the country's top advertisers. Ronald McDonald,[2] our best-known purveyor of hamburgers, French fries, and milkshakes, rivals Santa Claus and Mickey Mouse as our children's most familiar fantasy character.

3   How does an anthropologist, accustomed to explaining the life styles of diverse cultures, interpret these peculiar developments and attractions that influence the daily life of so many Americans? Have factors other than low cost, taste, fast service, and cleanliness — all of which are approximated by other chains — contributed to McDonald's success? Could it be that in consuming McDonald's products and propaganda, Americans are not just eating and watching television but are experiencing something comparable in some respects to a religious ritual? A brief consideration of the nature of ritual may answer the latter question.

4   Several key features distinguish ritual from other behavior, according to anthropologist Roy Rappaport. Foremost, are formal ritual events — stylized, repetitive, and stereotyped. They occur in special places, at regular times, and include liturgical orders — set

---

[1] processed potatoes: prepared in a factory, either frozen, canned, or dried
[2] Ronald McDonald: person dressed as a clown to promote McDonald's restaurants

---

94

sequences of words and actions laid down by someone other than the current performer.

5   Rituals also convey information about participants and their cultural traditions. Performed year after year, generation after generation, they translate enduring messages, values, and sentiments into observable action. Although some participants may be more strongly committed than others to the beliefs on which rituals are based, all people who take part in joint public acts signal their acceptance of an order that transcends their status as individuals.

6   In the view of some anthropologists, including Rappaport himself, such secular institutions as McDonald's are not comparable to rituals. They argue that rituals involve special emotions, nonutilitarian intentions, and supernatural entities that are not characteristic of Americans' participation in McDonald's. But other anthropologists define ritual more broadly. Writing about football in contemporary America, William Arens (*see* "The Great American Football Ritual," *Natural History*, October 1975) points out that behavior can simultaneously have sacred as well as secular aspects. Thus, on one level, football can be interpreted simply as a sport, while on another, it can be viewed as a public ritual.

7   While McDonald's is definitely a mundane, secular institution — just a place to eat — it also assumes some of the attributes of a sacred place. And in the context of comparative religion, why should this be surprising? The French sociologist Emile Durkheim long ago pointed out that some societies worship the ridiculous as well as the sublime. The distinction between the two does not depend on the intrinsic qualities of the sacred symbol. Durkheim found that Australian aborigines often worshiped such humble and non-imposing creatures as ducks, frogs, rabbits, and grubs — animals whose inherent qualities hardly could have been the origin of the religious sentiment they inspired. If frogs and grubs can be elevated to a sacred level, why not McDonald's?

8   I frequently eat lunch — and, occasionally, breakfast and dinner — at McDonald's. More than a year ago, I began to notice (and have subsequently observed more carefully) certain ritual behavior at these fast-food restaurants. Although for natives, McDonald's seems to be just a place to eat, careful observation of what goes on in any **outlet** in this country reveals an astonishing degree of formality and behavioral uniformity on the part of both staff and customers. Particularly impressive is the relative invariance in act and utterance that has developed in the absence of a distinct theological doctrine. Rather, the ritual aspect of McDonald's rests on twentieth-century technology — particularly automobiles, television, work locales, and the one-hour lunch.

9   The changes in technology and work organization that have contributed to the chain's growth in the United States are now taking place in other countries. Only in a country such as France,

which has an established and culturally enshrined cuisine that hamburgers and fish fillets **cannot hope** to displace, is McDonald's expansion likely to be retarded. Why has McDonald's been so much more successful than other businesses, than the United States Army, and even than many religious institutions in producing behavioral invariance?

emphatic form of cannot

10   Remarkably, even Americans traveling abroad in countries noted for their distinctive food usually visit the local McDonald's outlet. This odd behavior is probably caused by the same factors that urge us to make yet another trip to a McDonald's here. Wherever a McDonald's may be located, it is a home away from home. At any outlet, Americans know how to behave, what to expect, what they will eat, and what they will pay. If one has been unfortunate enough to have partaken of the often indigestible **pap dished out** by any turnpike restaurant monopoly,[3] the sight of a pair of McDonald's golden arches may justify a detour off the highway, even if the penalty is an extra toll.

undefined food, often soft, as in baby food / served

11   In Paris, where the French have not been especially renowned for making tourists feel at home, McDonald's offers sanctuary. It is, after all, an American institution, where only Americans, who are programmed by years of prior experience to salivate at the sight of the glorious hamburger, can feel completely at home. Americans in Paris can temporarily reverse roles with their hosts; if they cannot act like the French, neither can the French be expected to act in a culturally appropriate manner at McDonald's. Away from home, McDonald's, like a familiar church, offers not just hamburgers but comfort, security, and reassurance.

—feel comfort

12   An American's devotion to McDonald's rests in part on uniformities associated with almost all McDonald's: setting, architecture, food, ambience, acts, and utterances. The golden arches, for example, serve as a familiar and almost universal landmark, absent only in those areas where zoning laws prohibit garish signs. At a McDonald's near the University of Michigan campus in Ann Arbor, a small decorous sign — golden arches encircled in wrought iron — identifies the establishment. Despite the absence of the towering arches, this McDonald's, where I have conducted much of my fieldwork, **does not suffer** as a ritual setting. The restaurant, a contemporary brick structure that has been nominated for a prize in architectural design, is best known for its stained-glass windows, which incorporate golden arches as their focal point. On bright days, sunlight floods in on waiting customers through a skylight that recalls the clerestory of a Gothic cathedral. In the case of this McDonald's, the effect is to equate traditional religious symbols

focal point

garish / gaudy (tasteless)

does not lose money or its good reputation

---

[3] turnpike restaurant monopoly: chain of restaurants exclusively licensed to service toll highway travelers

and golden arches. And in the view of the natives I have interviewed, the message is clear.

13　When Americans go to a McDonald's restaurant, they perform an ordinary, secular, biological act—they eat, usually lunch. Yet, immediately upon entering, we can tell from our surroundings that we are in a sequestered place, somehow apart from the messiness of the world outside. Except for such anomalies as the Ann Arbor campus outlet, the town house McDonald's in New York City, and the special theme McDonald's[4] of such cities as San Francisco, Saint Paul, and Dallas, the restaurants rely on their arches, dull brown brick, plate-glass sides, and mansard roofs to create a setting as familiar as home. In some of the larger outlets, murals depicting "McDonaldland" fantasy characters, sports, outdoor activities, and landscapes surround plastic seats and tables. In this familiar setting, we do not have to consider the experience. We know what we will see, say, eat, and pay.

escape from the rest of the world

familiar, safe

menu-price same

14　Behind the counter, McDonald's employees are differentiated into such categories as male staff, female staff, and managers. While costumes vary slightly from outlet to outlet and region to region, such apparel as McDonald's hats, ties, and shirts, along with dark pants and shining black shoes, are standard.

standard
safe
ritual

15　The food is also standard, again with only minor regional variations.[5] (Some restaurants are selected to test such new menu items as "McChicken" or different milkshake flavors.) Most menus, however, from the rolling hills of Georgia to the snowy plains of Minnesota, offer the same items. The prices are also the same and the menu is usually located in the same place in every restaurant.

16　Utterances across each spotless counter are standardized. Not only are customers limited in what they can choose but also in what they can say. Each item on the menu has its appropriate McDonald's designation: "quarter pounder with cheese"[6] or "**filet-O-fish**" or "large fries." The customer who asks, "What's a Big Mac?" is as out of place as a southern Baptist at a Roman Catholic Mass.[7]

breaded fried fish

17　At the McDonald's that I frequent, the phrases uttered by the salespeople are just as standard as those of the customers. If I ask for a quarter pounder, the ritual response is "Will that be with cheese, sir?" If I do not order French fries, the agent automatically incants, "Will there be any fries today, sir?" And when I pick up

---

[4] special theme McDonald's: each with its own special design motif, but usually with the same cuisine

[5] regional variations: suited to the food preferences of local (regional) customers. An example would be tacos (pancake-style bread filled with chopped meat, chicken, or cheese and rolled up) in the Southwest.

[6] quarter pounder with cheese: a cheeseburger with one-fourth pound beef

[7] southern Baptist at a Roman Catholic Mass: analogy showing how a person of one religion would feel out of place at the ceremony of another religion

my order, the agent conventionally says, "Have a nice day, sir," followed by, "Come in again."

18   Nonverbal behavior of McDonald's agents is also programmed. Prior to opening the spigot of the drink machine, they fill paper cups with ice exactly to the bottom of the golden arches that decorate them. As customers request food, agents look back to see if the desired item is available. If not, they reply, "That'll be a few minutes, sir (or ma'am)," after which the order of the next customer is taken.

every single performance is same.

19   McDonald's lore of appropriate verbal and nonverbal behavior is even taught at a "seminary," Hamburger University, located in Elk Grove Village, Illinois, near Chicago's O'Hare airport. Managers who attend choose either a two-week basic "operator's course" or an eleven-day "advanced operator's course." With a 360-page *Operations Manual* as their bible, students learn about food, equipment, and management techniques—delving into such esoteric subjects as buns, shortening, and carbonization. Filled with the spirit of McDonald's, graduates take home such degrees as bachelor or master of hamburgerology[8] to display in their outlets. Their job is to **spread the word**—the secret success formula they have learned—among assistant managers and crew in their restaurants.

communicate their knowledge

20   The total McDonald's ambience invites comparison with sacred places. The chain stresses clean living and reaffirms those traditional America values that transcend McDonald's itself. Max Boas and Steve Chain, biographers of McDonald's board chairman, Ray Kroc, report that after the hundredth McDonald's opened in 1959, Kroc leased a plane to survey likely sites for the chain's expansion. McDonald's would invade the suburbs by locating its outlets near traffic intersections, shopping centers, and churches. Steeples figured prominently in Kroc's plan. He believed that suburban churchgoers would be preprogrammed consumers of the McDonald's formula—quality, service, and cleanliness.

21   McDonald's restaurants, nestled beneath their transcendent arches and the American flag, would enclose immaculate restrooms and floors, counters and stainless steel kitchens. Agents would sparkle, radiating health and warmth. Although **to a lesser extent** than a decade ago, management scrutinizes employees' hair length, height, nails, teeth, and complexions. Long hair, bad breath, stained teeth, and pimples are anathema. Food containers also defy pollution; they are used only once. (In New York City, the fast-food chain Chock Full O' Nuts foreshadowed this theme long ago and took it one step further by assuring customers that their food was never touched by human hands.)

less often

22   Like participation in rituals there are times when eating at

---

[8] bachelor or master of hamburgerology: reference to earning a college degree in the study of hamburgers

McDonald's is not appropriate. A meal at McDonald's is usually confined to ordinary, everyday life. Although the restaurants are open virtually every day of the year, most Americans do not go there on Thanksgiving, Easter, Passover, or other religious and quasireligious days. Our culture reserves holidays for family and friends. Although Americans neglect McDonald's on holidays, the chain reminds us through television that it still endures, that it will welcome us back once our holiday is over.

23   The television presence of McDonald's is particularly obvious on holidays, whether it be through the McDonald's All-American Marching Band[9] (two clean-cut high school students from each state) in a nationally televised Thanksgiving Day parade or through sponsorship of sports and family entertainment programs.

24   Although such chains as Burger King, Burger Chef, and Arby's compete with McDonald's for the fast-food business, none rivals McDonald's success. The explanation reflects not just quality, service, cleanliness, and value but, more importantly, McDonald's advertising, which skillfully appeals to different audiences. Saturday morning television, for example, includes a steady dose of cartoons and other children's shows sponsored by McDonald's. The commercials feature several McDonaldland fantasy characters, headed by the clown Ronald McDonald, and often stress the enduring aspects of McDonald's. In one, Ronald has a time machine that enables him to introduce hamburgers to the remote past and the distant future. Anyone who noticed the shot of the McDonald's restaurant in the Woody Allen film *Sleeper,* which takes place 200 years hence, will be aware that the message of McDonald's as eternal has gotten across. Other children's commercials gently portray the conflict between good (Ronald) and evil (Hamburglar).[10] McDonaldland's bloblike Grimace[11] is hooked on milkshakes, and Hamburglar's addiction to simple burgers regularly culminates in his confinement to a "patty wagon,"[12] as Ronald and Big Mac restore and preserve the social order.

25   Pictures of McDonaldland appear on cookie boxes and, from time to time, on durable plastic cups that are given away with the purchase of a large soft drink. According to Boas and Chain, a McDonaldland amusement park, comparable in scale to Disneyland,[13] is planned for Las Vegas. Even more obvious are children's chances to meet Ronald McDonald and other McDonaldland char-

---

[9] All-American Marching Band: high rank of accomplishment for high school bands

[10] Hamburglar: word pun using "hamburger" and "burglar" (robber)

[11] bloblike Grimace: purple blob cartoon figure used to advertise McDonald's, like milkshakes

[12] "patty wagon": word play combining *patty* (one hamburger) and *paddy wagon* (police van)

[13] Disneyland: enormous playground in California, named after Walt Disney (1901–1966), American producer of children's films

acters **in the flesh**. Actors portraying Ronald scatter their visits, usually on Saturdays, among McDonald's outlets throughout the country. A Ronald can even be rented for a birthday party or for Halloween trick or treating.[14]

in person

26   McDonald's adult advertising has a different, but equally effective, theme. In 1976, a fresh-faced, sincere young woman invited the viewer to try breakfast — a new meal at McDonald's — in a familiar setting. In still other commercials, healthy, clean-living Americans **gambol** on ski slopes or in mountain pastures. The single theme running throughout all the adult commercials is personalism. McDonald's, the commercials tell us, is not just a fast-food restaurant. It is a warm friendly place where you will be graciously welcomed. Here, you will feel at home with your family, and your children will not get into trouble. The word *you* is emphasized — "You deserve a break today"; "You, you're the one"; "We do it all for you." McDonald's commercials say that you are not just a face in the crowd. At McDonald's, you can find respite from a hectic and impersonal society — the break you deserve.

adult ad.

play (not gamble)

personalize

every people is important

27   Early in 1977, after a **brief flirtation with** commercials that **harped on** the financial and gustatory benefits of eating at McDonald's, the chain introduced one of its most curious incentives — the "Big Mac attack." Like other extraordinary and irresistible food cravings, which people in many cultures attribute to demons or other spirits, a Big Mac attack could strike anyone at any time. In one commercial, passengers on a jet forced the pilot to land at the nearest McDonald's. In others, a Big Mac attack had the power to give life to an inanimate object, such as a suit of armor, or restore a mummy to life.

short term experience with / emphasized

28   McDonald's advertising typically de-emphasizes the fact that the chain is, after all, a profit-making organization. By stressing its program of community projects, some commercials present McDonald's as a charitable organization. During the Bicentennial year, commercials reported that McDonald's was giving 1,776 trees to every state in the union. Brochures at outlets echo the television message that, through McDonald's, one can sponsor a carnival to aid victims of muscular dystrophy. In 1976 and 1977 McDonald's managers in Ann Arbor persuaded police officers armed with metal detectors to station themselves at restaurants during Halloween to check candy and fruit for hidden pins and razor blades.[15] Free coffee was offered to parents. In 1976, McDonald's sponsored a

put family image.

give money

---

[14] Halloween trick or treating: October 31 holiday custom in which young children in costume go house-to-house asking, "Trick or treat?" Neighbors usually give them candy, fruit, or coins.

[15] check candy and fruit for hidden pins and razor blades: In recent years (dating from the 1970s), criminally inclined persons have maliciously offered trick-or-treating children these dangerous items concealed inside harmless-looking goodies.

radio series documenting the contributions Blacks have made to American history.

29 McDonald's also sponsored such family television entertainment as the film *The Sound of Music*, complete with a prefatory, sermonlike address by Ray Kroc. Commercials during the film showed Ronald McDonald picking up after litterbugs and continued with the theme, "We do it all for you." Other commercials told us that McDonald's supports and works to maintain the values of American family life—and went so far as to suggest a means of strengthening what most Americans conceive to be the weakest link in the nuclear family,[16] that of father-child. "Take a father to lunch," kids were told.

30 Participation in McDonald's rituals involves temporary subordination of individual differences in a social and cultural collectivity. By eating at McDonald's, not only do we communicate that we are hungry, enjoy hamburgers, and have inexpensive tastes but also that we are willing to adhere to a value system and a series of behaviors dictated by an exterior entity.[17] In a land of tremendous ethnic, social, economic, and religious diversity, we proclaim that we share something with millions of other Americans.

31 Sociologists, cultural anthropologists, and others have shown that social ties based on kinship, marriage, and community are growing weaker in the contemporary United States. Fewer and fewer people participate in traditional organized religions. By joining sects, cults, and therapy sessions,[18] Americans seek many of the securities that formal religion gave to our ancestors. The increasing cultural, rather than just economic, significance of McDonald's, football, and similar institutions is intimately linked to these changes.

32 As industrial society shunts people around, church allegiance declines as a unifying moral force. Other institutions are also taking over the functions of formal religions. At the same time, traditionally organized religions—Protestantism, Catholicism, and Judaism—are reorganizing themselves along business lines. With such changes, the gap between the symbolic meaning of traditional religions and the realities of modern life widens. Because of this, some sociologists have argued that the study of modern religion must merge with the study of mass culture and mass communication.

33 In this context, McDonald's has become one of many new and powerful elements of American culture that provide common expectations, experience, and behavior—overriding region, class,

---

[16] the weakest link in the nuclear family: the so-called "weakest" member of the immediate family. This is, of course, advertising persuasion.

[17] an exterior entity: Kottak is referring to McDonald's here.

[18] sects, cults, and therapy sessions: nontraditional opportunities for spiritual and psychological experiences

formal religious affiliation, political sentiments, gender, age, ethnic group, sexual preference, and urban, suburban, or rural residence. By incorporating—wittingly or unwittingly—many of the ritual and symbolic aspects of religion, McDonald's has carved its own important niche in a changing society in which automobiles are ubiquitous and where television sets outnumber toilets.

Discussion Points

1. Why does Kottak use the word "rituals" in the title of his essay?
2. What tone does the author use in this piece? What is his personal opinion of McDonald's?
3. What features do most fast-food chains have in common?
4. How does Kottak justify considering McDonald's as a sacred ritual?
5. Interpret "from the ridiculous to the sublime" in the context of societal objects of worship.
6. In what way does Kottak relate McDonald's to twentieth-century technology?
7. Describe Hamburger University (location, purpose, curriculum).
8. According to the writer, what makes McDonald's more successful than its competitors?
9. Define "Big Mac attack."
10. Interpret Kottak's final commentary on American culture (paragraph 33, lines 6–9).

Composition Topics

Choose one of these themes on which to develop a two-page essay:

1. Compare and contrast McDonald's to a popular fast-food restaurant chain in your country.
2. If you enjoy eating in fast-food restaurants, explain why you do. If you do not, reveal why not.
3. If you just became manager of a McDonald's, what changes would you institute? Consider the menu, service, decor, and personnel.
4. If you decided to establish a new chain of fast-food restaurants, what features would make yours different from the existing ones? And what name would you select?

Research Ideas

To better understand the background of this essay, prepare a written report on one of the following areas:

1. American Eating Habits, Post–World War II
2. Fast-Food Restaurants, Origin and Development
3. McDonald's

BUREAU OF EMPLOYMENT SECURITY

CHAPTER 12

◆ *The Invisible Poor*

BY MICHAEL HARRINGTON

About the Author:

MICHAEL HARRINGTON (1928–   )

Michael Harrington has won a variety of awards for his political science writings. A political science professor at Queens College in New York City, Harrington is credited with many sociopolitical works. Here is a partial listing of them: *The Other America* (1963), *Fragments of the Century* (1973), *The Vast Majority: A Journey to the World's Poor* (1977), *The Next America: The Decline and Rise of the United States* (1981), *The New American Poverty* (1984), and *The Next Left: The History of a Future* (1987).

Setting the Scene

Public knowledge of and concern for poverty came into clear focus with the advent of the Depression[1] in the 1930s. It was that catastrophic time which transformed America's haphazard attention to those living below the so-called American Standard of Living into one of national alarm and action. In his second inaugural address in 1937, President Roosevelt[2] proclaimed that one-third of the population was not properly housed, not adequately clothed, and not sufficiently fed. As social scientists collected data on poverty-level citizens, the massive problem was brought into sharper focus. In his 1963 book *The Other America*, from which the essay that follows is excerpted, Harrington presented shocking statistics to substantiate the existence of wide-scale poverty in the decade of the 1960s. Harrington's work helped to define the problem, and in 1967, President Johnson[3] declared "an unconditional war on poverty in America." For some in the United States, that unfortunate condition is still a fact of life despite governmental attempts to diminish poverty.

Pre-Reading Considerations

1. What images come to mind when you contemplate poverty?
2. Do you believe that poverty can be eliminated?
3. In your opinion, is poverty always identifiable?

[1] Depression: starting in the year 1929, the worst period in the economy of the U.S., marked by severe unemployment
[2] President Roosevelt: Franklin Delano (1882–1945), term from 1933–45
[3] President Johnson: Lyndon Baines (1908–1973), term from 1963–69

The Invisible Poor

MICHAEL HARRINGTON

1   The millions who are poor in the United States tend to become increasingly invisible. Here is a great mass of people, yet it takes an effort of the intellect and will even to see them.

2   I discovered this personally in a curious way. After I wrote my first article on poverty in America, I had all the statistics down on paper. I had proved to my satisfaction that there were around 50,000,000 poor in this country. Yet, I realized I did not believe my own figures. The poor existed in the Government reports; they were percentages and numbers in long, close columns, but they were not part of my experience. I could prove that the other America existed, but I had never been there.

3   There are perennial reasons that make the other America an invisible land.

4   Poverty is often **off the beaten track**. It always has been. The *not where most* ordinary tourist never left the main highway, and today he rides *people regularly go* interstate turnpikes. He does not go into the valley of Pennsylvania where the towns look like movie sets of Wales in the thirties.[1] He does not see the company houses[2] in rows, the rutted roads (the poor always have bad roads whether they live in the city, in towns, or on farms), and everything is black and dirty. And even if he were to pass through such a place by accident, the tourist would not meet the unemployed men in the bar or the women coming home from a runaway sweatshop.[3]

5   Then, too, beauty and myths are perennial masks of poverty. The traveler comes to the Appalachians[4] in the lovely season. He sees the hills, the streams, the foliage — but not the poor. Or perhaps he looks at a run-down mountain house, and, remembering Rousseau[5] rather than seeing with his eyes, decides that 'those people' are truly fortunate to be living the way they are and that they are lucky to be exempt from the strains and tensions of the

---

[1] movie sets ... thirties: These showed economically depressed mining areas in Wales, such as those dotting the valleys of Pennsylvania.

[2] company houses: housing provided by the main employer in town; often of subsistence quality

[3] runaway sweatshop: factory-type job location, where typically the wages are low, conditions terrible, hours long, and workload grueling

[4] Appalachians: mountain range extending from southeastern Canada down the eastern portion of the U.S. into Alabama

[5] Rousseau: Henri (1844–1910), French painter

---

middle class. The only problem is that 'those people,' the quaint inhabitants of those hills, are undereducated, underprivileged, lack medical care, and are in the process of being forced from the land into a life in the cities, where they are misfits.

6   These are normal and obvious causes of the invisibility of the poor. They operated a generation ago; they will be functioning a generation hence. It is more important to understand that the very development of American society is creating a new kind of blindness about poverty. The poor are increasingly slipping out of the very experience and consciousness of the nation.

7   If the middle class never did like ugliness and poverty, it was at least aware of them. 'Across the tracks'[6] was not a very long way to go. There were forays into the slums at Christmas time; there were charitable organizations that brought contact with the poor. Occasionally, almost everyone passed through the Negro ghetto or the blocks of tenements, if only to get downtown to work or to entertainment.

8   Now the American city has been transformed. The poor still inhabit the miserable housing in the central area, but they are increasingly isolated from contact with, or sight of, anybody else. Middle-class women coming in from Suburbia on a rare trip may **catch the merest glimpse** of the other America on the way   *see only a little* to an evening at the theater, but their children are segregated in suburban schools. The business or professional man may drive along the fringes of slums in a car or bus, but it is not an important experience to him. The failures, the unskilled, the disabled, the aged, and the minorities are right there, across the tracks, where they have always been. But hardly anyone else is.

9   In short, the very development of the American city has removed poverty from the living, emotional experience of millions upon millions of middle-class Americans. Living out in the suburbs, it is easy to assume that ours is, indeed, an affluent society.

10   This new generation of poverty is compounded by a well-meaning ignorance. A good many concerned and sympathetic Americans are aware that there is much discussion of urban renewal. Suddenly, driving through the city, they notice that a familiar slum has been torn down and that there are towering, modern buildings where once there had been tenements or hovels. There is a warm feeling of satisfaction, of pride in the way things are working out: the poor, it is obvious, are being taken care of.

---

[6] 'Across the tracks': reference to the economically less privileged section of a town or city, usually on one side of the railroad tracks

11   The irony in this . . . is that the truth is nearly the exact opposite to the impression. The total impact of the various housing programs in postwar America has been to squeeze more and more people into existing slums. . . . Clothes make the poor invisible too: America has the best-dressed poverty the world has ever known. For a variety of reasons, the benefits of mass production have been spread much more evenly in this area than in many others. It is much easier in the United States to be decently dressed than it is to be decently housed, fed, or doctored. Even people with terribly depressed incomes can look prosperous.

12   This is an extremely important factor in defining our emotional and existential ignorance of poverty. In Detroit the existence of social classes became much more difficult to discern the day the companies put lockers in the plants. From that moment on, one did not see men in work clothes on the way to the factory, but citizens in slacks and white shirts. This process has been magnified with the poor throughout the country. There are tens of thousands of Americans in the big cities who are wearing shoes, perhaps even a stylishly cut suit or dress, and yet are hungry. It is not a matter of planning, though it almost seems as if the affluent society had given out costumes to the poor so that they would not offend the rest of society with the sight of rags.

13   Then, many of the poor are the wrong age to be seen. A good number of them (over 8,000,000) are sixty-five years of age or better; an even larger number are under eighteen. The aged members of the other America are often sick, and they cannot move. Another group of them **live out their lives** in loneliness and   *live until they die*
frustration: they sit in rented rooms, or else they stay close to a house in a neighborhood that has completely changed from the old days. Indeed, one of the worst aspects of poverty among the aged is that these people are **out of sight and out of mind**, and   *unseen and*
alone.   *forgotten*

14   The young are somewhat more visible, yet they too stay close to their neighborhoods. Sometimes they **advertise** their poverty   *reveal*
through a lurid tabloid story about a gang killing. But generally they do not disturb the quiet streets of the middle class.

15   And finally, the poor are politically invisible. It is one of the cruelest ironies of social life in advanced countries that the dispossessed at the bottom of society are unable to speak for themselves. The people of the other America do not, **by far and**   *generally*
large, belong to unions, to fraternal organizations, or to political parties. They are without lobbies[7] of their own; they put forward

---

[7] lobbies: political support/action groups

no legislative program. As a group, they are atomized. They have no face; they have no voice.

16   Thus, there is not even a cynical political motive for caring about the poor, as in the old days. Because the slums are no longer centers of powerful political organizations, the politicians need not really care about their inhabitants. The slums are no longer visible to the middle class, so much of the idealistic urge to fight for those who need help is gone. Only the social agencies[8] have a really direct involvement with the other America, and they are without any great political power.

17   To the extent that the poor have a spokesman in American life, that role is played by the labor movement. The unions have their own particular idealism, an ideology of concern. More than that, they realize that the existence of a reservoir of cheap, unorganized labor is a menace to wages and working conditions throughout the entire economy. Thus, many union legislative proposals — to extend the coverage of minimum wage and social security, to organize migrant farm laborers — **articulate** the needs of the poor.   *make known, express*

18   That the poor are invisible is one of the most important things about them. They are not simply neglected and forgotten as in the old rhetoric of reform; what is much worse, they are not seen.

Discussion Points

1. Why does the average American or typical tourist to the U.S. not see the poverty in this country?
2. When middle class travelers pass through poor rural areas, what is their immediate reaction to "those people"?
3. Explain the term *across the tracks* and describe the interaction that takes place between the two separated social classes.
4. What effect has urban renewal had on the middle-class American's view of poverty?
5. Explain Harrington's assertion: "America has the best-dressed poverty the world has ever known."
6. How did the installation of lockers in Detroit factories affect the identification of worker classes?
7. What does the author mean when he writes that many poor people are "the wrong age to be seen"?
8. How do some youths "advertise their poverty"?
9. According to the author, what is the relationship between the labor movement and the poor?

---

[8] social agencies: governmental or private organizations that function to assist the poor with food, housing, and medical needs

Composition Topics

The following are three topics related to "The Invisible Poor." Choose one of them on which to develop a two-page composition.

1. Present a personal account of your knowledge of poverty. Compare and contrast the invisible aspect of poverty in the United States with poverty found in another country.
2. If you were a social worker, would you advise a poor family to become more visible? Furnish reasons for your decision, and create a hypothetical family as the focal point of your writing.
3. Relate your view of the relationship between organized labor and unemployment.

Research Ideas

"The Invisible Poor" can be more readily appreciated after researching one of these topics. Prepare a two-page report for the one you choose:

1. The Labor Movement in the U.S.
2. Migrant Farm Workers
3. Poverty in the U.S.
4. Teenage Gang Wars
5. Urban Renewal

CHAPTER 13

◆ *Football Red and Baseball Green*

BY MURRAY ROSS

About the Author:
MURRAY ROSS
(1942–   )

Murray Ross was born in California and attended school both there and in Massachusetts. At present, he is professor of theater arts at the University of Colorado in Colorado Springs.

Setting the Scene

Both football and baseball have enjoyed growing popularity since their precursors were introduced into the United States. Football, a descendant of soccer and rugby, acquired most of its present-day features in a game between Harvard and Yale universities in 1876. That match was characterized by running with the ball, tackling opponents and overall strenuous physical performance. Modern American football combines physical prowess with added intellectual strategy. Although critics lambaste the sport for its violence, they do recognize that that element of the game accounts for much of its audience loyalty.

In its early stages, U.S. baseball, derived from the English game of rounders, had various names: "goal ball," "round ball," the "New England game," and "base ball." In 1869, the first professional team was established: the Cincinnati Red Stockings. The two present-day major leagues were organized thereafter: the National League in 1876 and the American League in 1901. Baseball has been a source of entertainment for millions of people and has produced numerous folk heroes. But baseball has had its critics, too, who accuse the leagues of engaging in "big business" instead of offering a sport to the public.

Murray Ross analyzes the spell that baseball and football have cast over their respective fans.

Pre-Reading Considerations

1. As a spectator sport, which do you prefer—baseball or football?
2. Do you consider football a violent sport?
3. Why do you think some people favor baseball, and others football?

Football Red and Baseball Green

MURRAY ROSS

1   The Super Bowl, the final game of the professional football season, draws a larger television audience than any of the moon walks or Tiny Tim's[1] wedding. This revelation is one way of indicating just how popular spectator sports are in this country. Americans, or American men anyway, seem to care about the games they watch as much as the Elizabethans[2] cared about their plays, and I suspect for some of the same reasons. There is, in sport, some of the rudimentary drama found in popular theater: familiar plots, type characters, heroic and comic action **spiced** *mixed with,* **with** new and unpredictable variations. And common to watching *including* both activities is the sense of participation in a shared tradition and in shared fantasies. If sport exploits these fantasies, without significantly transcending them, it seems no less satisfying for all that.

2   It is my guess that sport spectating involves something more than the vicarious pleasures of identifying with athletic prowess. I suspect that each sport contains a fundamental myth which it elaborates for its fans, and that our pleasure in watching such games derives in part from belonging briefly to the mythical world which the game and its players bring to life. I am especially interested in baseball and football because they are so popular and so uniquely *American*; they began here and unlike basketball they have not been widely exported. Thus whatever can be said, mythically, about these games would seem to apply to our culture.

3   Baseball's myth may be the easier to identify since we have a greater historical perspective on the game. It was an instant success during the Industrialization,[3] and most probably it was a reaction to the squalor, the faster pace and the dreariness of the new conditions. Baseball was old-fashioned right from the start; it seems conceived in nostalgia, in the resuscitation of the Jeffersonian dream.[4] It established an artificial rural environment, one removed from the toil of an urban life, which spectators could be admitted to and temporarily **breathe in**. Baseball is a *pastoral* sport, and I *experience* think the game can be best understood as this kind of art. For

[1] Tiny Tim: (c. 1930–   ), stage name of Herbert B. Khaury, popular singer in the 1960s and 1970s
[2] Elizabethans: those living in England during the reign of Queen Elizabeth I (reigned 1558–1601)
[3] Industrialization: also named Industrial Revolution, usually dated in late eighteenth century and marked by the introduction of power-driven machinery
[4] Jeffersonian dream: reference to the egalitarian philosophy of Thomas Jefferson (1743–1826), third president of the U.S., term from 1801–09

baseball does what all good pastoral does — it creates an atmosphere in which everything exists in harmony.

4   Consider, for instance, the spatial organization of the game. A kind of controlled openness is created by having everything fan out from home plate, and the crowd sees the game through an arranged perspective that is rarely violated. Visually this means that the game is always seen as a constant, rather calm whole, and that the players and the playing field are viewed in relationship to each other. Each player has a certain position, a special area to tend, and the game often seems to be as much a dialogue between the fielders[5] and the field as it is a contest between players themselves; will that ball get through the hole? Can that outfielder run under that **fly**? As a moral genre, pastoral asserts the virtue of communion with nature. As a competitive game, baseball asserts that the team which best relates to the playing field (by hitting the ball in the right places) will win.

a ball hit high into the air

5   I suspect baseball's space has a subliminal function too, for topographically it is a sentimental mirror of older America. Most of the game is played between the pitcher and the hitter in the extreme corner of the playing area. This is the busiest, most sophisticated part of the ball park, where something is always happening, and from which all subsequent action originates. From this urban corner we move to a supporting infield, active but a little less crowded, and from there we come to the vast stretches of the outfield. As is traditional in American lore, danger increases with distance, and the outfield action is often the most spectacular in the game. The long throw, the double off the wall,[6] the leaping catch — these plays take place in remote territory, and they belong, like most legendary feats, to the frontier.

6   Having established its landscape, pastoral art operates to eliminate any reference to that bigger, more disturbing, more real world it has left behind. All games are to some extent insulated from the outside by having their own rules, but baseball has a circular structure as well which furthers its comfortable feeling of self-sufficiency. By this I mean that every motion of extension is also one of return — a ball hit outside is a *home* run,[7] a full circle. Home — familiar, peaceful, secure — it is the beginning and end. You must go out and come back; only the completed movement is **registered**.

scored

7   Time is a serious threat to any form of pastoral. The genre poses a timeless world of perpetual spring, and it does its best to silence the ticking of clocks which remind us that in time the

---

[5] fielders: the three positions that are in the outer area of the baseball field
[6] double off the wall: On this play, the ball hits the back wall, enabling the batter to advance to second base.
[7] home run: a hit that lets the batter score when all the bases, including the home plate, are reached within the same play

green world fades into winter. One's sense of time is directly related to what happens in it, and baseball is so structured as to stretch out and ritualize whatever action it contains. Dramatic moments are few, and they are almost always isolated by the routine **texture** of normal play. It is certainly a game of climax *feel* and drama, but it is perhaps more a game of repeated and predictable action: the foul balls,[8] the walks,[9] the pitcher fussing around on the mound, the lazy fly ball to centerfield. This is, I think, as it should be, for baseball exists as an alternative to a world of too much action, struggle and change. It is a merciful release from a more grinding and insistent tempo, and its time, as William Carlos Williams[10] suggests, makes a virtue out of idleness simply by providing it:

> The crowd at the ball game
> is moved uniformly
> by a spirit of usefulness
> Which delights them . . .

8   Within this expanded and idle time the baseball fan is **at liberty** *free* to become a ceremonial participant and a lover of style. Because the action is normalized, how something is done becomes as important as the action itself. Thus baseball's most delicate and detailed aspects are often, to the spectator, the most interesting. The pitcher's windup, the anticipatory crouch of the infielders, the quick waggle of the bat as it poises for the pitch — these subtle miniature movements are as meaningful as the home runs and the strikeouts.[11] It somehow matters in baseball that all the tiny rituals are observed: the shortstop[12] must kick the dirt and the umpire must brush the plate[13] with his pocket broom. In a sense baseball is largely a continuous series of small gestures, and I think it characteristic that the game's most treasured moment came when Babe Ruth[14] pointed to where he subsequently hit a home run.

9   Baseball is a game where the little things mean a lot, and this, together with its clean serenity, its open space, and its ritualized action is enough to place it in a world of **yesterday**. Baseball *the past* evokes for us a past which may never have been ours, but which we believe was, and certainly that is enough. In the Second World

---

[8] foul balls: those that land outside the foul lines
[9] walks: After four inaccurate pitches to him (her), a batter is permitted to walk to first base; these "free" moves are termed "walks."
[10] William Carlos Williams: (1883–1963) American author
[11] strikeouts: an out in baseball resulting from a batter's being charged with three strikes (unsuccessful attempts to hit the ball)
[12] shortstop: one of the team positions
[13] plate: the object that marks "home," the starting *and* finishing place of the game
[14] Babe Ruth: George Herman Ruth (1895–1948) a baseball champion with the New York Yankees team

War, supposedly, we fought for "Baseball, Mom and Apple Pie,"[15] and considering what baseball means that phrase is a good one. We fought then for the right to believe in a green world of tranquility and uninterrupted contentment, where the little things would count. But now the possibilities of such a world are more remote, and it seems that while the entertainment of such a dream has an enduring appeal, it is no longer sufficient for our fantasies. I think this may be why baseball is no longer our preeminent national pastime, and why its myth is being replaced by another more appropriate to the new realities (and fantasies) of our time.

10   Football, especially professional football, is the embodiment of a newer myth, one which in many respects is opposed to baseball's. The fundamental difference is that football is not a pastoral game; it is a heroic one. One way of seeing the difference between the two is by the juxtaposition of Babe Ruth and Jim Brown,[16] both legendary players in their separate genres. Ruth, baseball's most powerful hitter, was a hero maternalized (his name), an epic figure destined for a second immortality as a candy bar.[17] His image was impressive but comfortable and altogether human: round, dressed in a baggy uniform, with a schoolboy's cap and a bat which looked tiny next to him. His spindly legs supported a Santa-sized [18] torso, and this comic disproportion would increase when he was in motion. He ran delicately, with quick, very short steps, since he felt that stretching your stride slowed you down. This sort of superstition is typical of baseball players, and typical too is the way in which a personal quirk or mannerism mitigates their awesome skill and makes them poignant and vulnerable.

11   There was nothing funny about Jim Brown. His muscular and almost perfect physique was emphasized further by the uniform which armored him. Babe Ruth had a tough face, but boyish and innocent; Brown was an expressionless mask under the helmet. In action he seemed invincible, the embodiment of speed and power in an inflated human shape. One can describe Brown accurately only with superlatives, for as a player he was a kind of Superman,[19] undisguised.

12   Brown and Ruth are caricatures, yet they represent their games. Baseball is part of a comic tradition which insists that its participants be humans, while football, in the heroic mode, asks that its players be more than that. Football converts men into gods, and suggests that magnificence and glory are as desirable as happi-

---

[15] "Baseball, Mom and Apple Pie": This slogan contains three traditionally American references, and as a whole, signifies American patriotism.

[16] Jim Brown: (1936–) Cleveland Browns (Ohio) player

[17] candy bar: "Baby Ruth" is the name of the candy bar named after Babe Ruth.

[18] Santa-sized: as large as Santa Claus, the jolly, bearded man symbolizing Christmas in some cultures

[19] Superman: the super-powerful character created in comic books and also in motion pictures

ness. Football is designed, therefore, to impress its audience rather differently than baseball.

13   As a pastoral game, baseball attempts to close the gap between the players and the crowd. It creates the illusion, for instance, that with a lot of hard work, a little luck, and possibly some extra talent, the average spectator might well be playing; not watching. For most of us can do a few of the things the ball players do: catch a pop-up, field a ground ball, and maybe get a hit once in a while. Chance is allotted a good deal of play in the game. There is no guarantee, for instance, that a good pitch will not be looped over the infield, or that a solidly batted ball will not turn into a double play. In addition to all of this, almost every fan feels he can make the manager's decision for him, and not entirely without reason. Baseball's statistics are easily calculated and rather meaningful; and the game itself, though a subtle one, is relatively lucid and comprehendible.

14   As a heroic game football is not concerned with a shared community of near-equals. It seeks almost the opposite relationship between its spectators and players, one which stresses the distance between them. We are not allowed to identify directly with Jim Brown any more than we are with Zeus,[20] because to do so would undercut his stature as something more than human. The players do much of the distancing themselves by their own excesses of speed, size and strength. When Bob Brown, the giant all-pro tackle says that he could "block King Kong[21] all day," we look at him and believe. But the game itself contributes to the players' heroic isolation. As George Plimpton[22] has graphically illustrated in *Paper Lion*, it is almost impossible to imagine yourself in a professional football game without also considering your imminent humiliation and possible injury. There is scarcely a single play that the average spectator could hope to perform adequately, and there is even a difficulty in really understanding what is going on. In baseball what happens is **what meets the eye**, but in football each action   *what one sees* is the result of eleven men acting simultaneously against eleven other men, and clearly this is too much for the eye to totally comprehend. Football has become a game of staggering complexity, and coaches are now **wired in to** several "spotters"[23] during the   *in electronic* games so they can find out what is happening.   *communication with*

15   If football is distanced from its fans by its intricacy and its "superhuman" play, it nonetheless remains an intense spectacle. Baseball, as I have implied, dissolves time and urgency in a green expanse, thereby creating a luxurious and peaceful sense of leisure.

[20] Zeus: the king of the gods in Greek mythology

[21] King Kong: American motion picture "star"—a super-sized gorilla

[22] George Plimpton: (1927–) author and media personality. In *Paper Lion*, he wrote about his training experiences with a football team.

[23] "spotters": persons assigned to either defense or offense as observers of plays. These spotters communicate the action to announcers.

As is appropriate to a heroic enterprise, football reverses this procedure and converts space into time. The game is ideally played
in an oval stadium, not in a "park," and the difference is the
elimination of perspective. This makes football a perfect television
game, because even **at first hand** it offers a flat, perpetually moving   *in person (not on*
foreground (wherever the ball is). The eye in baseball viewing   *TV)*
opens up; in football it **zeroes in**. There is no democratic vista in   *focuses on one point*
football, and spectators are not asked to relax, but to concentrate.
You are encouraged to watch the drama, not a medley of ubiquitous
gestures, and you are constantly reminded that this event is taking
place in time. The third element in baseball is the field; in football
this element is the clock. Traditionally heroes do reckon with
time, and football players are no exceptions. Time in football is
wound up inexorably until it reaches the breaking point in the
last minutes of a close game.[24] More often than not it is the clock
which emerges as the real enemy, and it is the sense of time
running out that regularly produces a pitch of tension uncommon
in baseball.

16   A further reason for football's intensity is that the game is
played like a war. The idea is to win by going through, around
or over the opposing team and the battle lines, quite literally, are
drawn on every play. Violence **is somewhere at the heart of** the   *determined / is an*
game, and the combat quality is reflected in football's army lan-   *essential part of*
guage ("blitz," "trap," "zone," "bomb," "trenches," etc.). Coaches
often sound like generals when they discuss their strategy. Woody
Hayes of Ohio State, for instance, explains his quarterback option
play as if it had been conceived in the Pentagon:[25] "You know,"
he says, "the most effective kind of warfare is siege. You have to
attack on broad fronts. And that's all the option is—attacking on
a broad front. You know General Sherman[26] ran an option through
the south."

17   Football like war is an arena for action, and like war football
leaves little room for personal style. It seems to be a game which   *does not include*
projects "character" more than personality, and for the most part   *much room for*
football heroes, publicly, are a rather similar **lot**. They tend to   *group*
become personifications rather than individuals, and, with certain
exceptions, they are easily read emblematically as embodiments of
heroic qualities such as "strength," "confidence," "perfection,"
etc.—clichés really, but forceful enough when represented by the
play of a Dick Butkus, a Johnny Unitas or a Bart Starr. Perhaps
this simplification of personality results in part from the heroes'
total identification with their mission, to the extent that they
become more characterized by their work than by what they intrin-
sically "are." **At any rate** football does not **make allowances for**   *Anyway / excuse*

[24] close game: one in which both teams have nearly the same score, and either might win
[25] Pentagon: headquarters of the U.S. Department of Defense in Washington, D.C.
[26] General Sherman: William Tecumseh (1820–1891), general in the U.S. Army

the idiosyncrasies that baseball actually seems to encourage, and as a result there have been few football players as uniquely crazy or human as, say, Casey Stengel[27] or Dizzy Dean.[28]

18   A further reason for the underdeveloped qualities of football personalities, and one which gets us to the heart of the game's modernity, is that football is very much a game of modern technology. Football's action is largely interaction, and the game's complexity requires that its players mold themselves into a perfectly coordinated unit. Jerry Kramer, the veteran guard and author of *Instant Replay*,[29] writes how Lombardi would work to develop such integration:

> He makes us execute the same plays over and over, a hundred times, two hundred times, until we do every little thing automatically. He works to make the kick-off team perfect, the punt-return team perfect, the field-goal team perfect. He ignores nothing. Technique, technique, technique, over and over and over, until we feel like we're going crazy. But we win.

Mike Garrett, the halfback, gives the player's version:

> After a while, you train your mind like a computer — put the ideas in, and the body acts accordingly.

19   As the quotations imply, pro football is insatiably preoccupied with the smoothness and precision of play execution, and most coaches believe that the team which makes the fewest mistakes will be the team that wins. Individual identity thus comes to be associated with the team or unit that one plays for to a much greater extent than in baseball. To use a reductive analogy, it is the difference between *Bonanza*[30] and *Mission Impossible*.[31] Ted Williams[32] is mostly Ted Williams, but Bart Starr is mostly the Green Bay Packers. The latter metaphor is a precise one, since football heroes stand out not because of purely individual acts, but because they epitomize the action and style of the groups they are connected to. Kramer cites the obvious if somewhat self-glorifying historical precedent: "Perhaps," he writes, "we're living in Camelot."[33] Ideally a football team should be what Camelot was supposed to have been, a group of men who function as equal parts of a larger whole, dependent on each other for total meaning.

20   The humanized machine as hero is something very new in sport,

---

[27] Casey Stengel: (1890–1975) New York Yankees manager
[28] Dizzy Dean: (1911–1974) St. Louis (Missouri) pitcher
[29] Lombardi: Vince (1913–1970), Green Bay (Wisconsin) Packers coach
[30] *Bonanza*: television program in a western setting, popular in the 1960s
[31] *Mission Impossible*: modern-style detective TV program, popular in the 1970s
[32] Ted Williams: (1918–) Boston Red Sox player
[33] Camelot: a place of idyllic happiness (taken after King Arthur's court location)

for in baseball anything **approaching** a machine has always been   *even a little bit*
suspect. The famous Yankee[34] teams of the fifties were almost   *similar to*
flawlessly perfect and never very popular. Their admirers **took**   *tried hard*
pains to romanticize their precision into something more natural
than plain mechanics—Joe DiMaggio,[35] for instance, was the
"Yankee Clipper." Even so, most people hoped fervently the Brooklyn Dodgers[36] (the "bums")[37] would thrash them in every World
Series.[38] To take a more recent example, the victory of the Mets[39]
in 1969 was so compelling **largely** because it was at the expense   *mainly*
of a superbly **homogenized** team, the Baltimore Orioles, and it   *mixed*
was accomplished by a somewhat random collection of inspired
leftovers. In baseball, machinery seems tantamount to villainy,   *rejected players*
whereas in football this smooth perfection is part of the expected
integration a championship team must attain.

21   It is not surprising, really, that we should have a game which
asserts the heroic function of a mechanized group, since we have
become a country where collective identity is a reality. Football
as a game of groups is appealing to us as a people of groups, and
for this reason football is very much an "establishment" game[40]—since
it is in the corporate business and governmental structures that
group America is most developed. The game comments on culture,
and vice versa:

> President Nixon,[41] an ardent football fan, got a football team
> picture as an inaugural anniversary present from his cabinet.[42] . . .
>   Superimposed on the faces of real gridiron players were the
> faces of cabinet members. (A.P.)

This is not to say that football appeals only to a certain class, for
group America is visible everywhere. A sign held high in the San
Francisco Peace Moratorium[43] . . . read: "49er Fans[44] against War,
Poverty and the Baltimore Colts."

---

[34] Yankee: New York Yankees team (baseball)
[35] Joe DiMaggio: (1914–   ) New York Yankees player
[36] Brooklyn Dodgers: baseball team; relocated in 1958 to Los Angeles, California, and now named
the Los Angeles Dodgers
[37] "bums": originally, the fans' shout to Dodgers when they played poorly; later, a term of endearment
[38] World Series: season-end culminating competition between the respective winning teams of
the American and National Leagues
[39] Mets: New York Mets (baseball team)
[40] "establishment" game: a game that appeals to those who are in control of current policies and
hold decision-making positions in big corporations
[41] President Nixon: Richard Milhous (1913–   ), term of office from 1969–74
[42] cabinet: group of close presidential assistants. These are the secretaries of the various depart-
ments, e.g., of State.
[43] San Francisco Peace Moratorium: In late 1969, 1970, and 1971, San Francisco was a site of
massive anti-war demonstrations (against American involvement in the Vietnam Conflict).
[44] 49er Fans: of the San Francisco 49ers team

22   Football's collective pattern is only one aspect of the way in which it seems to echo our contemporary environment. The game, like our society, can be thought of as a cluster of people living under great tension in a state of perpetual flux. The potential for sudden disaster or triumph is as great in football as it is in our own age, and although there is something ludicrous in equating interceptions[45] with assassinations and long passes with moonshots,[46] there is also something valid and appealing in the analogies. It seems to me that football does successfully reflect those salient and common conditions which affect us all, and it does so **with** *trying to make /* **the end of making** us feel better about them and our **lot**. For one *conditions and* thing, it makes us feel that something can be released and con- *status* nected in all this chaos; out of the accumulated pile of bodies something can emerge — a runner breaks into the clear or a pass finds its way to a receiver. To the spectator plays such as these are human and dazzling. They suggest to the audience what it has hoped for (and been told) all along, that technology is still a tool and not a master. Fans get living proof of this every time a long pass is completed; they see at once that it is the result of careful planning, perfect integration and an effective "pattern," but they see too that it is human and that what **counts** as well is man, his *is important* desire, his natural skill and his "grace under pressure." Football metaphysically yokes heroic action and technology by violence to suggest that they are mutually supportive. It's a doubtful proposition, but **given** how we live it has its attractions. *considering*

23   Football, like the space program, is a game in the grand manner, yet it is a rather sober sport and often seems to lack that positive, comic vision of which baseball's pastoral mannerisms are a part. It is a winter game, as those fans who saw the Minnesota Vikings play the Detroit Lions one Thanksgiving[47] were graphically reminded. The two teams played in a blinding snowstorm, and except for the small flags in the corners of the end zones, and a patch of mud wherever the ball was downed, the field was totally obscured. Even through the magnified television lenses the players were difficult to identify; you saw only huge shapes come out of the gloom, thump against each other and fall in a heap. The movement was repeated endlessly and silently in a muffled stadium, interrupted once or twice by a **shot** of a **bare-legged girl** who *television image/* fluttered her pompons in the cold. The spectacle was **by turns** *cheerleader /* pathetic, compelling and absurd; a kind of theater of oblivion. *alternately*

24   Games such as this are **by no means** unusual, and it is not *not*

---

[45] interceptions: tactic of interrupting and capturing a forward pass, thus transferring the control of action from one team to the other
[46] moonshots: the launching of space crafts onto the moon
[47] Thanksgiving: Day, national holiday in November

difficult to see why for many football is a gladiatorial sport[48] of pointless bludgeoning played by armored monsters. However accurate this description may be, I still believe that even in the worst of circumstances football can be a liberating activity. In the game I have just described, for instance, there was one play, the turning point[49] of the game, which more than compensated for the sluggishness of most of the action. Jim Marshall, the huge defensive end (who hunts on dogsleds during the off season),[50] intercepted a pass deep in his own territory and rumbled upfield like a dinosaur through the mud, the snow, and the opposing team, lateraling at the last minute to another lineman who took the ball in for a touchdown. It was a supreme moment because Marshall's principal occupation is falling on quarterbacks, not catching the ball and running with it. His triumphant jaunt, something that went unequaled during the rest of the that dark afternoon, was a hearty burlesque of the entire sport, an occasion for epic laughter in bars everywhere (though especially in Minnesota), and it was more than enough to rescue the game from the snowbound limbo it was in.

25   In the end I suppose both football and baseball could be seen as varieties of decadence. In its preoccupation with mechanization, and in its open display of violence, football is the more obvious **target** for social moralists, but I wonder if this is finally more "corrupt" than the seductive picture of sanctuary and tranquillity that baseball has so artfully drawn for us. Almost all sport is vulnerable to such criticism because it is not strictly ethical in intent, and for this reason there will always be room for puritans[51] like the Elizabethan John Stubbes who howled at the "wanton fruits which these cursed pastimes bring forth." As a long-time dedicated fan of almost anything athletic, I confess myself out of sympathy with most of this; which is to say, I guess, that I am vulnerable to those fantasies which these games support, and that I find happiness in the company of people who feel as I do.

object of critical attack

26   A final note. It is interesting that the heroic and pastoral conventions which underlie our most popular sports are almost classically opposed. The contrasts are familiar: city versus country, aspirations versus contentment, activity versus peace and so on. Judging from the rise of professional football we seem to be slowly relinquishing that unfettered rural vision of ourselves that baseball so beautifully mirrors, and we have come to cast ourselves in a genre more reflective of a nation confronted by contrast and un-

[48] gladiatorial sport: ancient Roman sport (public entertainment) featuring a person fighting to the death

[49] turning point: when a significant change occurs

[50] off season: when football is not being played

[51] puritans: those adhering to a strict moral code of behavior

avoidable challenges. Right now, like the Elizabethans, we seem to share both heroic and pastoral yearnings, and we reach out to both. Perhaps these divided needs **account** in part **for** the enormous *explain* attention we as a nation now give to spectator sports. For sport provides one place where we can have our football and our baseball too.

Discussion Points

1. Explain the author's comparison between American sports fans and Elizabethan theatergoers.
2. Why did Ross select baseball and football for the subjects of this essay?
3. According to Ross, in what way is baseball a pastoral sport?
4. Define the concept of time in baseball. How does this contrast with football time?
5. Why does Ross call football an heroic game?
6. Which is characterized by violence, baseball or football? Give examples.
7. How does the author fit baseball and football into their respective historical periods?
8. What is your reaction to Ross's classifying football and baseball as "varieties of decadence"?
9. Interpret the title of this essay.
10. Based solely on Ross's portrayals of baseball and football, which sport appeals to you more? Why?

Composition Topics

From the following five themes, choose one on which to prepare a two-page composition:

1. Identify your country's national sport. Present an analysis of its characteristics and popularity.
2. Name and detail your favorite spectator sport by describing its main characteristics and explaining why it appeals to you.
3. According to Ross, sports reflect culture. Present evidence to support this theory. To make your case, you may refer to baseball, football, or any other sport.
4. Provide an analysis of the role of violence in popular sports. Specify the sports and describe the violence in them.
5. Consider a popular sports figure of your country. Analyze the reasons for his or her popularity.

Research Ideas

To enhance your understanding of "Football Red and Baseball Green," write a one-page investigative paper each on two of the following topics:

1. Baseball in the U.S.
2. Jim Brown
3. Dizzy Dean
4. Joe DiMaggio
5. Football in the U.S.
6. Green Bay Packers
7. The Mets
8. The New York Yankees
9. Babe Ruth
10. Casey Stengel
11. Johnny Unitas
12. Ted Williams

CHAPTER 14

◆ *Portrait of an American: Ralph Nader*

BY WILLIAM MANCHESTER

**About the
Author:**
WILLIAM
MANCHESTER
(1922–   )

William Manchester's career has been a diversified one. He has been
a professor of history and English; has served as a foreign and war
correspondent; and is a celebrated writer of novels, short stories, and
historio-political works. Among his published writings are the following: *Disturber of the Peace* (1951), *The Glory and the Dream: A Nar-
rative History of America, 1932–1972* (1975), *Goodbye, Darkness: A
Memoir of the Pacific War* (1980), *One Brief Shining Moment: Remembering Kennedy* (1983), and *The Last Lion* (1988).

**Setting
the Scene**

The subject of Manchester's essay is Ralph Nader, regarded by many
as a hero in the consumer movement. Also known as consumerism,
this movement is defined as the organizations, activities, and attitudes
of consumers in their relationship to the distribution of goods and
services. Ralph Nader's 1966 book *Unsafe at Any Speed* (together with
Rachel Carson's[1] benchmark *Silent Spring* earlier in that decade) led
to a revival of consumer interest in the United States. Previous cycles
of consumerism in the 1900s occurred at the opening of the century
and again in the 1930s, but neither of these movements was sustained.
By contrast, the Nader-Carson-activated cycle seems to be enjoying a
longer-term viability and has forced new legislation, manufacturing
changes, and increased concern about the environment. Because "prevention better than cure" is the guiding philosophy of the new consumer movement, consumer education has become a vital component
in this movement. Buyers are cautioned to assess the safety and dura-
bility of goods, as well as general good value for their money. They
also receive advice as to how to complain when products are defective
or inferior. Manchester's portrait of Nader traces his subject's career
as a consumer advocate.

**Pre-Reading
Considerations**

1. Is automobile safety of great importance to you?
2. Do you ever worry about the purity of the food you eat?
3. Are you concerned about the quality of your environment?

---

[1] Rachel Carson: (1907–1964) American scientist and writer. Her *Silent Spring* launched the
environmentalist movement.

Portrait of an American: Ralph Nader
WILLIAM MANCHESTER

1   In the Connecticut manufacturing city of Winsted his Lebanese immigrant father was the local populist,[1] a familiar American type. Customers at Nadra Nader's Highland Sweet Shop, a restaurant and bakery, complained that the proprietor never let them eat in peace. Nadra was always lecturing them about the wrongs, the inequities, the injustices of the system. Like many immigrants, he was a more ardent Democrat[2] than the natives. He went on about the crimes of the Interests[3] and was forever threatening to sue them. In time everyone there **tuned him out**, with one exception: his youngest son Ralph.

stopped listening to him

2   In 1938, at the age of four, Ralph Nader was a tiny spectator when lawyers harangued juries in the local courthouse. At fourteen he became a daily reader of the *Congressional Record*.[4] He won a scholarship to Princeton,[5] where he refused to wear white bucks or other symbols of sartorial conformity and staged a protest against the spraying of campus trees with **DDT**. He was locked so often in the university library after hours that he was given a key. Characteristically he responded by denouncing the administration for callous disregard of the other students' legal rights. In 1955 he was elected to Phi Beta Kappa,[6] graduated magna cum laude,[7] and admitted to Harvard Law School,[8] which he described as a "high-priced tool factory" turning out servants of power.

dichloro-diphenyl trichloro-ethane, an insecticide

3   His reputation as a puritan[9] grew. He foreswore the reading of novels; they were a waste of time. So were movies; he would limit himself to two a year. He scorned plays, tobacco, alcohol, girls, and parties. At Harvard he also quit driving automobiles, but here

[1] populist: representative of the local people, believing in their rights
[2] Democrat: a member of the Democratic Party (U.S.), which traditionally stands for the rights of the common (middle-class and lower-class) people
[3] Interests: big businesses and other powerful people
[4] *Congressional Record*: official record of the business of the U.S. Congress
[5] Princeton: university in New Jersey
[6] Phi Beta Kappa: national honor society dedicated to high scholastic distinction at an American college or university
[7] magna cum laude: (Lat.) "with great distinction," an honor that may be awarded at the time of graduation
[8] Harvard Law School: part of Harvard University in Cambridge, Massachusetts
[9] puritan: adhering to a very strict moral code

his motive was different. He had become interested in auto injury cases, and after some research in car technology at nearby MIT[10] he wrote an article for the *Harvard Law Record* entitled "American Cars: Designed for Death."

4   The problem continued to bother him. Throughout his career he was to be concerned with the protection of the human body — from unsafe natural gas pipelines, food additives, tainted meat, pollution, mining health hazards, herbicides, unwholesome poultry, inadequate nursing homes, and radiation emission from color TVs — but the auto threat was basic. He opened a private law practice in Hartford[11] (which rapidly became a source of free legal advice for the poor) and continued to urge stronger car safety regulations on local governments. Early in 1964 he took his campaign to Washington, where Assistant Secretary of Labor Daniel Patrick Moynihan hired him as a fifty-dollar-a-day consultant to the Labor Department.

5   Working with Connecticut's Senator Abraham Ribicoff, Nader **turned out** a two-hundred-page brief calling for auto safety legis- *produced* lation **with teeth**. A General Motors engineer became the first of *strict* his many secret contacts in industry by pointing out the Chevrolet Corvair's tendency to flip over. In November 1965 Nader's first book, *Unsafe at Any Speed: The Designed-in Dangers of the American Automobile*, called the Corvair "one of the nastiest-handling cars ever built" and charged that the industry had taken "four years of the model and 1,124,076 Corvairs before they decided to do something."

6   *Unsafe at Any Speed*, which sold 450,000 copies in **cloth and** *hardcover and* **paper,** brought its author before a Ribicoff committee on February *paperback* 10, 1966, as an expert witness on hazardous autos. Three weeks later Nader became a national figure when he accused General Motors of harassing him with private detectives, abusive telephone calls, and women who tried to entice him into compromising situations. A GM operative admitted under oath that he had been instructed by his superiors "to **get something** somewhere **on** this *find out some crime* guy . . . get him **out of their hair** . . . shut him up." Nader filed *or fault / away from* suit for 26 million dollars and collected $280,000. Like his book *them* royalties, the money went to **the cause;** when the National Traffic *of consumer safety* and Motor Vehicle Safety Act was passed that summer the *Washington Post*[12] declared that "Most of the credit for making possible this important legislation belongs to one man — Ralph Nader . . . a one-man lobby[13] for the public prevailed over the nation's most powerful industry."

[10] MIT: Massachusetts Institute of Technology in Cambridge, Massachusetts
[11] Hartford: city in Connecticut
[12] *Washington Post*: newspaper in Washington, D.C.
[13] one-man lobby: an interest group petitioning the legislators on one or more issues. In this case, the group consisted of only Ralph Nader.

7   Nader set himself up as a **watchdog** of the National Traffic   *monitor*
Safety Agency and then **went after** the meat packers; the result   *began to investigate*
was the Wholesome Meat Act of 1967. He broadened his attack
on exploiters of the consumer to include the Food and Drug
Administration, Union Carbide smokestacks,[14] think tanks,[15]
unsafe trucks, pulp and paper mills, property taxes, bureaucrats,
consumer credit, banks, and supermarkets. One observer said,
"Ralph is not a consumer champion. He is just plain against
consumption."

8   Unlike the muckrakers of the Lincoln Steffens era,[16] Nader
acquired a conservative constituency. At a time of anarchy and
disorder he believed in **working within the system.** He was a   *according to existing*
linear thinker, an advocate of law and industrial order. Stockbrokers   *rules and*
contributed to his causes. Miss Porter's School[17] sent him volunteer   *procedures*
workers. He was acquiring lieutenants now — "Nader's Raiders," a
reporter dubbed them — and they were mostly white upper-middle-
class graduates of the best schools, with names like Pullman cars:[18]
Lowell Dodge, William Harrison Wellford, Reuben B. Robertson
III, and William Howard Taft IV. One of them, Edward F. Cox,
became a son-in-law of President Nixon.

9   He installed them in cubbyhole offices in the National Press
Building furnished with secondhand desks, chairs bought at
rummage sales,[19] apple crate files, and shelves made from planks
and bricks. He worked them a hundred hours a week and paid
them poverty-level salaries. Royalties from the books they turned
out went into his campaigns. They didn't complain; he himself
was earning $200,000 a year and spending $5,000.

10 He lived in an $80-a-month furnished room near Dupont Circle,
paid $97 a month office rent, and had no secretary. People gave
him briefcases; he turned them into files and traveled with his
papers in a sheaf of manila envelopes. His black shoes were scuffed,
the laces broken and knotted. He wore a gray rumpled suit, frayed
white shirts, and narrow ties which had been **out of style** for   *no longer*
years. Standing six feet four inches, with wavy black hair and a   *fashionable*
youthful face, he was compared by *Newsweek*[20] to a "Jimmy Stewart
hero in a Frank Capra movie."[21] His only unusual expense was

[14] Union Carbide smokestacks: where the pollutants emerge into the environment
[15] think tanks: groups of researchers
[16] muckrakers of the Lincoln Steffens era: journalists who delved into controversial issues. Steffens (1866–1936) was an American journalist and editor.
[17] Miss Porter's School: a college preparatory school for girls (grades 9–12), founded in 1843 and located in Farmington, Connecticut
[18] with names like Pullman cars: Some train cars were named after celebrated Americans, so these names were famous ones.
[19] rummage sales: informal sales of miscellaneous, usually used items
[20] *Newsweek*: a weekly news magazine
[21] Jimmy Stewart hero in a Frank Capra movie: reference to the main character (played by actor Jimmy Stewart), named "Mr. Smith," who was a fledgling politician in Washington, D.C. Capra was the movie's director.

his telephone bill. It was enormous. He was paying for calls from his volunteer spies in industry.

11 Most of his income came from lecture fees. Each week he received fifty invitations to speak; he accepted 150 a year, charging as much as $2,000. He became known as the most **long-winded**   *talkative* speaker since Walter Reuther,[22] rarely relinquishing the lectern before an hour and forty-five minutes. There was never any flourish at the end. He would simply stop talking and pivot away. College audiences gave him wild ovations, but he never turned back to acknowledge them. If asked to autograph a book he would curtly reply, "No." A friend said, "Ralph is so afraid of being turned into a movie star, of having his private life romanticized, that he has renounced his own private life."

12 He was an impossible customer. To a waitress he would say when ordering, "Is the ham sliced for each sandwich? Is that genuine or processed cheese? Do *you* eat sugar? You do? Let me tell you something—it's absolutely useless, no food value." To an airline stewardess he said, "The only thing you should be proud to serve on this whole plane is the little bag of nuts. And you should take the salt off the nuts." When Allegheny Airlines had the temerity to **bump** him from a flight on which he had a   *remove* confirmed reservation, he filed suit and was awarded $50,000 in punitive damages, half for him and half for the consumer group he had been unable to address because of the missed flight.

13 Asked by Robert F. Kennedy[23] why he was "doing all this," he answered, "If I were engaged in activities for the prevention of cruelty to animals, nobody would ask me that question." His ultimate goal, he said, was "nothing less than the qualitative reform of the industrial revolution," and he refused to be lured from it by any bait. Nicholas von Hoffman[24] and Gore Vidal[25] proposed him for the Presidency. He said, "I'm not interested in public office. The biggest job in this country is citizen action. Politics follows that."

14 **Yet for all** his evangelism,[26] his devotion to the public good,   *Despite* and his monastic life, Nader's impact on society was questionable. At times he seemed to know it. "We always fail," he said once. "The whole thing is limiting the degree of failure." His audiences appeared to regard him as a performer. They applauded him, but it was as though they were applauding an act. Few of them felt compelled to get involved, to follow his example or even his advice. They **went right on** driving big Detroit cars, eating processed   *continued*

---

[22] Walter Reuther: (1907–1970) American labor leader
[23] Robert F. Kennedy: (1925–1968) American politician and brother of President John F. Kennedy
[24] Nicholas von Hoffman: (1929–) American journalist
[25] Gore Vidal: (1925–) American biographer and novelist
[26] evangelism: fervent preaching

foods,[27] **coating** themselves with expensive cosmetics and smoking poisonous cigarettes.

applying on the surface

15   In a pensive moment he reflected that "A couple of thousand years ago in Athens, a man could get up in the morning, wander around the city, and inquire into matters affecting his well-being and that of his fellow citizens. No one asked him 'Who are you with?'" Americans of the 1970s did not inquire about him; they knew. Yet they themselves remained uncommitted. The painful fact—excruciating for him—was that **however loud** their cheers for Ralph Nader, however often they said that they were for him, in this Augustan age of materialism they were not really with him.

no matter how loud

[27] processed foods: frozen, dried, sometimes precooked and packaged commercially. Many of these processes involve the use of harmful additives.

Discussion Points

1. How did Nader's father influence his son's career choice?
2. Describe Nader's earliest proconsumer activities.
3. Which investigative publication brought Nader national fame?
4. What tactics did General Motors use against Nader?
5. Define the role of "watchdog."
6. Describe the physical setup of Nader's organization.
7. How do college audiences react to Nader's speeches?
8. What is Nader's view on politics?
9. How does Nader respond to success and failure in his profession?

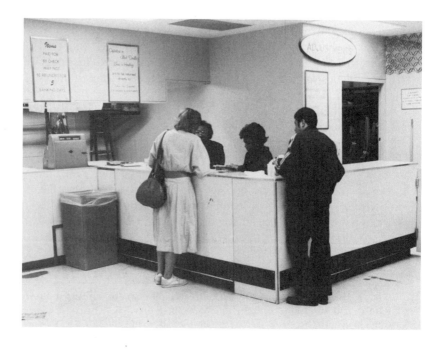

Composition Topics

The following four themes are related to the essay on Ralph Nader. Write a two-page composition on one of them.

1. Some people think of Ralph Nader as a national hero. Others consider him an eccentric nuisance. Take one of these stands and support it with examples furnished by Manchester. If possible, supplement the essay's points with independent research.
2. Compare and contrast Ralph Nader to a consumer advocate in your country. Depict the investigative projects spearheaded by that Nader counterpart.
3. Based on the revealing conversations between Nader and a waitress and a stewardess, characterize Nader's life-style.
4. Imagine yourself to be one of Nader's Raiders. What products or organizations would you choose to investigate and why? Indicate what the rewards and frustrations of such a work assignment might be.

Research Ideas

Try to gain a fuller understanding of Ralph Nader's contributions to American society by researching and preparing a report on one of these topics:

1. Agricultural Pesticides
2. Automobile Safety
3. Consumer Advocacy
4. Food Additives and Preservatives
5. Industrial Wastes

♦ *Sullivan's Death*

BY PHILIP CAPUTO

About the Author:

PHILIP CAPUTO
(1941–   )

Philip Joseph Caputo has won numerous awards for his work as a foreign correspondent assigned to Rome, Beirut, Moscow, and Vietnam. Caputo's experiences as a member of the Marine Corps (until 1967) and as a war correspondent have shaped his literary themes. Besides *A Rumor of War* (1977), from which the following essay derives, Caputo has authored these books: *Horn of Africa* (1980), *Del Corso's Gallery* (1983), and *Indian Country* (1987).

Setting the Scene

U.S. involvement in Vietnam's civil conflict dates from the 1950s, when American military advisers were sent to South Vietnam to assist with war strategy against their North Vietnamese adversaries. By 1964, American combat troops had joined the advisers in that war-torn Southeast Asian country. At home, there was growing opposition to American military support in South Vietnam, and as a result, some American soldiers at the front had ambivalent feelings about their own participation. As must be natural in a young soldier's mind, the priority of combat was weighed against the possibility of death. In "Sullivan's Death," Caputo focuses on immediate reactions and delayed afterthoughts of combatants faced with daily death.

Pre-Reading Considerations

1. What is your impression of the psychological effects of combat duty?
2. Have you or someone close to you witnessed war casualties?
3. Do you have personal knowledge of death?

135

Sullivan's Death
PHILIP CAPUTO

1   I did not feel like talking to anyone. Sullivan was much on my mind. Hugh John Sullivan, dead at the age of twenty-two and before he had had the chance to see his son. Colby had been right; it was **bound** to happen. But I wondered why it had to *destined* happen to a decent young man who always had a joke to tell, not to some cynical old veteran. I wondered why it had to happen to a husband and father, and why it had to happen in the way it did. Like many inexperienced soldiers, I **suffered from the** *had the* **illusion** that there were good ways to die in war. I thought grandly *misconception* in terms of noble sacrifices, of soldiers offering up their bodies for a cause or to save a comrade's life. But there had been nothing sacrificial or ceremonial about Sullivan's death. He had been sniped while filling canteens in a muddy jungle river.

2   I saw him as Lemmon had described him, lying on his back with the big, bloody hole in his side. I imagined that his face must have looked like the faces of the dead Viet Cong[1] I had seen the month before: mouth opened, lips pursed in a skull-like grin, eyes staring blankly. It was painful to picture Sullivan like that; I had **grown** so used to seeing his living face. That is when *become* I felt for the first time, sitting in the **mess** over a greasy tray of *dining area* greasy food, the slimy, hollow-cold fear that is the fear of death; the image of Sullivan's dead face had suddenly changed into an image of my own. That could be me someday, I thought. I might look like that. If it happened to him, there's no reason it can't happen to me. I did not think it necessarily would happen, but I realized it could. Except in an abstract sense, the chance of being killed had never occurred to me before. As a young, healthy American raised and educated in peacetime, or what passes for peacetime in this century, I had been incapable of imagining myself sick or old, **let alone** dead. Oh, I had thought about death, but *without even* only as an event that would happen far in the future, so far that *thinking of* I had been unable to consider it as a real possibility. Well, it had suddenly become a possibility, and a proximate one for all I knew. That was the thing: I could not possibly know or suspect when it would come. There was only a slight chance of being killed in a headquarters unit, but Sullivan probably had not felt any intimations of mortality when he walked down to that river, a

---

[1] Viet Cong: guerrilla members of the Vietnamese communist movement

string of canteens jangling in his hand. Then the sniper centered the cross hairs on his telescopic sight, and all that Sullivan had ever been or would ever be, all of his thoughts, memories, and dreams were annihilated in an instant.

3   I came to understand why Lemmon and the others had seemed so distant. It had nothing to do with my no longer belonging to the battalion. It was, rather, the detachment of men who find themselves living in the presence of death. They had lost their first man in battle, and, with him, the youthful confidence in their own immortality. Reality had caught up with them, with all of us. As Bradley put it later that evening: "I guess the splendid little war is over."

4   Some combat veterans may think I am **making too much of** a single casualty. Later, I was to see fairly active fighting, and I know that experiencing heavy or constant losses tends to diminish the significance of one individual's death. But at the time we lost Sullivan, casualties were still light; it was the "expeditionary" period of the war, a period that lasted **roughly** from March to September 1965. The loss of even one man was an extraordinary event. Perhaps, too, we were less emotionally prepared for death and wounds than those who came later; the men who fought in Vietnam at this time had joined the service in peacetime, before the **toll** built up to a daily announcement. A small statistic illustrates what I mean: One-Three's[2] total losses between March and August of 1965 amounted to about one hundred and ten killed and wounded, or ten percent. During one battle in April 1966, a single company from that same battalion lost one hundred and eight men in only one hour. But most important, in this early period the men in One-Three were very close to one another. They had been together for years and assumed they would remain together until the end of their enlistments. Sergeant Sullivan's death shattered that assumption. It upset the sense of unity and stability that had pervaded life in the battalion. One-Three was a corps in the old sense of the word, a body, and Sullivan's death represented the amputation of a small part of it. The corps would go on living and functioning without him, but it was aware of having lost something irreplaceable. Later in the war, that sort of feeling became rarer in infantry battalions. Men were killed, evacuated with wounds, or rotated home at a constant rate, then replaced by other men who were killed, evacuated, or rotated in their turn. By that time, a loss only meant a gap in the line that needed filling.

exaggerating the importance of

approximately

count

---

[2] One-Three: name of military unit

Discussion Points

1. In the author's opinion, why was Hugh John Sullivan a particularly sad choice to be a war casualty?
2. Describe the illusion that Caputo and other inexperienced soldiers held about war.
3. What psychological effect did Sullivan's death have on the author?
4. Compare war casualties in 1965 to those in 1966. How did this difference affect the soldiers' attitude toward death?
5. What did Sullivan's death represent to the One-Three corps?

Composition Topics

Select one of the following topics on which to compose a two-page paper:

1. Describe the illusions you have about war. From personal experience and/or media presentations, do you regard your concepts of war to be realistic? Explain your answer fully.
2. Caputo writes about the psychological change produced by the increase in battle casualties. Compare this effect to the impact of numerical increase in another area of human experience, for example, first "A" grade, tenth athletic award, etc.
3. Portray a personal association you have had with death. This might have been in a military setting or other context. Trace the psychological effect this experience had on you.

Research Ideas

To broaden your understanding of "Sullivan's Death," produce a two-page research report on one of these subject areas:

1. Philip Caputo
2. Military Esprit de Corps
3. The Psychology of Death
4. The Psychology of War
5. The Vietnam War

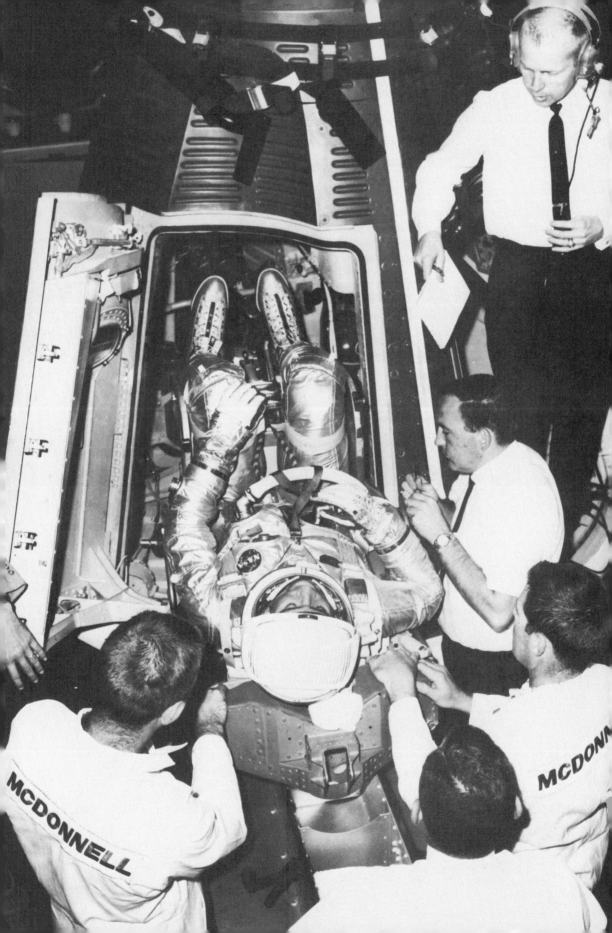

C H A P T E R **16**

◆ *The Right Stuff*

BY TOM WOLFE

About the Author: Virginia-born Thomas Kennerly Wolfe, Jr., is a highly regarded New
Journalist who began his career as a newspaper reporter. Until 1987,
TOM WOLFE Wolfe wrote predominantly about contemporary American culture, as
(1931–   ) in the following works: *The Electric Kool-Aid Acid Test* (1968), *Radical
Chic and Mau-Mauing the Flak Catchers* (1970), *Mauve Gloves and
Madmen* (1976), *In Our Time* (1980), and *The Purple Decades* (a
collection of 20 essays, 1982). In 1987, Wolfe departed from this non-
fiction trend and penned his first novel, *The Bonfire of the Vanities*.
The essay presented here, "The Right Stuff," is excerpted from his 1979
book of the same title.

**Setting the
Scene** Notwithstanding many early aerodynamic achievements developed in
the United States, the 1957 launching of the Soviet Sputnik satellite
startled Americans into a period of self-evaluation. They feared the
consequences of Soviet leadership in space technology. After much
competitive squabbling among the three branches of the U.S. military
(as to which one should be assigned space exploration projects), in
1958, the government established a separate agency, the National Aeronautics and Space Administration (NASA) for this enterprise. One of
the main elements in American space technology is pride, and Wolfe's
essay zeroes in on this element as it relates to astronaut training.

**Pre-Reading
Considerations**
1. Have you ever wanted to be an astronaut?
2. What type of training do you think an astronaut goes through?
3. What qualifications do you believe an astronaut should have?

The Right Stuff

TOM WOLFE

1   A young man might go into military flight training believing that he was entering some sort of technical school in which he was simply going to acquire a certain set of skills. Instead, he found himself all at once enclosed in a fraternity. And in this fraternity, even though it was military, men were not rated by their outward rank as ensigns, lieutenants, commanders, or whatever. No, herein the world was divided into those who **had it** and those who did not. This quality, this *it*, was never named, however, nor was it talked about in any way.

possessed the basic qualification of character

2   As to just what this ineffable quality was . . . well, it obviously involved bravery. But it was not bravery in the simple sense of being willing to risk your life. The idea seemed to be that any fool could do that, if that was all that was required, just as any fool could throw away his life in the process. No, the idea here (in the all-enclosing fraternity) seemed to be that a man should have the ability to go up in a hurtling piece of machinery and **put his hide on the line** and then have the moxie, the reflexes, the experience, the **coolness**, to pull it back in **the last yawning moment** —and then to go up again *the next day*, and the next day, and every next day, even if the series should prove infinite— and, ultimately, in its best expression, do so in a cause that means something to thousands, to a people, a nation, to humanity, to God. Nor was there *a test* to show whether or not a pilot had this righteous quality. There was, instead, a seemingly infinite series of tests. A career in flying was like climbing one of those ancient Babylonian pyramids made up of a dizzy progression of steps and ledges, a ziggurat, a pyramid extraordinarily high and steep; and the idea was to prove at every foot of the way up that pyramid that you were one of the elected and anointed ones who had *the right stuff* and could move higher and higher and even— ultimately, God willing, one day—that you might be able to join that special few at the very top, that elite who had the capacity to bring tears to men's eyes, the very Brotherhood of the Right Stuff itself.

risk his life

emotional control/ the last possible moment

3   None of this was to be mentioned, and yet it was acted out in a way that a young man could not fail to understand. When a new flight (i.e., a class) of trainees arrived at Pensacola,[1] they were brought into an auditorium for a little lecture. An officer would tell them: "Take a look at the man on either side of you."

[1] Pensacola: city in Florida

Quite a few actually swiveled their heads this way and that, in the interest of appearing diligent. Then the officer would say: "One of the three of you is not going to **make it**!" — meaning not **get his wings**. That was the opening theme, the *motif* of primary training. We already know that one-third of you do not have the right stuff — it only remains to find out who.

succeed

qualify for pilot duty

4   Furthermore, that was the way it turned out. At every level in one's progress up that staggeringly high pyramid, the world was once more divided into those men who had the right stuff to continue the climb and those who had to be *left behind* in the most obvious way. Some were eliminated in the course of the opening classroom work, as either not smart enough or not hardworking enough, and were left behind. Then came the basic flight instruction, in single-engine, propeller-driven trainers, and a few more — even though the military tried to make this stage easy — were **washed out** and left behind. Then came more demanding levels, one after the other, formation flying, instrument flying, jet training, all-weather flying, gunnery, and at each level more were washed out and left behind. By this point easily a third of the original candidates had been, indeed, eliminated . . . from the ranks of those who might prove to have the right stuff.

disqualified

5   In the Navy, in addition to the stages that Air Force trainees went through, the neophyte always had waiting for him, out in the ocean, a certain grim gray slab; namely, the deck of an aircraft carrier; and with it perhaps the most difficult routine in military flying, carrier landings. He was shown films about it, he heard lectures about it and he knew that carrier landings were hazardous. He first practiced **touching down** on the shape of a flight deck painted on an airfield. He was instructed to touch down and **gun right off**. This was safe enough — the shape didn't move, at least — but it could do terrible things to, let us say, the gyroscope of the soul.[2] *That shape! — it's so damned small!* And more candidates were washed out and left behind. Then came the day, without warning, when those who remained were sent out over the ocean for the first of many days of reckoning with the slab[3]. The first day was always a clear day with little wind and a calm sea. The carrier was so steady that it seemed, from up there in the air, to be resting on pilings, and the candidate usually made his first carrier landing successfully, with relief and even *élan*. Many young candidates looked like terrific aviators up to that very point — and it was not until they were actually standing on the carrier deck that they first began to wonder if they had the proper stuff, after all. In the training film the flight deck was a grand piece of gray geometry, perilous, to be sure, but an amazing abstract shape as

landing

take off immediately

[2] the gyroscope of the soul: instrument for balancing the spirit (figurative use)
[3] reckoning with the slab: practicing landing on and taking off from the deck

one looks down upon it on the screen. And yet once the newcomer's two feet were on it . . . Geometry—my God, man, this
is a . . . skillet! It heaved, it moved up and down underneath his
feet, it pitched up, it pitched down, it rolled to port (this great
beast rolled!) and it rolled to starboard, as the ship moved into   *the aircraft carrier*
the wind and, therefore, into the waves, and the wind kept sweep-
ing across, sixty feet up in the air out in the open sea, and there
were no railings whatsoever. This was a skillet!—a frying pan!—a
short-order grill![4]—not gray but black, smeared with skid marks
from one end to the other and glistening with pools of hydraulic
fluid and the occasional jet-fuel slick, all of it still hot, sticky,
greasy, runny, virulent from God knows what traumas—
still ablaze!—consumed in detonations, explosions, flames, com-
bustion, roars, shrieks, whines, blasts, horrible shudders, fracturing
impacts, as little men in **screaming** red and yellow and   *bright*
purple and green shirts with black Mickey Mouse[5] helmets over
their ears skittered about on the surface as if for their very lives
(you've said it now!), hooking fighter planes onto the catapult
shuttles so that they can explode their afterburners and be slung
off the deck in a **red-mad** fury with a kaboom! that pounds through   *violently angry*
the entire deck—a procedure that seems absolutely controlled,
orderly, sublime, however, compared to what he is about to watch
as aircraft return to the ship for what is known in the engineering
stoicisms of the military as "recovery and arrest." To say that an
F-4[6] was coming back onto this heaving barbecue from out of the
sky at a speed of 135 knots . . . that might have been the truth
in the training lecture, but it did not begin to **get across**   *communicate*
the idea of what the newcomer saw from the deck itself, because
it created the notion that perhaps the plane was gliding in. On
the deck one knew differently! As the aircraft came closer and
the carrier heaved on into the waves and the plane's speed did
not diminish and the deck did not grow steady—indeed, it pitched
up and down five or ten feet per greasy heave—one experienced
a neural alarm that no lecture could have prepared him for: This
is not an airplane coming toward me, it is a brick with some poor
sonofabitch[7] riding it (someone much like myself!), and it is not
gliding, it is falling, a thirty-thousand-pound brick, headed not for
a stripe on the deck but for me—and with a horrible smash! it
hits the skillet, and with a blur of momentum as big as a freight
train's it hurtles toward the far end of the deck—another blinding

---

[4] short-order grill: type of stove used for quick meals: grilled sandwiches, hamburgers
[5] Mickey Mouse helmets: These helmets have insulated ear pieces (to protect ears from intense
noise) which resemble Mickey Mouse's ears.
[6] F-4: a type of airplane
[7] some poor sonofabitch: someone looked upon with pity (a modified spelling of "son of a bitch,"
a profane term usually used in anger or with malice)

storm! — another roar as the pilot pushes the throttle up to full
military power and another smear of rubber screams out over the
skillet — and this is nominal! — quite okay! — for a wire stretched
across the deck has grabbed the hook on the end of the plane as
it hit the deck tail down, and the smash was the rest of the
fifteen-ton **brute** slamming onto the deck, as it tripped up, so that   *airplane*
it is now straining against the wire at full throttle, in case it hadn't
held and the plane had "boltered" off the end of the deck and
had to struggle up into the air again. And already the Mickey
Mouse helmets are running toward the fiery **monster** . . .   *airplane*

6   And the candidate, looking on, begins to *feel* that great heaving
sun-blazing deathboard of a deck wallowing in his own vestibular
system — and suddenly he finds himself backed up against his own
limits. He ends up going to the flight surgeon with so-called
conversion symptoms. Overnight he develops blurred vision or
numbness in his hands and feet or sinusitis so severe that he
cannot tolerate changes in altitude. On one level the symptom is
real. He really cannot see too well or use his fingers or stand the
pain. But somewhere in his subconscious he knows it is a plea
and a **beg-off**; he shows not the slightest concern (the flight   *expression of with-*
surgeon notes) that the condition might be permanent and affect   *drawal or refusal*
him in whatever life awaits him outside the arena of the right stuff.

7   Those who remained, those who qualified for carrier duty — and
even more so those who later on qualified for *night* carrier duty —
began to feel a bit like Gideon's warriors.[8] *So many have been left
behind!* The young warriors were now treated to a deathly sweet
and quite unmentionable sight. They could gaze at length upon
the crushed and wilted pariahs who had washed out. They could
inspect those who did not have that righteous stuff.

8   The military did not have very merciful instincts. Rather than
packing up these poor souls and sending them home, the Navy,
like the Air Force and the Marines, would try to make use of
them in some other role, such as flight controller. So **the**   *the disqualified*
washout has to keep taking classes with the rest of his group,   *trainee*
even though he can no longer touch an airplane. He sits there
in the classes staring at sheets of paper with cataracts of sheer
human mortification over his eyes while the rest **steal looks** at   *look subtly or*
him . . . this man reduced to an ant, this untouchable, this poor   *indirectly*
sonofabitch. And in what test had he been found **wanting**? Why,   *deficient*
it seemed to be nothing less than *manhood* itself. Naturally, this
was never mentioned, either. Yet there it was. *Manliness, manhood,
manly courage* . . . there was something ancient, primordial,
irresistible about the challenge of this stuff, no matter what a
sophisticated and rational age one might think he lived in.

[8] Gideon's warriors: fighters with Gideon, an early Hebrew

**Discussion
Points**

1. Define "the right stuff."
2. Trace the different wash-out levels facing the trainees.
3. How did the training film image of the aircraft carrier compare to the actual carrier?
4. What kinds of symptoms did the training pilots develop following their real aircraft carrier maneuvers? Were these symptoms real or imagined? Explain.
5. What duties were customarily assigned to the washouts?
6. How did the qualified candidates relate to the washouts?
7. One training officer told the recruits, "One of the three of you is not going to make it!" What psychological effect do you think these words had?
8. Now that females have entered the ranks of astronaut training and duty, how do you react to Wolfe's use of the terms *manhood* and *manly courage* to describe astronaut qualities?

Composition Topics

Of the following four topics, select one on which to prepare a two-page composition:

1. Consider a personal experience that involved several levels of qualification. Compare and contrast your experience to that portrayed by Wolfe.
2. Express your views on the Navy's handling of the training washouts. Would you recommend any modifications in these procedures? Justify your suggestions.
3. Name and characterize at least two other professional fields you believe require "the right stuff." Explain your choices fully.
4. In your native country, which profession is considered as exclusive as space travel is in the United States? Provide an account of the qualifications and training of the career you have named.

Research Ideas

To gain a wider knowledge of the historical backdrop to "The Right Stuff," investigate one of these topics for a two-page background paper:

1. The Apollo Missions
2. Astronaut Training
3. John Glenn
4. Space Travel

PART III

Changing Roles and Perspectives

Changing roles and perspectives is the central theme of the eight essays that comprise Part III of this book. "Marks," a poem by Linda Pastan (1932–), was chosen to introduce this final group of essays because it so aptly expresses modern disenchantment with traditional role assignment. In "Marks," a woman is besieged with critical performance evaluations (marks) by immediate members of her family. Deeply frustrated in her multiple roles, the woman fights back by abandoning her role assignment. Part III offers further illustrations of role assessment and abandonment, along with instances of modified points of view on other contemporary issues.

Marks
LINDA PASTAN

My husband gives me an A
for last night's supper,
an **incomplete** for my ironing,   *grade withheld*
a B plus **in bed.**   *pending completion*
My son says I am average,   *of assignment / for*
an average mother, but if   *conjugal performance*
I **put my mind to** it
I could improve.   *concentrate on,*
My daughter believes   *try hard at*
in Pass/Fail[1] and tells me
I pass. Wait 'til they learn
I'm dropping out.[2]

[1] Pass/Fail: more modern grading system that eliminates marks of "A," "B," etc. and, instead, indicates either passing or failing
[2] dropping out: This usually refers to permanently leaving school before completing the course requirements necessary for graduation, but here it means abandoning the traditional female duties of being a mother and a housewife.

C H A P T E R **17**

◆ *You Are What You Say*

BY ROBIN LAKOFF

About the
Author:
ROBIN
LAKOFF
(1942–   )

Robin Lakoff, born in New York, was a textbook editor before joining the Department of Linguistics at the University of California at Berkeley. In her field of linguistics, Lakoff is highly regarded as a leader in the specific area of Generative Semantics. Among her works, Lakoff is credited with *Language and Woman's Place* (1975) and *Face Value: The Politics of Beauty* (with Raquel L. Scherr, 1984).

Setting
the Scene

Can a woman be a "chairMAN" of a committee? Are females included in histories of "MANkind"? Is it a compliment for a female to be designated "mistress"? What is a "farmerette"? Why are first-year collegians of both genders termed "freshMEN"? Why has "Ms." been added to the list of English titles? And does "Roberta" know that her parents chose for her a feminine version of the male name "Robert"? Lakoff, as well as other writers abreast of the changes that the feminist movement has engendered, pinpoints the so-called "double standard" or sexism that exists in the English language. Her essay is both serious and engaging, as she methodically goes about addressing the linguistic dilemmas that are posed here.

Pre-Reading
Considerations

1. Have you ever noted linguistic differences in the ways males and females express themselves?
2. When you were a child, were you taught that certain words and phrases were either "boys' talk" or "girls' talk"?

You Are What You Say

ROBIN LAKOFF

1   "Women's language" is that pleasant (dainty?), euphemistic, never-aggressive way of talking we learned as little girls. Cultural bias was built into the language we were allowed to speak, the subjects we were allowed to speak about and the ways we were spoken of. Having learned our linguistic lesson well, we go out in the world, only to discover that we are communicative cripples—**damned** if we do, and damned if we don't.

criticized, faulted

2   If we refuse to talk "like a lady," we are ridiculed and criticized for being unfeminine. ("She thinks like a man" is, at best, a left-handed compliment.)[1] If we do learn all the **fuzzy-headed**, unassertive language of our sex, we are ridiculed for being unable to think clearly, unable to take part in a serious discussion, and therefore unfit to hold a position of power.

silly, unclear

3   It doesn't take much of this for a woman to begin feeling[2] she deserves such treatment because of inadequacies in her own intelligence and education.

4   "Women's language" shows up in all levels of English. For example, women are encouraged and allowed to make far more precise discriminations in naming colors than men do. Words like *mauve, beige, ecru, aquamarine, lavender,* and so on, are **unremarkable** in a woman's active vocabulary, but **largely** absent from that of most men. I know of no evidence suggesting that women actually *see* a wider range of colors than men do. It is simply that fine discriminations of this sort are relevant to women's vocabularies, but not to men's; to men, who control most of the interesting affairs of the world, such distinctions are trivial—irrelevant.

common

mostly

5   In the area of syntax, we find similar gender-related peculiarities of speech. There is one construction, in particular, that women use conversationally far more than men: the tag question. A tag is midway between an outright statement and a yes-no question; it is less assertive than the former, but more confident than the latter.

6   A *flat statement* indicates confidence in the speaker's knowledge and is fairly certain to be believed; a *question* indicates a lack of knowledge on some point and implies that the gap in the speaker's knowledge can and will be remedied by an answer. For example, if, at a Little League[3] game, I have had my glasses off, I can

---

[1] left-handed compliment: praise that is either insincere or doubtful
[2] It doesn't take much ... feeling: after receiving several of these critical and/or insincere comments, a woman begins to feel
[3] Little League: children's baseball team organization

From Robin Lakoff, "You Are What You Say," from *Ms.* Magazine, July 1974. Reprinted by permission of the author.

legitimately ask someone else: "Was the player out at third?" A *tag question*, being intermediate between statement and question, is used when the speaker is stating a claim, but lacks full confidence in the truth of that claim. So if I say, "Is Joan here?" I will probably not be surprised if my respondent answers "no"; but if I say, "Joan is here, isn't she?" instead, **chances are I am** already *I am probably* biased in favor of a positive answer, wanting only confirmation. I still want a response, but I have enough knowledge (or think I have) to predict that response. A tag question, then, might be thought of as a statement that doesn't demand to be believed by anyone but the speaker, a way of giving leeway, of not forcing the addressee **to go along** with the views of the speaker.   *to agree*

7   Another common use of the tag question is in small talk when the speaker is trying to elicit conversation: "Sure is hot here, isn't it?"

8   But in discussing personal feelings or opinions, only the speaker normally has any way of knowing the correct answer. Sentences such as "I have a headache, don't I?" are clearly ridiculous. But there are other examples where it is the speaker's opinions, rather than perceptions, for which corroboration is sought, as in "The situation in Southeast Asia is terrible, isn't it?"

9   While there are, of course, other possible interpretations of a sentence like this, one possibility is that the speaker has a particular answer in mind — "yes" or "no" — but is reluctant to state it **baldly**.   *directly* This sort of tag question is much more apt to be used by women than by men in conversation. Why is this the case?

10   The tag question allows a speaker to avoid commitment, and thereby avoid conflict with the addressee. The problem is that, by so doing, speakers may also give the impression of not really being sure of themselves, or looking to the addressee for confirmation of their views. This uncertainty is reinforced in more subliminal ways, too. There is a peculiar sentence intonation-pattern, used almost exclusively by women, as far as I know, which changes a declarative answer into a question. The effect of using the rising inflection typical of a yes-no question is to imply that the speaker is seeking confirmation, even though the speaker is clearly the only one who has the requisite information, which is why the question was put to her in the first place:

(Q) When will dinner be ready?
(A) Oh . . . around six o'clock . . . ?

11   It is as though the second speaker were saying, "Six o'clock — if that's okay with you, if you agree." The person being addressed is put in the position of having to provide confirmation. One likely consequence of this sort of speech-pattern in a woman is that, often unbeknownst to herself, the speaker builds a reputation

of tentativeness, and others will refrain from **taking her seriously** or *believing what she says* trusting her with any real responsibilities, since she "can't make up her mind," and "isn't sure of herself."

12   Such idiosyncrasies may explain why women's language sounds much more "polite" than men's. It is polite to leave a decision open, not impose your mind, or views, or claims, on anyone else. So a tag question is a kind of polite statement, in that it does not force agreement or belief on the addressee. In the same way a request is a polite command, in that it does not force obedience on the addressee, but rather suggests something be done as a favor to the speaker. A clearly stated order implies a threat of certain consequences if it is not followed, and — even more impolite — implies that the speaker is in a superior position and able to enforce the order. By **couching** wishes in the form of a request, on *disguising to soften or weaken* the other hand, a speaker implies that if the request is not carried out, only the speaker will suffer; noncompliance cannot harm the addressee. So the decision is really left up to the addressee. The distinction becomes clear in these examples:

> Close the door.
> Please close the door.
> Will you close the door?
> Will you please close the door?
> Won't you close the door?

13   In the same ways as words and speech patterns used by women undermine her image, those used to describe women make matters even worse. Often a word may be used **of both** men and women *for both* (and perhaps of things as well); but when it is applied to women, it assumes a special meaning that, by implication rather than outright assertion, is derogatory to women as a group.

14   The use of euphemisms has this effect. A euphemism is a substitute for a word that has acquired a bad connotation by association with something unpleasant or embarrassing. But almost as soon as the new word comes into common usage, it **takes on** *receives* the same old bad connotations, since feelings about the things or people referred to are not altered by a change of name; thus new euphemisms must be constantly found.

15   There is one euphemism for *woman* still very much alive. The word of course, is *lady*. *Lady* has a masculine counterpart, **namely** *which is* *gentlemen*, occasionally shortened to *gent*. But for some reason *lady* is very much commoner than *gent(leman)*.

16   The decision to use *lady* rather than *woman*, or vice versa, may considerably alter the sense of a sentence, as the following examples show:

> (a) A woman (lady) I know is a dean at Berkeley.
> (b) A woman (lady) I know makes amazing things out of shoelaces and old boxes.

17   The use of *lady* in (a) imparts a frivolous, or nonserious, tone
to the sentence: the matter under discussion is not one **of great**   *very important*
moment. Similarly, in (b), using *lady* here would suggest that the
speaker considered the "amazing things" not to be serious art, but
merely a hobby or an aberration. If *woman* is used, she might be
a serious sculptor. To say *lady doctor* is very condescending, since
no one ever says *gentleman doctor* or even *man doctor*. For example,
mention in the *San Francisco Chronicle* of January 31, 1972, of
Madalyn Murray O'Hair as the *lady atheist* reduces her position to
that of a scatterbrained eccentric. Even *woman atheist* is scarcely
defensible: sex is irrelevant to her philosophical position.

18   Many women argue that, on the other hand, *lady* carries with
it overtones recalling the age of chivalry: conferring exalted stature
on the person so referred to. This makes the term seem polite at
first, but we must also remember that these implications are
perilous: they suggest that a "lady" is helpless, and cannot do
things by herself.

19   *Lady* can also be used to infer frivolousness, as in titles of
organizations. Those that have a serious purpose (not merely that
of enabling "the ladies" to spend time with one another) cannot
use the word *lady* in their titles, but less serious ones may. Compare
the *Ladies' Auxiliary* of a men's group, or the *Thursday Evening
Ladies' Browning and Garden Society* with *Ladies' Liberation* or *Ladies'
Strike for Peace*.[4]

20   What is **curious** about this split is that *lady* is in origin a   *interesting*
euphemism—a substitute that puts a better face on something
people find uncomfortable—for *woman*. What kind of euphemism
is it that subtly denigrates the people to whom it refers? Perhaps
lady functions as a euphemism for *woman* because it does not
contain the sexual implications present in *woman*: it is not
"embarrassing" in that way. If this is so, we may expect that, in
the future, *lady* will replace woman as the primary word for the
human female, since *woman* will have become too blatantly sexual.
That this distinction is already made in some contexts at least is
shown in the following examples, where you can try replacing *woman*
with *lady*:

    (a) She's only twelve, but she's already a woman.
    (b) After ten years in jail, Harry wanted to find a woman.
    (c) She's my woman, see, so don't **mess around** with her.   *act too friendly
or forward*

21   Another common substitute for *woman* is *girl*. One seldom hears
a man past the age of adolescence referred to as a boy, **save** in   *except*
expressions like "going out with the boys," which are meant to
suggest an air of adolescent frivolity and irresponsibility. But

---

[4] *Ladies'... Peace*: In the names of the third and fourth groups mentioned, only the word *Women's*
(and not Ladies') is accepted usage.

women of all ages are "girls": one can have a **man**—not a boy— *assistant to* Friday, but only a **girl**—never a woman or even a lady—**Friday**; *the boss* women have girlfriends, but men do not—in a nonsexual sense— have boyfriends. It may be that this use of *girl* is euphemistic in the same way the use of *lady* is: in stressing the idea of immaturity, it removes the sexual connotations lurking in *woman*. *Girl* brings to mind irresponsibility: you don't send a girl to do a woman's errand (or even, for that matter, a boy's errand). She is a person who is both too immature and too far from real life to be entrusted with responsibilities or with decisions of any serious or important nature.

22   Now let's take a pair of words which, in terms of the possible relationships in an earlier society, were simple male-female equivalents, analogous to *bull:cow*. Suppose we find that, for independent reasons, society has changed in such a way that the original meanings now are irrelevant. Yet the words have not been discarded, but have acquired new meanings, metaphorically related to their original senses. But suppose these new metaphorical uses are no longer parallel to each other. By seeing where the parallelism **breaks down**, we discover something about the different roles *no longer is* played by men and women in this culture. One good example of *parallel* such a divergence through time is found in the pair, *master:mistress*. Once used with reference to one's power over servants, these words have become unusable today in their original master-servant sense as the relationship has become less prevalent in our society. But the words are still common.

23   Unless used with reference to animals, *master* now generally refers to a man who has acquired consummate ability in some field, normally nonsexual. But its feminine counterpart cannot be used this way. It is practically restricted to its sexual sense of "paramour." We start out with two terms, both **roughly** paraphras- *approximately* able as "one who has power over another." But the masculine form, once one person is no longer able to have absolute power over another, becomes usable metaphorically in the sense of "having power over *something*." *Master* requires as its object only the name of some activity, something inanimate and abstract. But *mistress* requires a masculine noun in the possessive to precede it. One cannot say: "Rhonda is a mistress." One must be *someone's* mistress. A man is defined by what he does, a woman by her sexuality, that is, in terms of one particular aspect of her relation- ship to men. It is one thing to be an *old master* like Hans Holbein,[5] and another to be an *old mistress*.

24   The same is true of the words *spinster* and *bachelor*—gender words for "one who is not married." The resemblance ends with the definition. While *bachelor* is a neuter term, often used as a

---

[5] Hans Holbein: the Elder (1465-1524), of father-and-son German painters having this name

compliment, *spinster* normally is used pejoratively, with connotations of prissiness, fussiness, and so on. To be a bachelor implies that one has the choice of marrying or not, and this is what makes the idea of a bachelor existence attractive, in the popular literature. He has been pursued and has successfully eluded his pursuers. But a spinster is one who has not been pursued, or at least not seriously. She is old, unwanted goods. The metaphorical connotations of *bachelor* generally suggest sexual freedom; of *spinster*, puritanism or celibacy.

25   These examples could be multiplied. It is generally considered a *faux pas*, in society, to congratulate a woman on her engagement, while it is correct to congratulate her fiancé. Why is this? The reason seems to be that it is impolite to remind people of things that may be uncomfortable to them. To congratulate a woman on her engagement is really to say, "Thank goodness! **You had a close call!** For the man, on the other hand, there was no such danger. His choosing to marry is viewed as a good thing, but not something essential.

(Fr.) social mistake

You were almost out of luck!

26   The linguistic double standard holds throughout the life of the relationship. After marriage, bachelor and spinster become man and wife, not man and woman. The woman whose husband dies remains "John's widow"; John, however, is never "Mary's widower."

27   Finally, why is it that salesclerks and others are so quick to call women customers "dear," "honey," and other terms of endearment they really **have no business using**? A male customer would never **put up with** it. But women, like children, are supposed to enjoy these endearments, rather than being offended by them.

should not be using

tolerate

28   In more ways than one, it's time to speak up.

Discussion Points

1. According to Lakoff, what lesson in communication did girls used to learn?
2. What typically happens when women do not talk "like a lady" in conversation with men?
3. What point does the author make regarding gender differences in question formation? Do you agree with her observation?
4. Explain the psychological impression that the use of tag questions makes.
5. Is there a sociolinguistic distinction between *lady* and *woman*? Explain your answer.
6. Distinguish between the uses of *girl* and *boy*.
7. Trace the evolution of the word *master*, and contrast its use with that of *mistress*.
8. What are the denotations and connotations of *spinster* and *bachelor*?
9. Why is it incorrect to congratulate a woman on her engagement to be married, but correct to do so with a man?
10. How do store clerks address you?

Composition Topics

Write a two-page paper on one of the following topics:

1. Using Lakoff's essay as a starting point, elaborate on the gender differences found in your native language. Highlight those that contain unequal connotations. Analyze the incidence of sexism in your language.
2. Provide an analysis of the contrasting language lessons girls and boys receive at home in your culture. Include translated examples. As you develop your paper, consider Lakoff's "she thinks like a man" and "she talks like a lady" references.
3. Compare and contrast the linguistic double standard relating to the way professional men and women are designated in your society with that depicted by Lakoff.

Research Ideas

In order to gain a fuller understanding of "You Are What You Say," prepare an investigative report of two pages on one of the research topics that follow:

1. Assertiveness Training for Women
2. Cultural Bias Toward Unmarried Females
3. Polite Language
4. Sexism in the English Language

CHAPTER **18**

◆ *Cop-out Realism*

BY NORMAN COUSINS

About the Author:
NORMAN
—COUSINS
(1912–   )

Norman Cousins has had a long and illustrious career in journalism and teaching. After more than three decades as editor of the literary magazine *The Saturday Review*, Cousins withdrew from that post in 1978. His association with that publication continues, however, as he holds the title of editor emeritus. Simultaneously, Cousins is serving as adjunct professor at University of California's Los Angeles Medical School. The author has earned myriad professional awards and honors. Among Cousins's more recent publications are the following: *Human Options: An Autobiographical Notebook* (1981), *The Physician in Literature* (1982), *Albert Schweitzer's Mission: Healing and Peace* (1985), and *The Pathology of Power* (1987).

Setting the Scene

The decade of the 1960s included "copping out" and "dropping out," which were acts of defiance against Establishment[1] rules and entrenched traditions. Some attribute this defiance to the parental and societal permissiveness of that decade, while others regard the anti-Establishment movement as the cause of the decade's permissiveness. What emerged in the late sixties was a counter-culture movement, known as the "hippie" movement. The hippies (also named "flower children") advocated peace (they were against U.S. involvement in the Vietnam Conflict), individualism, sexual freedom, and antimaterialism. Their credo was to do anything that felt good and did not hurt anybody. In "Cop-out Realism," Cousins reflects on the changes that took place in the sixties, those changes in personal behavior and society at large.

Pre-Reading Considerations

1. Do you support legalized gambling?
2. In your opinion, should high school students be forbidden to smoke on school grounds?
3. From your observations, would you say that parents have tended to surrender their authority over their children in recent times?

---

[1] Establishment: reference to the government and the customs and traditions that are practiced at a particular time in history

Cop-out Realism

NORMAN COUSINS

1   On all sides, one sees evidence today of cop-out[1] realism —
ostensible efforts to be sensible in dealing with things as they are
but that turn out to be a **shucking** of responsibility.   *shirking*

2   Example: Until fairly recently, off-track betting[2] was illegal in
New York State. Gambling on horses was regarded as a disguised
form of stealing, run by professional gamblers who preyed upon
people who could least afford to lose. Also outlawed was the
numbers game,[3] in which people could bet small amounts of money
on numbers drawn from the outcome of the day's horse races.

3   Attempts by government to **drive out** the gambling syndicates   *remove or chase*
had only indifferent results. Finally, state officials decided that,   *away*
since people were going to throw their money away despite
anything the law might do to protect them, the state ought to
take over off-track betting and the numbers racket.

4   It is now possible to assess the effect of that legalization. The
first thing that is obvious is that New York State itself has become
a predator in a way that the Mafia[4] could never hope to match.
What was intended as a plan to control gambling has become a
high-powered device to promote it. The people who can least
afford to take chances with their money are not only not dissuaded
from gambling but are actually cajoled into it by the state. Millions
of dollars are being spent by New York State on lavish advertising
on television, on radio, in buses, and on billboards. At least the
Mafia was never able publicly to glorify and extol gambling with
taxpayer money. And the number of poor people who were hurt
by gambling under the Mafia is miniscule compared to the number
who now lose money on horses with the urgent **blessings** of New   *encouragement*
York State.

5   A second example of cop-out realism is the way some communities are dealing with cigarette-smoking by teenagers and pre-
teenagers. Special rooms are now being set aside for students who
want to smoke. No age restrictions are set; freshmen have the
same **lighting-up** privileges as seniors.   *smoking*

6   The thinking behind the new school policy is similar to the
"realism" behind New York's decision to legalize off-track betting
and the numbers game. It is felt that since the youngsters are
going to smoke anyway, the school might just as well make it

[1] cop-out: characterized by abandonment of responsibility
[2] off-track betting: horse or dog-race betting that takes place away from the racetrack
[3] numbers game: lottery based on published numbers
[4] Mafia: a Sicilian (Italian) secret criminal society

possible for them to do it **in the open** rather than feel compelled *publicly*
to do it furtively in back corridors and washrooms.

7   Parents and teachers may **pride themselves on** their "realism" *be proud of*
in such approaches. What they are actually doing is finding a
convenient rationalization for failing to uphold their responsibility.
The effect of their supposedly "realistic" policy is to convert a ban
into a benediction. By sanctioning that which they deplore, they
become part of the problem they had the obligation to meet.
What they regard as common sense turns out to be **capitulation**.   *surrender*

8   Pursuing the same reasoning, why not set aside a corner for a
bar where students can buy alcoholic beverages? After all, teenage
drinking is a national problem, and it is far better to have the
youngsters drink out in the open than to have them feel guilty
about stealing drinks from the cupboard at home or contriving to
snatch their liquor outside the home. Moreover, surveillance can
be exercised. Just as most public bars will not serve liquor to
people who are hopelessly drunk, so the school bartender could
withhold alcohol from students who can hardly stand on their feet.

9   It is not **far-fetched** to extend the same "reasoning" to marijuana.   *implausible*
If the youngsters are going to be able to put their hands on the
stuff anyway, why shouldn't they be able to buy it legally and
smoke it openly, perhaps in the same schoolroom that has been
converted into a smoking den?

10   We are not reducing the argument to an absurdity; we are
asking that parents and teachers **face up to** the implications of   *confront*
what they are doing.

11   The school has no right to jettison standards just because of
difficulties in enforcing them. The school's proper response is not
to abdicate but to extend its efforts in other directions. It ought
to require regular lung examinations for its youngsters. It ought
to schedule regular sessions with parents and youngsters at which
reports on these examinations can be considered. It ought to bring
in cancer researchers who can run films for students showing the
difference between the brackish, pulpy lungs caused by cigarette
smoking and the smooth pink tissue of healthy lungs. The schools
should schedule visits to hospital wards for lung cancer patients.
In short, educators should take the U.S. Surgeon-General's report[5]
on cigarettes seriously.

12   In all the discussion and debate over cigarette smoking by
children, one important fact is generally overlooked. That fact is
that a great many children *do not* smoke. The school cannot ignore
its obligation to these youngsters just because it cannot persuade
the others not to smoke. It must not give the nonsmokers the
impression that their needs are secondary or that the school has

---

[5] U.S. Surgeon-General's report: The Surgeon-General is the nation's highest health officer, who
publishes health warnings, one of which was about the risk of cigarette smoking.

placed a seal of approval on a practice that is condemning millions of human beings to a fatal disease.

13   Still another example of cop-out realism is the policy of many colleges and universities of providing common dormitories and common washrooms for both sexes. The general idea seems to be that it is unrealistic to expect young people not to sleep together. Besides, it is probably reasoned, if people are old enough to vote they are old enough to superintend their own sleeping habits. So, the thinking goes, the school might just as well[6] allow them to share the same sleeping and toilet facilities.

14   The trouble with such policies is that they put the school in the position of lending itself to the breakdown of that which is most important in healthy relations between the sexes — a respect for privacy and dignity. No one ever need feel ashamed of the human body. But that doesn't mean that the human body is to be displayed or handled like a slab of raw meat. Sex is one of the higher manifestations of human sensitivity and response, not an impersonal sport devoid of genuine feeling. The divorce courts are filled to overflowing with cases in which casual, mechanistic attitudes toward sex have **figured in** marital collapses. For the school to foster that casualness is for it to become an agent of de-sensitization in a monstrous default.   *contributed to*

15   The function of standards is not to serve as the basis for mindless repressive measures but to give emphasis to the realities of human experience. Such experience helps to identify the causes of un-necessary pain and disintegration. Any society that ignores the lessons of that experience may be in **a bad way**.   *trouble*

Discussion Points

1. What is "cop-out realism"?
2. Describe the author's first example of cop-out realism. Discuss the official (of New York State) rationale on this subject.
3. What is Cousins's attitude toward school-approved cigarette-smoking? How does he view parental role in this matter? What is the typical role of parents in your community?
4. What hypothetical example of cop-out realism does Cousins propose?
5. What policies and plans does Cousins recommend for schools in the area of smoking and health education? How did your high school handle this issue?
6. What criticism does the author level at U.S. colleges and universities? Do you agree or disagree with allowing students to "superintend their own sex habits"?
7. Interpret the closing paragraph of Cousins's essay.

---

[6] the school might just as well: it would be equally advisable for the school to (Cousins is being sarcastic here)

Composition Topics

Prepare a two-page composition on one of the following topics:

1. Using Cousins's illustrations as a springboard, offer at least two of your own examples of modern-day cop-out realism. Present the pro and con sides to each of the issues you cite.
2. According to Cousins, parents have abandoned their responsibility toward establishing and monitoring behavioral standards for their children. Have you observed this erosion of parental authority that he portrays? Interpret parental responsibility as you perceive it. Wherever possible, compare and contrast U.S. standards to those of your society.
3. In the author's opinion, U.S. colleges and universities allow students too much freedom in their dormitories. Compare and contrast American collegiate residency to that in another country. Express and justify your preferences on this matter.

Research Ideas

To better understand the cultural and historical background of "Cop-out Realism," prepare a two-page research report on one of these topics:

1. Dormitory Life on U.S. College Campuses
2. Drinking Laws in the U.S.
3. Legalized Gambling: Social Consequences
4. Sex Education in American Schools
5. Smoking in U.S Public Schools
6. U.S. Surgeon-General's Report on Cigarette Smoking

CHAPTER 19

◆ *The Belated Father*

BY ELLEN GOODMAN

About the Author:

ELLEN
GOODMAN
(1941–   )

Massachusetts-born Ellen Holtz Goodman is a syndicated[1] newspaper columnist for the "Boston Globe." She is also highly respected for her radio and television commentaries and for her work as an author and a researcher. In 1980, Goodman won the coveted Pulitzer Prize[2] for excellence in journalism. Here is a partial listing of her published works, many of which treat social and political issues relating to women and the family: *Close to Home* (1979), *At Large* (1981), *Turning Points* (1982), and *Keeping in Touch* (1985).

Setting the Scene

Between 1940 and 1945, World War II forced American women to leave home and go to work in order to help the war effort. Women's earnings replaced the men's income, lost while they were in military service. Working mothers had to maintain their traditional homemaking function simultaneously with their new wage-earner role. An increase in the divorce rate, the influence of the women's liberation movement[3] in the sixties and the emergence of children's legal rights were other major factors that contributed to the evolution of parental roles. Many females desired to develop their own careers and, as mothers, began to share the parenting responsibility with their husbands. In "The Belated Father," Goodman introduces the theme of shifting parental roles in contemporary American society.

Pre-Reading Considerations

1. Do you believe in shared child-rearing responsibilities between mother and father?
2. Have you observed changes in parental roles since you were a child?
3. Do your parents function in so-called traditional or modern roles?

---

[1] syndicated: sold to and published in local papers throughout the country
[2] Pulitzer Prize: annual prize awarded in various fields of achievement, such as literature; established in 1918 by the will of Joseph Pulitzer, an American publisher
[3] women's liberation movement: a political direction reactivated energetically in the 1960s in the U.S. to promote equality of opportunity and legal rights for females

The Belated Father

ELLEN GOODMAN

1   There is a small clipping, no more than 2 square inches, that has been in my file marked "Fathers" since last fall. It's a simple story about a judge in western Massachusetts who, when confronted with a fifteen-year-old kid in trouble, made an unusual judgment. He sentenced the father to thirty days of dinner at home.

2   There are some other things in the folder. One is a letter to an advice column[1] from a woman whose husband has never kissed their baby son because he said, "I feel funny kissing a guy." Behind that letter is a statistic: "Ten percent of the children in this country live in fatherless homes."

3   There is also a quote from a novel about the children of the sixties,[2] written by Stephen Koch. It says, "Who among those fiery sons, with their vague and blasted eyes,[3] really **connected with** his father; who even knew, **let alone admired** what the father did in that invisible city[4] of his? Fatherhood meant delivering, or not delivering, checks. It meant not being around, or being unwelcome when around. It meant either shouting or that soul-crushing silence most deeply installed in the soul of any **red-blooded** American boy: Dad mute behind his newspaper."

> *had a close relationship with / without our even considering their admiring*

> *healthy and normal*

4   I wish there were something else in the file folder, some story; some **role model** you could applaud.

> *example of a role*

5   There are so many young fathers who don't want to be like their own dads. They feel awkward when they find themselves alone with their fathers today. They **flip through their own mental files** on the subject. There is Father Knows Best and Father Knows Nothing,[5] Father as Pal, and Father as Trans-parent.[6] There is

> *try to remember*

---

[1] advice column: newspaper article devoted to answering readers' letters that contain social or psychological dilemmas and questions

[2] children of the sixties: Depending upon the age of the "children" in this reference, Koch might be writing about the "hippies" of that decade — those teenagers (and older) who dropped out of society and opted for a life-style of antimaterialism, sexual permissiveness, and drugs.

[3] vague and blasted eyes: possible reference to drug-taking symptoms

[4] invisible city: reference to father's unavailability

[5] Father Knows Best/Father Knows Nothing: Father Knows Best refers to a popular television series of the 1950s; Father Knows Nothing is the author's wordplay contrasting the Father Knows Best program title.

[6] Trans-parent: the writer's own term for a parent in a transitional parental role

---

even an occasional full-time father — who trips in all the pitfalls of full-time mothers.

6   None of these **will do.** They don't fit. They don't feel right. So these sons are trying to devise their own role models, to be their own first generation. They are becoming — what shall we call them? — working fathers.

is acceptable

7   Margaret Mead[7] has written that "human fatherhood is a social invention." Maybe so. But they are re-inventing it. They want to be involved in the full range of their children's lives, to know which days the kids have to wear sneakers for **gym** and which kid would starve before he'd eat cauliflower.[8]

physical education class (from gymnasium)

8   They are learning to deal with kids when they are crying or dirty or hungry. As one father said, "When I was a kid, my father would play ball with me, but the minute I hurt my knee, we'd both call for my mother. I don't want to divide my kids like that."

9   He wants the kind of relationship that is only woven in the intimacy of daily, time-consuming routines during which you "learn" what they call intuition — the second sense that tells you one kid is worried and another is sad, and the difference between a cry that is tired and one that is hungry or hurt. These fathers don't want to be Sunday events.[9]

10   On the other hand, they have new guilts. They feel guilty if they miss the school play and guilty if they are tired or out of town. They can't **push it down** justifying their absence with the need to **Make It,** or with the notion that children are women's work.

convince themselves have a successful career

11   They wonder: "Can I be a successful worker and a successful father?" Their bosses are usually men of their father's generation whose offices are geared to full-time mothers and absent fathers. If they refuse overtime will they get ahead? What if they can't travel their way to a better job?

12   At the office they suddenly find themselves wondering, Did the babysitter **show?** I wonder if that **bully** in the playground is bothering Bobby again? Finally they wonder whether they have enough energy left over from work and fathering for their own lives and plans and marriages.

arrive (short for show up) / big, rough boy who intimidates the smaller, weaker ones

13   And when they describe all this, all this that is so new to them, they notice their wives quietly smiling. These fathers, you see, are becoming — well, how should we put it? Like us.

---

[7] Margaret Mead: (1901–1978) American anthropologist

[8] would starve before he'd eat cauliflower: reference to children's dislike of certain foods

[9] Sunday events: reference to the custom of a father's being so busy professionally during the work week that he has only Sunday to interrelate with his children

Discussion Points

1. Do you feel that thirty days of dinner at home, the sentence given by the Massachusetts judge, was an appropriate punishment? Explain your answer and interpret the underlying assumption of the penalty.

2. What aspect of contemporary American culture does the court's punishment (see preceding point number 1) reflect?

3. Explain the relationship between parental affection toward their children and the statistic Goodman provides in paragraph 2.

4. What is the significance of the reference to "Dad mute behind his newspaper"? Is this image familiar to you? Explain your answer.

5. Compare and contrast the following father types presented in the essay: full-time father, Father Knows Nothing, Father Knows Best, Father as Pal, and Father as Trans-parent. Does your father fit into any of these categories? Explain your answer.

6. Why are many young fathers trying to create a new style of fatherhood?

7. What part does intuition play in being a parent?

8. Describe the guilt feelings that some modern fathers have.

9. Name some of the worries that new fathers are now experiencing.

Composition Topics

Select one of the following themes on which to base a two-page paper:

1. Describe how the father's role has changed over the years in your society. Compare and contrast those changes with the ones depicted by Goodman.
2. Write a composition based on the subject of parental guilt. In your family, how do your parents express their guilt? Elaborate upon your answer.
3. Portray how parental affection is demonstrated in your culture. Analyze what effect it has on children's behavior. Compare and contrast your portrayal to that which Goodman provides in her essay. You may base your comparison on the essay and personal observations.
4. Express your ideas about fatherhood. Include your definition of parental success.

Research Ideas

In order to broaden your knowledge of the cultural and historical issues that are an important part of "The Belated Father," prepare a two-page investigative report on one of these topics:

1. American Family Structure
2. Children's Rights Under the U.S. Constitution
3. Divorce in the United States
4. Fatherhood in the Eighties
5. Feminism in the United States
6. Parenting in the Eighties
7. Women's Liberation Movement
8. American Working Women (Post–World War II)

◆ *Does Total Woman Add Up?*

BY ANNE TAYLOR FLEMING

**About the
Author:**
ANNE TAYLOR
FLEMING

Anne Taylor Fleming is a well-known journalist and media commentator. Her articles are published regularly in prominent magazines, and
she makes frequent guest commentaries on the "MacNeil-Lehrer News-
hour," a nightly television news program.

**Setting
the Scene**

The feminist movement in the United States attained considerable
momentum in the sixties, and it forced both men and women into
conscious definition of their roles in society. As a consequence, some
women felt better about their career orientation (as men have traditionally felt), while some men understood the importance of sharing in
child-rearing responsibilities. The term *Superwoman* was popularized
to describe "the modern woman" in her multiple roles: wife, mother,
and professional. In this essay, Fleming questions the concreteness of
feminist gains in light of popular guidebooks that instruct females in
the "art" of being alluring.

**Pre-Reading
Considerations**

1. How do you define *feminism* and *femininity*?
2. How do you assess the status of the Women's Movement today?
3. What is your reaction to gender equality in the work place and at
   home?

Does Total Woman Add Up?

ANNE TAYLOR FLEMING

"For an experiment I put on pink baby-doll pajamas[1] and white
boots after my bubble bath. I must admit that I looked foolish and felt
even more so. When I opened the door that night to greet Charlie, I
was unprepared for his reaction. My quiet, reserved, nonexcitable
husband took one look, dropped his briefcase on the doorstep, and
chased me around the dining room table. We were **in stitches** by the   *laughing very hard*
time he caught me, and breathless with that old feeling of romance."

1   In the first of her many costumes—cowgirl **get-ups** and pirate   *costumes*
plumes followed the pyjamas—Marabel Morgan, author of the
excerpt above from her bestseller, *The Total Woman* (Fleming H.
Revell Co., publisher), laid siege, apparently successfully, to her
husband's flagging libido. I did not read her book when it was
published a few years ago, fearing that it would enrage me, inflame
my fledgling feminism.[2] Lately, my feminism **taken for granted**, I   *not noticed or*
read it. It's really a very funny book. The idea that, nightly, as   *appreciated*
I sit in jeans and tired T-shirt watching the news, millions of   *sufficiently*
Total Women are in those moments meeting their husbands at
the door in **see-through** aprons and fish-net whatevers[3] makes me   *transparent*
laugh, a **not-at-all unkind** laugh. We all have our small, quiet,   *sympathetic*
and not so quiet ways to try to keep our loves or lusts alive; and,
if costuming works for some, why not?

2   Many women would disagree, rather violently, and would maintain that physical costuming is, for women, emotional costuming—
posturing, pretending to feel something one does not feel, sexual
pleasure being the prime example—the very thing they have tried
to fight. Despite my sympathy for black stockings, I do not like
emotional posturing, particularly my own, and I do well understand
that anti-Morgan venom of the Liberated Woman.

3   Ms. Morgan's message is, finally, **stockings aside**, quite naughty.   *without consider-*
Underneath her costumes and her compassion for the work-weary   *ation of the*
male—a compassion for which, like the playclothes, I have   *stockings*
sympathy—there hides a **hard-hearted** seductress who, bare-   *unemotional*
bottomed, wiggles her **will** over her husband. In return for her   *wishes, preferences*
costume parades, in return for her adulation of his superior muscles,
mental and physical, Ms. Morgan gets goodies from her husband—a
bottle of perfume, a new refrigerator, and good loving. The Total

[1] baby-doll pajamas: very feminine pajamas made of a lightweight fabric. The top features short,
puffy elasticized sleeves and scoop neck, and the bottoms are short with bloomer-type legs.
[2] feminism: organized activity on behalf of women's rights and interests
[3] fish-net whatevers: different articles of apparel made of a coarse open-mesh fabric

From Ann Taylor Fleming, "Does Total Woman Add Up?" *Vogue*, August 1977. Courtesy *Vogue*.
Copyright© 1977 by the Condé Nast Publications Inc.

Woman course is ultimately just a Weight Watchers[4] for the psyche or sex life—to Ms. Morgan the two are the same.

4   Arrayed against Morgan, and enraged at her, are legions of liberating women whose self-help manuals have titles like *The New Assertive Woman*. The aim of these books, which is also quite funny, is exactly the same aim as Ms. Morgan's: that is, to teach women how to tone up their **flabby wills**. It is merely a difference of technique that divides these authors. Where Ms. Morgan advocates costumes and coyness, the Assertiveness Trainers advocate unmasked directness and assertiveness. Being assertive apparently means being "**straight**," hitting just the right balance between being coy, or "feminine," and being fierce. A typical exercise for the aspiring Assertor goes like this: A man you've been dating for a few weeks is, as his ardor is increasing, beginning to bore you and you don't want to see him anymore. You: *weakness in communicating their true desires* *direct*

   (a) tell him you'd prefer not to see him, feeling that you've been honest?
   (b) feel a sudden attack of flu coming on?
   (c) continue to be the object of his affections, because leaving would really hurt his ego?
   (d) tell him that he bores you **to tears**, and that even if you were both marooned on a desert island, you would camp out on the opposite shore?   *very much*

5   Now, anyone knows that (a) is the right, nice, "assertive" answer, but I have strong latent leanings toward (d)—the thoroughness of it—and know that I would actually answer (b). That, according to the authors, makes me a coward—though not as big a one as I would be by answering (c) and continuing to see this man. Then I would be falling into "The Compassion Trap." That's the worst thing I could do.

6   I do have considerably more respect for the Assertiveness Trainers, despite their often silly questions and sillier senses of humor (**Putdown**: "Are you a Women's Libber?"[5] Assertive retort: "Is Libber something you serve with bacon or onions?"), than I do for Marabel Morgan. Many woman do need to find their **voice**. But, essentially, I find both **wanting**, both wooing women away from following their own instincts, from doing what is comfortable. Women, with their new freedoms—hence new uncertainties—are being wooed by these rival zealots. It is the war of The Total Women, the chest-forward brigade, versus the Assertive Women, the chin-forward brigade.   *an insult* *audible opinion lacking*

[4] Weight Watchers: a commercial organization offering weight reduction through special diets and physical activities

[5] Woman's Libber: proponent of the Women's Liberation Movement. The word play here is the substitution of *libber* for *liver*.

7   It is as if women must make a choice: costumes or no, **doormat** *a yielding, subser-*
or **door opener, hand holder** or **fist clencher.** It is as if women *vient person / a*
must declare allegiance to one side or the other, abdicate the right *liberated female /*
to their confusion, undergo a certain sudden clarification of *a sympathetic, com-*
emotion. It is as if women should stop knowing that the **lines are** *forting person / an*
always blurred, that being strong and being soft overlap as much *assertive person /*
as being male and being female. Why shouldn't everyone be *issue is never*
everything—men soft and sad, women strong and sassy, then vice *clearly defined*
versa, as one's mood or instinct dictates? Why, in fact, shouldn't
we all be soft all of the time if possible? Soft does not mean meek;
strong does not mean tough. Surely, meekness and toughness are
equally wasteful. The insidious presumption in all of these books
is that life is a battle in which one must have a resolute repertoire
of behavior in order to survive or triumph. Why behave? Behavior
is a **corset** invented by psychosocialists to keep people **hemmed in,** *restraint (figurative*
hence classifiable. Why not laugh, cry, shriek in pain or joy, woo, *use) / restricted*
reject, caress, or covet as one's instincts indicate? Now that I've
weeded out—with help from the Women's Movement[6]—the *eliminated through*
cramping coyness of my girlhood days, why shed my remaining *a sifting process*
reticences for which I've developed a certain perverse fondness?

Discussion   1. Explain the origin of the essay's title.
Points   2. What is Fleming's opinion of Marabel Morgan's *The Total
                      Woman?*
                   3. What is the purpose of books like *The New Assertive Woman?*
                   4. Define "The Compassion Trap."
                   5. Distinguish between the chest-forward and chin-forward brigades.
                   6. Why does Fleming resent the apparent recommendation that
                      women find an emotional classification for themselves?
                   7. Interpret Fleming's question "Why behave?" (paragraph 7).

[6] Women's Movement: political movement advocating equal rights for women

Composition Topics

Select one of the following themes on which to base a two-page paper:

1. Outline the ways in which Fleming reveals herself to be a feminist.
2. Portray a feminist you know (it may be yourself). Provide examples that typify this person's (your) feminist philosophy.
3. Take sides in the Morgan-Fleming "total woman" controversy. Support your viewpoint with real-life examples.

Research Ideas

For a greater appreciation of the issues that underlie "Does Total Woman Add Up?" choose one of these subjects on which to prepare a two-page research report:

1. Assertiveness Training for Women
2. Feminism in the United States
3. *The Total Woman* by Marabel Morgan
4. The Women's Liberation Movement in the United States

CHAPTER 21

Masculinity: Style and Cult

BY HAROLD ROSENBERG

About the Author:
HAROLD ROSENBERG (1906–1978)

Harold Rosenberg distinguished himself not only as an author, but also as an art critic, a university lecturer, a poet, and a translator. He served as the *New Yorker* magazine's art critic for many years, during which time he authored several studies of prominent artists. Listed here are some of his publications: *Trance above the Streets* (collection of poems, 1942); *The Anxious Object: Art Today and its Audience* (1964); *Discovering the Present: Three Decades in Art, Culture, and Politics* (1973); and *Art on the Edge* (1975).

Setting the Scene

Rosenberg's essay is provocative, for it forces the reader to consider a variety of images of masculinity, and to attempt to identify and reconcile the trappings of virility with virility itself. Does a naturally masculine male have to flaunt his masculinity? Rosenberg addresses this question throughout his essay.

Pre-Reading Considerations

1. What is your definition of *masculinity*?
2. Which occupations do you associate with masculinity?

Masculinity: Style and Cult

HAROLD ROSENBERG

1   Societies of the past have admired different personifications of the manly virtues: the warrior, the patriarch, the sage; the lover, the seducer; Zeus[1] the Thunderer, Jehovah[2] the Lawgiver.

2   In America, masculinity is associated primarily with the outdoors, and with such outdoor trades as cattledriving, railroading, whaling, and trucking. The outdoor type is presumed to possess masculine character traits: toughness, resourcefulness, love of being alone, fraternity with animals, and attractiveness to women and the urge to abandon them. To the man of the open spaces is also attributed the **ultimate mark** of manliness, the readiness to die.   *most highly regarded trait*

3   From the outdoors America derives the boots, lumber jackets and shirts, sailor's caps, pipes, and guns that are its paraphernalia of masculinity. Oddly enough, in the United States, military and police uniforms do not confer masculinity, as they do among Cossacks[3] and Hussars.[4] One can as readily imagine women in our army uniform as men. To prove that he was all man, General Patton[5] had to augment his battle costume with a pearl-handled revolver. (It is true, however, that he wrote poetry and may have felt the need to overcome this handicap.)[6]

4   As to hair, masculinity is ambivalent. Long hair belongs to the style of frontier scouts and trappers, the most male of men. Yet "longhairs" is the name applied to intellectuals, a breed always suspected of sexual inauthenticity. Beards used to be a material evidence of maleness; today they are as frequently an appurtenance of masquerade.

5   In the last century the outdoors represented genuine hazards. It took self-reliance, identifiable with masculinity (though the pioneer mother had it, too), to venture very far from the farm or town.

6   Today there are still risky occupations—piloting spaceships, handling nuclear substances—but these trades have become increasingly technical and depersonalized. **As for** the rugged   *Regarding* outdoors, it is used chiefly for sports; and a vacation at a ranch

[1] Zeus: king of the gods in Greek mythology

[2] Jehovah: incorrect transliteration of Hebrew name for God, "Yahweh"

[3] Cossacks: Russian cavalry troops

[4] Hussars: Hungarian cavalry troops

[5] General Patton: George Smith (1885–1945), American general

[6] handicap: The author is sarcastically referring to the ability to write poetry as a character flaw that would require the performance of manly activities to counteract it.

From Harold Rosenberg, "Masculinity: Style and Cult," from *Discovering the Present: Three Decades in Art, Culture, and Politics* (Chicago: University of Chicago Press, 1973)©1973 by Harold Rosenberg. All rights reserved.

180

or ski lodge, or shooting lions in Kenya, is about as hazardous as a trip to the Riviera.

7   The outdoors, representing **once-hostile** nature, has been transformed into a stage set. Masculinity in the American sense has thus lost its locale and, perhaps, its reason for being. On the neonlighted lonesome prairie, masculinity is a matter of certain traditional costume details: the cowboy hat, jeans, and guitar. It has become clear that the traditional traits of the **man's man** (and the ladies' man)[7] can be put on, too. One *plays* manliness, with or without dark goggles.

hostile in the past

location

a virile man

8   Big-game hunters, mountain climbers, horsemen, and other representative male types are actors in a charade of nostalgia. Old masculine pursuits, like baseball or wrestling, when carried on at night under the glare of fluorescent tubes, come to resemble spectacles on television and **wind up** in the living room. In the epoch of the picture window,[8] outdoors and indoors have lost their separateness.

look back

end (up)

9   In modern mass societies the uniforms of all kinds of cults compete with one another. Masculinity is one of these cults, and to create an impression the practitioner of maleness must **stand out** in a crowd. Persons with other interests are not disposed to make an issue of their sex. Only psychiatrists and sociologists complain that boys and girls today look alike and are often mistaken for each other. Even tough adolescents, like members of big-city gangs, don't mind if their girls wear the same shirts and jeans as the men. All are more concerned with identifying themselves as outsiders[9] than as males and females.

be noticed

10   Masculinity today is a myth that has turned into a comedy. A ten-gallon hat still seems to bestow upon its wearer the old male attributes of taciturnity, resourcefulness, courage, and love of solitude. At the same time, the virility of the cowboy and the truck driver, like that of the iceman of yesterday, is a joke that everybody **sees through**.

able to have sex

understands the falseness of

11   A person uncertain of his sexual identity dresses up in boots, bandanna, and riding breeches not so much to fool the public as to **parade** his ambiguity. Those who have **gone over the line** may advertise their desires for male company by wearing a beard in addition to sheepskins.[10] Women can be masculine too, of course, in the degree necessary to make them irresistible to feminine men.

display / become a homosexual

12   Hemingway,[11] who constantly kept the issue of masculinity alive

---

[7] ladies' man: man who is attractive to females and is involved in romantic affairs

[8] picture window: one that is much larger than the standard size; usually has only a single pane so as to provide an unobstructed view to the outside, typically of an attractive outdoor scene.

[9] outsiders: those representing points of view that differ from the accepted, established ones

[10] sheepskins: leather pieces made of sheepskin

[11] Hemingway: Ernest Miller (1899–1961), American writer and journalist

in his writings, flaunted both the look of the outdoor man and his presumed character qualities of daring, self-detachment, contempt for the **over-civilized,** and eagerness to **court death.**

conformist / perform risky acts / masculine

13   Hemingway's **he-man** performance was, among other things, a means of combatting the American stereotype of the writer as a sissy. In the United States, the artist and man of ideas have always lived under the threat of having their masculinity impugned. Richard Hofstadter, in his *Anti-Intellectualism in American Life,* lists a dozen instances in which the "stigma of effeminacy" was branded upon intellectuals by political bullies,¹² ranging from Tammany Hall¹³ leaders in the nineteenth century, who attacked reformers as "political hermaphrodites," to Communist Party hacks in the 1930s, who denounced independent writers as "scented whores." Evidently, it has always been possible to convince the common man that his intellectual superiors **fall short of** him in manliness.

are inferior to

14   To the overhanging charge of being **contaminated** by a ladylike occupation, Hemingway responded by injecting the romance of masculinity into the making of literature. At least as far as he was concerned, the sexual legitimacy of the male writer was to be **put beyond question.** Besides **lining up with** traditional outdoor types, such as bullfighters and deep-sea fishermen, Hemingway's strategy included identification with the new activist male image of the Depression¹⁴ decade: the leather-jacketed revolutionist allied with the peasant and factory worker. One might say that each of his novels originated in a new choice of male makeup.

(figurative use of this word)

made doubtless identifying with

15   Unfortunately, demonstrating his own manhood was not enough for Hemingway. He found it necessary to challenge the masculinity of other writers. Like Theodore Roosevelt¹⁵ earlier in the century, he became an instance of the intellectual who slanders intellectuals generally, in the hope of **putting himself right with** the **regular guys.** During the Spanish Civil War¹⁶ he **forgot himself** to the extent of sneering publicly at Leon Trotsky¹⁷ for remaining at his typewriter in Mexico, implying that the former chief of the Red Army¹⁸ lacked the manliness to go to Spain and fight. He, himself, of course, went to Spain to write. In *For Whom the Bell Tolls* he identified himself with the dynamiter Jordan who also shook the earth by his love feats in a sleeping bag.

making himself acceptable to hetero- sexual males / lost emotional control

¹² political bullies: politicians who use their positions to intimidate others
¹³ Tammany Hall: headquarters of the Tammany Society, a New York City political organization, especially at the turn of the century
¹⁴ Depression: starting in the year 1929, the worst economic period in the U.S., marked by severe unemployment
¹⁵ Theodore Roosevelt: (1858–1919), U.S. President from 1901–09
¹⁶ Spanish Civil War: 1936–39
¹⁷ Leon Trotsky: (1879–1940) leader in the Russian Communist movement
¹⁸ Red Army: Russian Army

16   Thirty years ago not all of Hemingway's contemporaries were convinced that he had established his masculinity through displaying an appetite for violence, sex, and death. In *no thanks*, E.E. Cummings[19] translated Hemingway's romance of maleness back into the daydreams of boyhood:

> "what does little Ernest croon
> in his death at afternoon?
> (kow dow r 2 bul retoinis   *cow thou are to bull returnest*
> wus de woids uf lil Oinis"   *was the words of little Ernest*

To Cummings, Hemingway's heroics were not only childish ("lil Oinis") but feminine ("kow dow r").

17   The post-Hemingway he-man had labored under the handicap of a masculinity that is generally recognized to be a masquerade. The adventurer living dangerously has disintegrated into the **tongue-in-cheek** élan of James Bond.[20] Neither at work nor at home is maleness any longer endowed with glamour or privilege. The cosmonaut is less a birdman than a specialist **minding** his signals and dials. The father who has entered into a diapering partnership[21] with his wife has nothing in common with the patriarch. To the public of Norman Mailer[22] (more male?) the outdoor rig (Mailer in sea captain's cap on the **jacket** of *Advertisements for Myself*) and chronicles of supersex are suspect, both psychologically and as playing to the gallery.[23] It is no secret that a Bogartean toughness[24] with women may represent the opposite of male self-confidence.

joking

paying attention to

outer paper cover of a hardcover book

18   The mass media exploit the ambiguity of the male role and the sexual sophistication that goes with the increasing awareness of it. In male comedy teams, one of the partners almost invariably plays the "wife," confident that the audience will know when to smirk. Analysts of mass culture speak of the decline of the American male and of the "masculinity crisis" as topics capable of arousing libidinous responses. The public is given the image of luscious females starving **in vain** for the attention of men, and of men who, **egged on** and deprived by frigid seductresses, end by falling into each other's arms.

unsuccessfully
enticed

19   Masculinity-building is urged, a theme which the media are not

---

[19] E.E. Cummings: Edward Estlin (1894–1962), American poet
[20] James Bond: name of the romanticized lead character in modern British spy novels and films
[21] diapering partnership: one in which the father, as well as the mother, changes the baby's diapers
[22] Norman Mailer: (1923–) American author
[23] playing to the gallery: exaggerating gestures and projecting the voice so as to reach the farthest seats of the theatre
[24] Bogartean toughness: reference to the tough "bad guy" screen image of Hollywood film actor Humphrey Bogart (1899–1957)

slow to adapt for their own purposes. Masculinity is the alfalfa peddled in Marlboro Country.[25] It is the essence of worn leather laced with campfire smoke that provides the aroma of the man of distinction. It also comes in powder form, none genuine without the Shaggy Dog on the wrapping.

20 To those who resent the fact that their pretension to masculinity is not taken seriously, one means is available for gaining respect: violence. The victim of rape is not inclined to question the virility of her assailant.

21 The relation between masculinity that has been put into doubt and violence reveals itself most clearly in the recent history of the Civil Rights movement.[26] The black has derived from white America the lesson that physical force is the **mark** of manhood. *sign* White society is "the Man," whose insignia of power are the club, the whip, the **bloodhounds**. The presence of the Man impeaches *dogs that pursue or* the masculinity of the young black and demands that he prove *track down* himself. He becomes full grown when he resolves to fight the Man. To confront the Man, the black militant has resurrected the figure of the radical activist of the thirties, the model of Hemingway's he-man, honor-bound to risk his life in physical combat.

22 An article in the *New York Times Magazine* on the Black Panthers[27] is illustrated by photographs of its two leaders. Both wear the traditional leather jackets and berets of the Left fighters[28] of thirty years ago — these could be photographs of two Lincoln Brigade[29] volunteers. A statement by one of the Panthers touches the philosophical essence of the romantic conception of masculinity: to be a man one must dare to die. "The ghetto[30] black," said Bobby Seale,[31] "isn't afraid to **stand up to** the cops, because he *confront / police* already lives with violence. He expects to die any day." *officers*

23 In our culture all human attributes tend to be **over-defined** and *too defined* become a basis of self-consciousness. The behavioral sciences[32]

---

[25] Marlboro Country: the untamed western-looking background scenery used in Marlboro cigarette advertisements

[26] Civil Rights movement: political movement that began in the 1950s to achieve civil rights for black Americans

[27] Black Panthers: 1960s group of black Americans. The purpose of their organization was to aid impoverished Blacks; their militarylike garb and forceful leadership caused them to lose some public support.

[28] Left fighters: fighters for socialist causes

[29] Lincoln Brigade: private group of Americans who fought for the Nationalists in the Spanish Civil War (1936–39)

[30] ghetto: in the U.S., a confined living area for Blacks; boundaries originally imposed by laws of segregation, later by tradition

[31] Bobby Seale: Black Panther leader (1936–   )

[32] behavioral sciences: studies of human behavior, e.g., psychology

collaborate with the mass media in making a man **anxious** about   *nervous*
his sex status; both then provide him with models of aggressiveness
by which to correct his deficiencies. Yet the present uneasiness
about masculinity, **coupled** with theatrical devices for attaining it,   *combined*
may be more harmful than any actual curtailment of manliness
discovered by researchers and editorialists. The real damage may
lie in the remedy rather than the ailment, since the desire to have
one's masculinity acknowledged may lead, as we have seen, to
absurd postures and acts of force. It is hard to believe that
Americans would be worse off by becoming more gentle. Nor that
mildness in manners and social relations would make them less
manly. In the real world nothing is **altogether** what it is. True   *completely*
maleness is never without its vein of femininity. The Greeks
understood this and made it the theme of their tales of sexual
metamorphosis, the remarkable account of Hercules,[33] of all men,[34]
taking on temporarily the character of a woman and wearing   *adopting*
women's clothes. Total masculinity is an ideal of the frustrated,
not a fact of biology. With the cult of masculinity put aside,
maleness might have a better chance to develop in the United
States.

Discussion   1. Name the character traits that Rosenberg asserts are associated
Points   with American masculinity.
                 2. What are the traditional paraphernalia of masculinity?
                 3. What role does hair play in the masculine image?
                 4. What are some of today's risk-taking occupations? Do they
                    symbolize masculinity?
                 5. How does Rosenberg analyze Hemingway's use of the romance of
                    masculinity in the latter's novels?
                 6. How does Rosenberg characterize the post-Hemingway he-man?
                    Give examples.
                 7. In the context of the American Civil Rights movement, how has
                    "black America" viewed "white America's" use of physical force?
                 8. What is Rosenberg's definition of "total masculinity"? Does it
                    exist?

[33] Hercules: mythical Greek hero known for his superstrength
[34] of all men: one who would never be thought of in this context

Composition Topics

Select one of the following five topics on which to compose a two-page essay:

1. The author opines that in this country masculinity is characterized mainly by outdoor activities. Compare and contrast this image with the one that prevails in your society.
2. Rosenberg writes that violence is sometimes viewed as a sign of masculinity. Relate this viewpoint to your own, and provide supporting examples.
3. Long hair versus short hair is a controversial subject in the context of a male image. Comment on the impression hair length makes in your culture.
4. James Bond is an example of a media he-man. In terms of his "total masculinity," analyze his popularity.
5. If you have read a novel by Ernest Hemingway, present your analysis of any masculine character in his writings.

Research Ideas

In order to appreciate more fully the issues presented in Rosenberg's essay, consider one of the following topics on which to develop a two-page research paper:

1. Black Panthers
2. James Bond
3. Ernest Hemingway
4. Masculinity in the United States
5. Theodore Roosevelt

C H A P T E R **22**

Those Good Ole Boys

BY BONNIE ANGELO

About the Author:
BONNIE ANGELO

Bonnie Angelo, a successful newspaper journalist, was born in North Carolina. Among other testaments to her professional excellence, Angelo received an award for reporting civil rights events. She served as a reporter for various newspapers and one television network before settling in to her current assignment as London bureau chief for *Time* magazine.

Setting the Scene

An underlying question that Angelo might ask at the outset of her essay—but doesn't—is why there are so few women in public office in the United States when they comprise more than half the population. One of the explanations for this truism is the existence of the "good ole boy" network in government and politics. Angelo portrays the "good ole boy" with finesse and wit.

Pre-Reading Considerations

1. What is your definition of a "good ole boy"?
2. What social obstacles do you think female politicians in the United States confront?

Those Good Ole Boys

BONNIE ANGELO

1   It is Friday night at any of ten thousand **watering holes** of the   *bars*
small towns and crossroads hamlets of the South. The room is a
cacophony of the pingpong-dingdingding of the pinball machine,
the pop-fizz of another **round** of Pabst,[1] the **refrain** of *Red Necks,*   *order / tune*
White Socks and Blue Ribbon Beer[2] on the juke box, the insolent
roar of a **souped-up** engine outside and, above it all, the sound   *mechanically*
of easy laughter. The good ole boys have gathered for their fraternal   *altered to be*
ritual — the aimless diversion that they have elevated into a life-style.   *very powerful*

2   Being a good ole boy is not a consequence of birth or breeding;
it **cuts across** economic and social lines; it is a **frame of mind**   *transcends / attitude*
based on the premise that life is nothing to get serious about. A
glance at the brothers Carter[3] tells a lot. There is some confusion
about why Billy Carter seems in many respects the quintessential
good ole boy, while Brother Jimmy couldn't even fit into the more
polished subspecies of conscious good ole boys who abound in   *refined, dignified*
small-town country clubs.[4] Billy, amiable, full of jokes, his
REDNECK POWER[5] T shirt straining unsuccessfully to cover the
paunch, swigs a beer, carefree on a Sunday morning, as Jimmy
Carter, introspective, hard driving, teaches Sunday school. Jimmy
sometimes speaks wistfully of Billy's good-ole-boy ease.

3   Lightheartedness permeates the good ole boy's life-style. He
goes by nicknames like "Goober" or "Goat." He disdains neckties
as a form of snobbery; when he dresses up, it is to wear a decorated
T shirt with newish jeans or, for **state occasions**, a leisure suit[6]   *more formal events*
with a colored shirt. If discussions veer beyond football toward
substance, he **cuts them off** with funny stories.   *interrupts them*

4   The core of the good ole boy's world is with his buddies, the
comfortable, **hyperhearty**, all-male camaraderie, joshing and   *super jolly*
drinking and regaling one another with tales of assorted,
exaggerated prowess. Women are outsiders; when social events are
unavoidably mixed, the good ole boys cluster together at one end

---

[1] Pabst: a brand of beer
[2] *Red Necks, White Socks and Blue Ribbon Beer*: This song title refers to southern white males
who wear white socks and drink top-quality beer (especially the label Pabst Blue Ribbon).
[3] brothers Carter: Jimmy (James Earl) (1924–   ), American president from 1977–81, and his
brother Billy (not a politician)
[4] country clubs: suburban clubs for social life and recreation
[5] REDNECK POWER: slogan declaring both strength and group identity for the stereotypical
southern "good ole boy"
[6] leisure suit: a suit consisting of a shirt jacket and matching trousers, for informal wear

---

of the room, leaving wives at the other. The GOB's magic doesn't work with women; he feels insecure, threatened by them. In fact, he doesn't really like women, except in bed.

5   What he really loves is his automobile. He overlooks his wife with her hair up in pink rollers, sagging into an upside-down question mark in her tight slacks. But he lavishes attention on his Mercury **mistress**, Easy Rider shocks[8] oversize slickers, dual   *refers to the car* exhaust. He exults in tinkering with that beautiful engine, lying cool beneath the open hood, ready to respond, quick and fiery, to his touch. The automobile is his love and his sport.

6   Behind his devil-may-care lightheartedness, however, runs a strain of innate wisdom, an instinct about people and an unwavering loyalty that makes him the one friend you would turn to, not just because he's a drinking buddy who'll keep you laughing, but because, well, he's a good ole boy.

Discussion Points

1. Describe the typical atmosphere of a good ole boy "watering hole."
2. Delineate the differences between Jimmy and Billy Carter (according to Angelo). Which one could be classified as a good ole boy?
3. What are the good ole boy's preferences in clothing and leisure time activities?
4. How do good ole boys relate to females?
5. Describe the good ole boy's relationship to his car.
6. Name the good ole boy's positive traits.

---

[7] Mercury: a make of car

[8] Easy Rider shocks: shock absorbers for motorcycles. (An American film of the 1970s, called *Easy Rider*, told the story of motorcycle riders.)

Composition Topics

Read through the following themes and then select one on which to develop a two-page paper:

1. Compare and contrast the socializing of men and women at a good ole boy event with that of a social gathering in your community.
2. Given Angelo's characterization of the good ole boy, consider whether or not you could fit into his society. Provide a thoughtful explanation for your response to this hypothetical scene.
3. If you know a good ole boy, describe him and his life-style. Remember to relate the good ole boy traits outlined in this essay to the individual you have chosen to be the focus of your composition.

Research Ideas

For a more complete understanding of the cultural background of Angelo's essay, prepare a two-page research paper on one of the following topics:

1. Billy Carter
2. Good Ole Boys
3. The Role of Females in Southern Society (U.S.)
4. Female Politicians in the South (U.S.)

CHAPTER 23

♦ *You Haven't Come a Long Way, Baby: Women in Television Commercials*

BY CAROL CALDWELL

About the Author:
CAROL CALDWELL

Carol Caldwell's career covers assignments as an advertising copywriter and a free-lance literary commentator. Her magazine articles focus on popular culture, and she frequently writes about well-known personalities from the entertainment field.

Setting the Scene

With the advent of an invigorated women's liberation movement in the 1960s, the traditional roles of men and women were reexamined, not only in real life, but also in their representation in advertising. Were men and women unfairly and unrealistically stereotyped? Was the woman constantly characterized as the housewife striving to please her husband? And was the man always portrayed as judging his wife? At one time, the label of a can of beans depicted the contented face of a man, and the words adjacent to his smiling face were "husband-pleasin'." That same label underwent a change in the mid-1980s: the words "people-pleasin' " now appear in place of the former "husband-pleasin'." But Caldwell's findings are less heartening. Using the popular cigarette slogan, "You've Come a Long Way, Baby" (referring to progress in the women's liberation movement), Caldwell divulges the conclusions of her research in advance—by substituting "You *Haven't* Come" for "You've Come" in her title.

Pre-Reading Considerations

1. Do you think that females are realistically portrayed in television commercials?
2. Over the last few years, have you observed any changes in the way commercials characterize the family?

You Haven't Come a Long Way, Baby: Women in Television Commercials

CAROL CALDWELL

1   It's the beginning of the age of television, and all around it's black and white. Millions of minuscule scan dots collide in electronic explosion to create Woman in her Immaculate Kitchen. She is Alpha, Omega,[1] eternal and everlasting Mother Video, toasting and frying, cleansing and purifying, perfectly formed of fire and ice. Permanent-waved,[2] magenta-lipped, demurely collared and cuffed, cone-shaped from her tightly cinched waist down through yards and yards of material that brush coquettishly mid-calf, she is Betty Furness[3] for Westinghouse; and you can be *sure* if it's Westinghouse.[4]

2   The year is 1951. On the set of CBS-TV's *Studio One*, Furness has just captured the part to become America's first full-time product spokewoman on television. Advertising **execs** at Westinghouse are **taking a stab** at having someone other than the host sell their product; they reason (and quite correctly) that Furness, with her Brearly School cool and her Broadway glamor, is a figure thousands of women will admire and listen to. During the audition Betty alters the script supplied by the casting director. Later, she tells *Time* magazine that she ad-libbed the refrigerator routine because "it was written like men think women talk!"

short for executives
trying

3   1952. While John Daly, Bill Henry, and Walter Cronkite monitor Ike[5] and Adlai[6] at the conventions, Betty Furness opens and shuts forty-nine refrigerators, demonstrates the finer points of forty-two television sets, twenty-three dishwashers and twelve ovens for a total of four-and-a-half hours of air time. General Eisenhower is on the air approximately an hour and twenty minutes; Mr. Stevenson, fifty minutes.

---

[1] Alpha, Omega: These are the first and last letters of the Greek alphabet; they are used here to represent the beginning and the end.

[2] Permanent-waved: hair style featuring waves or curls artificially added to naturally straight hair

[3] Betty Furness: (1916–) prominent figure in early television commercials; later chosen to be a governmental spokesperson in the area of consumerism

[4] " ... and you can be *sure* if it's Westinghouse.": famous advertising slogan of Westinghouse electrical appliances, such as refrigerators

[5] Ike: nickname of Dwight David Eisenhower (1890–1969), American general during World War II and U.S. President from 1953–61

[6] Adlai: Adlai Ewing Stevenson (1900–1965), American lawyer, politician, and statesman who opposed Eisenhower in two presidential races

---

4   1956. Bright and **blondeened**, twenty-eight-year-old Julia *with dyed-blonde hair*
Meade is the commercial spokeswoman for Lincoln[7] on the *Ed
Sullivan Show*, for Richard Hudnut hair products on *Your Hit
Parade*, for *Life* magazine on John Daly's news show. She is **pulling** *earning*
down a hundred thousand dollars a year, which moves *Time* to
comment, "Julia (34-20-34)[8] is one of a dozen or so young women
on TV who find self-effacement enormously profitable." Howard
Wilson, a vice-president of Kenyon & Eckhardt, Lincoln's ad
agency, hired Julia for the spots with trepidation: a woman just
couldn't be convincing about such things as high torque, turbo
drive, and ball-joint suspensions. His fears, it turns out, were
unfounded, and Meade becomes the perky prototype for a whole
slew of carefully coiffed women selling cars — selling *anything* — by
means other than their technical knowledge. And so Julia Meade
begat Bess Myerson, who begat Anita Bryant, who begat Carmelita
Pope, who begat Florence Henderson, each wholesome, flawless,
clear of eye and enunciation, in short, sixty-second **reminders** of *commercials*
everything the American woman ought to be.

5   Times change, however, and eventually infant TV's ideal,
untouchable dozen spokeswomen were replaced by hundreds of
nameless actresses who portray **"the little woman"** in scenarios *housewife*
believed, by the agencies who create them, to be honest-to-God,
middle-American,[9] **slice-of-life** situations. As early as 1955, this *typical*
new wave of commercial realism got **a pat on the back** by the *approval*
industry's weekly trade paper, *Advertising Age*. Procter & Gamble
had just come out with a revolutionary new way to sell soap on
TV: "It is very difficult for a soap commercial to emerge from the
mass of suds, with every known variant on the familiar theme of
the woman holding up a box of 'X' soap powder with a grisly smile
pointing to a pile of clothes she has just washed. Cheer has come
up with the unique approach of dramatizing an everyday washing
problem from the poor woman's point of view with a sound-over
technique of stream of consciousness."[10]

6   That stream of consciousness flowed unchecked until Bill Free's
famous National Airlines "Fly Me" faux pas in 1971. Women
activists carried signs, **stormed** Free's and National's offices, read *entered*
proclamations, and permeated the media with protest. Free talks *bombastically*
of this trying and critical time with a humor and stoicism that
comes from a six-year perspective, and from no longer handling
the account. "The women's movement was identifying itself — and

[7] Lincoln: a make of car
[8] (34–20–34): referring to the bust, waist, and hip measurements of a female's shape
[9] middle-American: the average middle-class citizen
[10] sound-over technique of stream of consciousness: This technique features a background voice
saying the "thoughts" of the person(s) in the commercial.

our 'Fly Me' campaign was an opportunity for a public platform. We were deluged with letters and calls. I even got an absurd letter from one of the leaders of the movement (who must go unnamed) demanding that I surely planned the sexual innuendo in the word 'fly'—she meant as in men's trouser pants." He paused. "The ad community continues to demean women, far more subtly than in our campaign."

7   There are some easy hints at why this is so: Of the seventy-five thousand people currently employed in advertising, only 16.7 percent are women in other than clerical positions—not exactly an overwhelming voice. And, while advertising executives often live in the suburbs of large cities, they just as often tend to have a low regard for anyone who isn't an urbanite. As one New York agency executive quipped, "All I really know about the Middle America I sell to everyday is that it's the place I fly over to get to L.A."

8   But these notations still don't answer the question: Why have advertisers, who make their living keeping up with trends, been so slow to **get on board** with the women's revolution? Where was everybody the recent night David Brinkley **closed the book on** America's traditional homelife structure, citing the fact that a mere seven percent of our nation's homes still maintained the time-honored tradition of the everyday housewife. Mom has officially **flown the coop** just about everywhere, except on TV in the commercials.

follow the trend
terminated

abandoned the house

9   At a **roundtable** on women's advertising sponsored by the agency trade publication *Madison Avenue*, Harriet Rex, a vice-president at J. Walter Thompson, had this comment to make: "There's always been a lag between what is and what the ad business has codified as what 'is.'" And Rena Bartos, a senior VP at the same agency, said, "Advertising may be a mirror of society but somehow the image in that mirror is a little out of focus. It plays back a 1950s reflection in a 1970s world."

discussion

10   Madison Avenue's "little woman" is hardly new, and only partially improved. When feminists cite advertising that is "acceptable," it's invariably print ads. This isn't surprising, since magazine ads are prepared for specific subscribers whose personal backgrounds and attitudes have been carefully documented by the publication and noted by the agency. Television, on the other hand, commands a much larger and subsequently less definable audience.

11   So it is left to the advertisers and their agencies to define who television's consuming woman might be and what type of commercial she might like. The reward is compelling: Americans **heap** a total $9.2 billion every year **into the coffers of** the nation's top three TV advertisers—Procter & Gamble, Bristol-Myers, and General Foods. Still, the women portrayed aren't always to the

pay to

customer's liking, and last year agitated viewers marched en masse outside P&G headquarters in Cincinnati, suggesting in rather unladylike terms what to do with Mr. Whipple and his grocery store groupies.[11] Inside, P&G stockholders **took little heed, voting down** a suggestion that their commercial portrayal of women be reconsidered. *paid almost no attention and defeated*

12   Others in the business did listen. When the National Organization for Women sent all major advertising agencies a position paper[12] on the role of women in commercials, no one was surprised that most of the commercials on the air didn't **jibe with** the NOW requirements. *conform to* Several agencies, fearing intervention by the Federal Trade Commission, prodded their own regulatory outfit to consider the matter. The National Advertising Review Board formed a panel, including Patricia Carbine, publisher of *Ms.*; Joyce Snyder, coordinator of the task force on the image of women for NOW; the vice-presidents of broadcast standards for ABC and NBC; and a number of officers of sponsoring companies. A twenty-one page directive came out in 1975, in which the panel made a number of suggestions concerning ways in which advertisers could improve their portrayal of women. Here's what **came out in the wash**: *the conclusions were* "Advertising must be regarded as one of the forces molding society," the study asserted. "Those who protest that advertising merely reflects society must reckon with the criticism that much of the current reflection of women in advertising is out of date." Before airing a commercial, the panel urged advertisers to run down the NARB checklist, which included the following points:

- Are sexual stereotypes perpetuated in my ads? Do they portray women as weak, silly and over-emotional?
- Are the women portrayed in my ads stupid?
- Do my ads portray women as ecstatically happy over household cleanliness or deeply depressed because of their failure to achieve near-perfection in household tasks?
- Do my ads show women as fearful of not being attractive, of not being able to keep their husbands or lovers, fearful of in-law disapproval?
- Does my copy promise unrealistic psychological rewards for using the product?

13   Well now, does it? With these self-regulatory commandments in mind, I spent four weeks in front of daytime TV, **logging** current household product commercials and trying to determine just **where women stand** in the advertising scheme of things. During that *recording* *what the status of women is*

---

[11] Mr. Whipple and his grocery store groupies: Mr. Whipple is the name of a character portraying a grocer; his "groupies" are those (most often female) customers in the commercial who are his devoted, enthusiastic followers.

[12] position paper: a document that contains the position (point of view) of a person or company on a particular subject

time, Iris dickered with Rachel and Mac's teetering marriage, Beth died, Stacy miscarried, and Jennifer killed John's wife so they could finally be together.[13]

14   **Now a word from our sponsors.**   *And here comes a*
                                            commercial.

15   Ring around the collar lives.[14] After eight long years, the little woman is still exposing hubby and the kids to this awful embarrassment. It can strike virtually anywhere — in taxis, at ballgames, even on vacation doing the limbo.[15] Our lady of the laundry is always guilty, always lucky to have a next-door neighbor who knows about Wisk, the washday miracle, and always back in hubby's good, but wary, graces[16] by the happy ending. The Wisk woman faces the same unspoken commercial threat that the Geritol woman faces: "My wife, I think I'll keep her . . ." *if* she keeps in line.

16   Jim Jordan is president of Batten, Barton, Durstine and Osborn Advertising. Eight years ago, in a fit of cosmic inspiration, he came up with "ring around the collar" for his agency's client, Lever Bros. Since then, Jordan has run check-out-counter surveys on his commercials, asking shoppers who were purchasing Wisk, "You must be buying this product because you like the commercials." The reply he got was always the same: "Why no! I hate those commercials; but why should I hold that against the product?"

17   Jim Jordan echoes advertising's premier axiom: "The purpose of the commerical is not the aesthetic pleasure of the viewer — it's to sell the product." And Wisk is selling **like gangbusters**. He   *extremely well* doesn't believe "ring around the collar" commercials show women in an embarrassing light; and to assume that, he says, "would be giving commercials more credit than they deserve."

18   Perhaps. And perhaps his "ring around the collar" campaign is getting more credit than it deserves for selling Wisk. Take any commercial with a simple message, repeat it again and again, and the product, if it's good, will sell, even if the spot is mindless and annoying. It's fixing the name of the product in the consumer's mind with a quick, catchy phrase that's important.

19   The household slice-of-life commercial is one of the classic offenders of the NARB checklist. (Are sexual stereotypes perpetuated? You'd best believe it. Are the women portrayed stupid? **And how**). Crisco's current campaign is a flawless example   *Yes, indeed!*

---

[13] Iris . . . together: references to the story lines of daytime television drama

[14] Ring around the collar lives: The author means that the stereotypes found in this commercial are being perpetuated, namely, that the woman lives in fear of doing something her husband will disapprove of.

[15] limbo: an acrobatic dance form of the West Indies (Caribbean nations), where many Americans travel for the warm tropical climate and beautiful beaches, especially in the wintertime

[16] in hubby's good, but wary, graces: To be in one's "good graces" means to be "approved" by that person; the addition of "but wary" here signifies that the hubby (husband) is constantly judging his wife.

of this much-imitated genre, which has been developed and designed by Procter & Gamble. In it various long-suffering husbands and condescending neighbors are put through the heartache of greasy, gobby chicken and fries, all because some unthinking **corner cutter** spent "a few pennies less" on that mainstay of American cookery, lard. These pound-foolish[17] little women cause their loved ones to live through "disasters" and "catastrophes." At the cue word "catastrophe," our video crumples into wavy electronic spasms and thrusts us back to the scene of the crime: to that excruciating point in the Bicentennial picnic or the backyard cookout when Dad has to wrinkle his upper lip and take Mom aside for a little **set-to** about her greasy chicken. The moral, delivered by some unseen[18] pedantic male announcer, is plain: "Ladies who've learned—buy Crisco."[19]

frugal shopper

argument

20   These examples are, sad to say, still very much the rule for women's portrayals in thirty- and sixty-second spots. They occur with alarming regularity during the daytime hours, when stations may sell up to sixteen commercial minutes an hour. (The nighttime rate is a mere eight minutes, forty seconds per hour.) Now, you are probably not the average American who spends some six hours a day in front of the old boob tube[20] (which, when the maximum number of commercials per hour is computed, means over an hour and a half of product propaganda). And you probably are quite sure that commercials have absolutely no effect on you. Maybe they don't. But a shaken agency copywriter told me the first word his child spoke was "McDonald's"[21] and I've stood in a grocery line and watched while a mother, tired of her child's tears, lets him wander off and return—not with a candy bar, but with a roll of Charmin.[22] Make no mistake about it: the cumulative effects of commercials are awesome. As the NARB study argues: "An endless procession of commercials on the same theme, all showing women using household products in the home, raises very strong implications that women have no other interests except laundry, dishes, waxing floors, and fighting dirt in any form. . . . Seeing a great many such advertisements in succession reinforces the traditional stereotype that 'a woman's place is *only* in the home.'"

21   There have, in the past few years, been commercials that break the homebody mold. The Fantastik spray commercial, "I'm married

---

[17] pound-foolish: careless with large sums of money. The complete adage is "penny-wise and pound-foolish."

[18] unseen: person who is heard but not seen

[19] Crisco: a brand of vegetable oil

[20] old boob tube: television set, so-named to indicate the idiocy (*boob* is slang for *idiot*) of the programming

[21] McDonald's: fast-food restaurant chain

[22] Charmin: a brand of toilet paper

to a man, not a house" (which, incidentally, was written and produced by men), has reaped much praise, as has L'Oreal's[23] "I'm worth it" campaign. "Ten years ago, it would have been, 'John thinks I'm worth it,'" says Lenore Hershey, editor of *Ladies' Home Journal. Ms.'* Pat Carbine thinks United Airlines is flying right when they address women executives, "You're the boss." She also likes the Campbell's soup "working wife" commercial, in which a man scurries around the kitchen, preparing soup for his woman, but adds, "I'm afraid they took the easy route and resorted to total role reversal—making her look good **at the expense of the man.**"

and (making) him look bad

22   Indeed, Lois Wyse of Wyse Advertising fears that advertisers are not only failing to talk to today's women, but they're missing men as well. The reason for this, as she sees it, is research—the extensive demographic studies done on who buys what product. Last winter Wyse told *Madison Avenue*, "About twenty years ago we were all little Ozzies and Harriets[24] to all the people who do research, and now their idea of contemporizing is to make the Ozzies into Harriets and the Harriets into Ozzies."

23   Marketing research, with its charts and graphs and scientific jargon, has increased in importance over the last ten years or so, while creativity, the keystone to the Alka-Seltzer, Volkswagen, and Benson & Hedges campaigns of the sixties, has **taken the backseat.** Ask anybody in advertising why commercials still show the little woman bumbling around in a fearful daze, and you'll find the answer is always the same: "Because our research tells us it is so." Agencies devote hundreds of thousands of dollars to find out who's buying their client's stuff and why. And it's not just Mom up there on the charts and graphs. Marketing researchers dissect and analyze the buying habits, educational and income levels of every member of the family. They even know what we do with our leisure time, and **how much God we've got.**

received less attention

how religious we are

24   The subjective form of research is amorphously titled life-style research, explained by the respected *Journal of Marketing* in the following brave-new-world lingo:[25] "Life-style data—activities, interests, opinions—have proved their importance as a means of *duplicating* the consumer for the marketing researcher. . . ." And more: "Life-style attempts to answer questions like: What do women think about the job of housekeeping? Do they see themselves

---

[23] L'Oreal: a cosmetics manufacturer. "I'm worth it" was their hair dye slogan.

[24] Ozzies and Harriets: Ozzie and Harriet Nelson and their sons Ricky and David were in real life, as well as on radio and later on television (especially in the 1950s), a stereotypical American family. Even now (in the late 1980s) their television series, being reshown, reveals what a typical family life-style in the 1950s was like.

[25] brave-new-world lingo: reference to the language of a future world, as originated by writer Aldous Huxley (1894–1963) in his 1932 novel *Brave New World*

as **homebodies** or **swingers**? Life-style provides definitions like 'housewife role haters,' 'old-fashioned homebodies' and 'active affluent urbanites.'"

full-time housewives / those who socialize a lot

25   But life-style research is still **in its infancy** and very, very expensive. The trendiest and most attainable form of research going is called focus-group research, the grassroots movement[26] of advertising research. From lairs of hidden cameras and tape-recording devices, agency and client-types, despite the experts' warnings that focus-group samples are far too small to be projected on a national scale, eke out a vision of their consumer that almost invariably fits just the stereotype they had in mind in the first place, and proceed to advertise accordingly.

in its beginning stages

26   The theory, quite simply, is to get inside women's heads in order to get inside their pocketbooks. From Satellite Beach to Spokane,[27] fact-finding specialists are **retained at grand sums** to commune with the natives and document their particular buying habits. For instance:

hired at high salaries

27   The canned-meat industry's advertising wasn't paying off in the Southeast. Focus-group researchers were called in and groups of eight women were randomly selected from Memphis[28] neighborhoods. The women fit the product's profile[29]—in this case, all came from families with middle to lower-middle incomes. Each woman was paid ten dollars. On an assigned day each focus group would meet for a two-hour session at the suburban home of the researcher's field representative—a woman who **was a veteran of** several similar exercises. As the women took their seats around the dining room table, **loosening up** with coffee and homemade cake, the client and agency folk sat, out of sight, in the rumpus room,[30] carefully **scanning the meeting on closed-circuit monitors**. This is what they heard.

had had much experience with

relaxing

watching on a privately televised setup

MODERATOR: Do any of you ever buy canned meats?
VOICES: Oh yes. Yeah. Uh, huh.
MODERATOR: When do you buy them?
ANN: Well, my husband went to New Orleans,[31] so I bought a lot of canned goods. The children enjoy them.

---

[26] grassroots movement: one that takes place in rural areas and goes directly to the people (as opposed to a media campaign linked to powerful political centers)
[27] From Satellite Beach to Spokane: meaning all across the country, as these two places are at opposite points—great distances apart—in the U.S.
[28] Memphis: a city in Tennessee
[29] buyer profile: a biographical presentation of the typical consumer
[30] rumpus room: leisure or recreation room with informal furniture
[31] New Orleans: a city in Louisiana

LOU: Well, I bought Vienna sausage the other day 'cause the **Giant** had a special on it — seventy-nine cents a can — it's usually a dollar nine, a dollar nineteen. You could only get four at a time, so I went back twice that week.

grocery store

MODERATOR: Do you buy these for particular members of the family?

NORMA: If they didn't like it, I wouldn't buy it.

DELORES: Melvin loves the hot dog chili. And the baby — you can just stick a Vienna sausage in her hand and she'll go 'round happy all day.

MODERATOR: Do you read the labels on canned meats?

VOICES: Oh sure. Yes

NORMA: The children read the labels first and called my attention to it. When I saw it had things like intestines and things like that, I didn't want to buy potted meat any more.

LOU: Fats, tissues, organs. If you read the labels on this stuff — when they say hearts . . . I don't know. I don't like hearts.

VIRGINIA: Well, psychologically you're not **geared to** it.

accustomed to, ready for

ALMA: They could lie on the label a little bit. Just don't tell us so much. (Laugh.) It would taste pretty good, but . . . yeah, I'd rather not know.

MODERATOR: What do you think ought to be on the labels?

ANNE: I think you ought to know about the chemicals.

NORMA: I love to read calories on the side of a can.

DELORES: I wonder what all's in those preservatives?

IDA: The side of this Hormel can here says that this meat is made by the same company that makes Dial soap. Says Armour-Dial.

NORMA: At least you think it's clean.

DELORES: Some preservatives do taste like soap. . . .

IDA: I wouldn't be eating that stuff with them chemicals.

ANN: Well, if you worry about that, you're going to starve to death.

VIRGINIA: You'd never eat in a restaurant if you ever got back in the kitchen.

MODERATOR: Would you buy a product because of the advertising?

VOICES: No. No. Maybe.

IDA: My children love that Libby's — the one, "Libby's, Libby's, Libby's. . . . "

NORMA: Now, if there's young kids that go to the grocery store with you, everytime they'll pick up something . . . "Libby's, Libby's, Libby's."

DELORES: Every time I see Hormel chili . . . I think
about them people out at a fireside by the
beach eating that chili. One of them is playing
a guitar and they start singing.

VIRGINIA: Armour has a cute hot dog commercial, that's   *hot dogs*
where they're all marching around, **weenies**,
ketchup and mustard. . . .

IDA: Yeah. That's cute.

MODERATOR: Do any of you ever buy Spam?[32]

IDA: What's Spam?

ANNE: It's chopped something. Or pressed.

LOU: It's beaver board.[33]

MODERATOR: Beaver what?

28   Most researchers claim that their studies are only as good as
the people who interpret them. The interpreters are usually the
agency and clients who — many advertising executives will admit,
but only **off the record** — read their own product concerns into the   *told in confidence*
comments of the panelists. Quite often, complaints about daytime   *not to be quoted*
commercials ("They're awful!" "Ridiculous!" "Laughable") are
brushed aside. "You can formulate **breakthrough** approaches in   *ignored / creative,*
order to reach this new woman," Joan Rothberg, senior VP at   *new*
Ted Bates, told *Madison Avenue,* "and yet the traditional 'Ring
Around the Collar' approach wins out in terms of creating awareness and motivating people to buy the product."

29   One of the final research tests a commercial can go through
after it's been created and storyboarded[34] is the Burke test. One
day up at my old agency, the creative director, a writer, and an
art director came **blazing** through the halls with hats and horns,   *racing noisily*
announcing at **120 decibels**, "We Burked twenty-nine! We Burked   *very loudly*
twenty-nine!" Now this may sound to you as it did to me that
day, as if these people were talking in tongues.[35] What having
"Burked twenty-nine" actually means is the percentage the com-
mercial scored **in recall** after one viewing by a large audience.   *from what was*
The average number on the Burke scale for the particular product   *remembered*
my friends were testing was twenty-five — so you can understand
the celebration.

30   Because the agencies and their clients accept Burke scores as
valid, the scores become a powerful factor in what types of com-

---

[32] Spam: a cheap version of chopped and pressed ham

[33] beaver board: a fiberboard used for partitions and ceilings. The food is being criticized for
tasting like board.

[34] storyboarded: a panel or series of panels with sketches showing the sequence of action planned
for a television spot

[35] in tongues: as if under the influence of a delirious spell

mercials will run. It's no accident that the Burke company is located in Cincinnati, since Cincinnati is the **birthplace** of Crest, Crisco, Comet, Charmin, Cheer, Bonus, Bounce, Bounty, Bold, Lava, Lilt, Pampers, Prell, Downy, Dash, and Duz—in other words, Cincinnati is the home of the King Kong[36] of Household Cleanliness, Procter & Gamble. From high atop magnificent offices, P&G executives control daytime television and a goodly portion of prime time,[37] too. They are the top-dollar spender on TV, having put out $260 million last year alone in commercial time bought. They produce and have editorial control over five of the biggest soap operas[30] on TV: *As the World Turns*, *Another World*, *Edge of Night*, *Guiding Light*, and *Search for Tomorrow*, which reach some forty million women every day.

original place of manufacture

31   Procter & Gamble is the most blatant offender in perpetuating "the little woman" commercial stereotype. Because of its monopoly on both media and marketplace (it pulls in $3.6 billion every year) and because its research is the most expensive and extensive, P&G is the recognized leader and arbiter of format and content in household product commercials—where P&G goes, others will follow.

32   This does not spur innovation. In one P&G agency, the creative people have two formulae they use for "concepting" a commercial: regular slice-of-life (problem in the home, solution with the wonderful product) or what the agency guys call "2 C's in a K." The "K" stands for kitchen; the "C" is a **four-letter word**.

an obscene word for female

33   Once a commercial is written, tested, and approved by the client, it's got to be cast and shot. I asked Barbara Claman to talk about what agency people and their clients ask for when they're casting housewife roles. She should know: Barbara's built up one of the largest commercial casting agencies in the country. The day we talked **all hell was breaking loose** outside her office door. Scores of women and children had come to try out for a McDonald's commercial.

there was much noise and confusion

34   I wondered if agencies ever called for a P&G-type housewife for their commercials.

35   "Absolutely. She should be blond—or, if brunette, not too brunette. Pretty, but not too pretty. Midwestern in speech, middle-class looking, gentile. If they want to use blacks, they want *waspy* blacks."[39]

[36] King Kong: the larger-than-life gorilla "star" of Hollywood film.   In this reference, the author means that Procter & Gamble is a commercial giant (leader) in the manufacture of household cleansers.

[37] prime time: the most popular viewing hours

[38] soap operas: serialized dramas presented on radio and television; generally filled with complex human relationships and high emotion; SOAP opera because soap products (household cleansers) are advertised then

[39] *waspy* blacks: *waspy* is the adjective for the abbreviation WASP (white, Anglo-Saxon Protestant, the major ethnic-religious group in the U.S. population). Blacks who are "waspy" appear to have WASP traits.

36   "What about P&G-type husbands?"

37   "Same thing," Claman said. "But you'll find that the husband is getting to play the **asshole** more and more in American commercials."   *obscene word for* fool

38   "But do you see a change occurring? A trend in women's portrayals away from the traditional P&G type?"

39   "A little. I think they'd like to be a little more real. They're realizing, very slowly, that the working woman has a lot of money."

40   "What if they want a Rosie, a Madge, or a Cora—one of the Eric Hoffer[40] working-class philosopher-queens?"

41   Barbara laughed. "They'll say, 'Let's cast a ballsy one.' "[41]

42   "Are you offended by the roles they want to put women in? Do you try to change their thinking on this?"

43   "I'm totally offended. I'm tired of seeing women hysterical over dirt spots on their glasses. I get lady producers in here all the time. We've tried to change their minds about the roles. You see how successful we've been."[42]

44   Jane Green is another casting director in New York. She tells of a friend who was auditioning for a P&G spot in which the agency's creative people were trying to break out of the housewife mold.[43] They'd called interesting faces—real people who wore real clothes. A couple of hours passed and the P&G client was obviously agitated. He turned to the agency producer: "What are you people trying to **pull over on me?** The woman in this commercial   *trick me into accepting* needs to be *my* wife, in *my* bathroom in Cincinnati—not some   *modern, attractive* **hip little chickie**. Whom do you think we're selling to?"   *young woman*

45   One wonders. Recently an agency producer asked me and my cat Rayette to be in a kitty litter commercial. I arrived wearing blue jeans and a shirt, my usual at-home ensemble. The art director, who was wearing jeans himself, wasn't pleased: "Where is your shirtwaist?[44] I told the producer I wanted a *housewife* look in this commercial." I tried to explain that most women—housewives and otherwise—had left those McMullans and Villagers[45] back at the Tri Delt[46] House in '66. The **shoot** was postponed until we   *filming* found something that looked more housewifey.

46   Some commercial trends have passed: The damsel in distress[47] has, for the time being, retreated to her tower. (Remember the thundering White Knight? The mystical, spotless Man from Glad? Virile, barrel-chested Mr. Clean?) But others remain, the most blatantly offensive, perhaps, being those commercials using women

[40] Eric Hoffer: (1902–1983) American laborer, labor leader, and philosopher-writer
[41] ballsy one: crude reference to a masculine female, to one with strong character
[42] You see how successful we've been: The author is being sarcastic here; there has, in fact, been little to no success.
[43] break out of the mold: leave the tradition, try something new
[44] shirtwaist: traditional style dress (collar, button-down bodice, with short or long sleeves)
[45] McMullans and Villagers: trade names of dresses for young and youthful females
[46] Tri-Delt: This is the name of a sorority.
[47] damsel in distress: helpless female with a problem or in danger

as sex objects to entice the consumer into buying the product. Most agency people aren't allowed to comment on the scheme of things in such commercials (one **slip of the tongue** and that multimillion-dollar account might choose another, more circumspect agency). But Dwight Davis, **VP** and creative director on the Ford dealers' account with J. Walter Thompson in Detroit, says it's no secret Detroit is still the national **stronghold** of selling with sex. Why? The male is still the decision maker in car buying ("Our research tells us it is so"); and the auto is still an extension of the American male libido. So we've got Catherine Deneuve[48] **hawking** Lincoln-Mercurys. She circles the car in her long, slinky gown and slips inside to fondle the plush interior. Catherine **signs off**, sprawled across the hood of the car, with a seductive grrrrr. She is, as Davis describes the phenomenon, the car advertisers' "garnish on the salad."

verbal error

short for Vice President

main location

selling
ends the commercial

47   Commercials like this, and the little woman slice-of-life, are caricatures of themselves. That's precisely why Carol Burnett[49] and the people at *Saturday Night Live*[50] have so much fun with them. Even the new wave of women's commercials isn't spared. In a spoof Anne Beatts wrote for *Saturday Night*, a middle-class Mom, dressed not in a shirtwaist but a polyester pantsuit, rushes into the kitchen, crashing through a café-curtained dutch door. She starts to have a **heart-to-heart** with the camera: "I'm a nuclear physicist and Commissioner of Consumer Affairs." She starts to put her groceries away.

personal talk

48   "In my spare time I do needlepoint, read, sculpt, take riding lessons, and **brush up on** my knowledge of current events. Thursday's my day at the day-care center,[51] and then there's my work with the deaf; but I still have time left over to do all my own baking and practice my **backhand**, even though I'm **on call** twenty-four hours a day as a legal aid lawyer in Family Court. . . . " Our New-Wave Mom is still running on, all the time very carefully folding the grocery bags and stuffing them into a cabinet where literally hundreds of other carefully folded bags are stacked incredibly neatly, when the omniscient announcer comes in:

reinstate

tennis stroke /
available

49   "How does Ellen Sherman, Cleveland housewife, do it all? She's smart! She takes Speed. Yes, Speed—the tiny blue diet pill you don't have to be overweight to need."

50   If the "average" woman **is true to** her portrayal in commercials, we've got a pretty bitter pill to swallow.[52] But you know, we all know, commercials don't portray real life. Nice Movies' Dick

fits

---

[48] Catherine Deneuve: (1943–) French film star
[49] Carol Burnett: (1936–) American musical comedy, television, and movie star
[50] *Saturday Night Live*: TV show featuring satirical comedy
[51] day-care center: private establishment that cares for children of working parents while they are at work
[52] we've got a bitter pill to swallow: We have to accept this painful truth.

Clark,[53] who's done spots for Coca-Cola, Toyota, and Glade, points out, most commercials are "formula answers to advertising questions—bad **rip-offs** of someone else's bad commercials." They are bad rip-offs of their viewers too. But, someday, some bright young advertising prodigy will begin a whole new trend of commercials that don't **talk down**, don't demean or debase, and still sell soap or toothpaste or cars **like crazy**. And then everybody will be doing it. Double your money back, guaranteed.[54]

cheap imitations

use juvenile language / extremely well

51   Why am I so sure? Because, as Brinkley so neatly points out, only seven percent of our homes have the traditional resident Mom. Because there are more women doctors, engineers, copywriters, jockeys, linesmen, **you name it**, than ever before. Because women are becoming more selective in their buying habits. Because, quite simply, research tells me it is so.

et cetera

Discussion Points

1. What role did Betty Furness play on television?
2. Why was there negative reaction to the National Airlines "Fly Me" commercial?
3. Not counting clerical workers, what was the percentage of women employed in advertising at the time this essay was written? Tell how this statistic explains Caldwell's description of female stereotyping in commercials.
4. Detail the National Organization of Women's actions regarding women's roles in commercials.
5. Describe the 1975 National Advertising Review Board panel's checklist for advertisers.
6. Interpret "ring around the collar" and explain how this ad typifies female stereotyping in commercials.
7. How was L'Oreal's "I'm worth it" campaign a break with advertising tradition? Was it a success?
8. Define life-style research.
9. Summarize the two-hour session recorded in Memphis. Do you believe that was a typical conversation among consumers? Explain your answer.
10. Interpret "We Burked twenty-nine."
11. Describe the author's experience of auditioning for a part in a commercial.
12. What is a New-Wave Mom? And how did "Saturday Night Live" portray her?
13. What is Caldwell's prediction for the portrayal of females in future commercials? Do you agree with her forecast? Explain your answer.

---

[53] Dick Clark: (1929–   ) well-known television host of American pop music shows
[54] Double your money back, guaranteed: This slogan occasionally appears on consumer products; it means that if the customer is not satisfied with the item, twice the originally paid price will be refunded upon return of the unsatisfactory product.

Composition Topics

Read through the following writing themes and select one on which to develop a two-page paper:

1. Compare and contrast the role of women in American television commercials with those seen in your country. Be sure to comment on stereotyping.
2. If you were in the field of advertising, what changes would you institute in the portrayal of males and females in television spots?
3. Carefully view three current television commercials and analyze them critically for any stereotyping.

**Research
Ideas**

To gain a fuller appreciation of the world Caldwell writes about in her essay on advertising, investigate one of these topics and prepare a two-page paper on your findings:

1. Federal Trade Commission
2. Gender Stereotyping in Television Commercials
3. Madison Avenue
4. The National Advertising Review Board
5. The National Organization for Women
6. Women in American Advertising

CHAPTER 24

♦ *To Noble Companions*

BY GAIL GODWIN

About the Author:
GAIL GODWIN (1937–   )

Born in Alabama, Gail Kathleen Godwin has earned diversified credentials as a teacher, short-story writer, novelist, reporter, and consultant with the United States Travel Service in London. The following is a partial listing of her books: *The Perfectionists* (1970), *Glass People* (1972), *Dream Children* (collection of stories, 1976), *A Mother and Two Daughters* (1982), and *A Southern Family* (1987).

Setting the Scene

The author presents a thoughtful portrait of friendship in "To Noble Companions." It is somewhat unconventional, yet charming. Through personal anecdotes, Godwin illustrates her viewpoint on the essence of friendship.

Pre-Reading Considerations

1. What is your definition of *friendship*?
2. Are you more inclined to divulge good or bad news to your closest friends?

To Noble Companions

GAIL GODWIN

1   The dutiful first answer seems programmed into us by our meager expectations: "A friend is one who will be there in times of trouble." But I believe this is a skin-deep answer to describe skin-deep friends. There is something irresistible about misfortune to human nature, and standbys for setbacks and sicknesses (as long as they are not too lengthy, or contagious) can usually be found. They can be *hired*. What I value is not the "friend" who, looming sympathetically above me when I have been dashed[1] to the ground, appears gigantically generous in the hour of my **reversal**; more *misfortune* and more I desire friends who will endure my ecstasies with me, who possess wings[2] of their own and who will fly with me. I don't mean this as arrogance (I am too superstitious to indulge long in that trait), and I don't fly **all that** often. What I mean is that I *very* seek (and occasionally find) friends with whom it is possible to **drag out** all those beautiful, old, outrageously aspiring costumes *bring out* and rehearse together for the Great Roles;[3] persons whose qualities groom me and train me up for love. It is for these people that I reserve the glowing hours, too good not to share. It is the existence of these people that reminds me that the words "friend" and "free" grew out of each other. (**OE** *freo*, not in bondage, noble, glad; *Old English* OE *freon*, to love; OE *freond*, friend.)

2   When I was in the eighth grade, I had a friend. We were shy and "too serious" about our studies when it was becoming fashionable with our classmates to acquire the social graces.[4] We said little at school, but she would come to my house and we would sit down with pencils and paper, and one of us would say: "Let's start with a train whistle today." We would sit quietly together and write separate poems or stories that **grew out of** a *were inspired by* train whistle. Then we would read them aloud. At the end of *and developed from* that school year, we, too, were transformed into social creatures and the stories and poems stopped.

3   When I lived for a time in London, I had a friend. He was in despair and I was in despair, but our friendship was based on the small flicker of foresight in each of us that told us we would be sorry later if we did not explore this great city because we had

---

[1] dashed: thrown (a figurative, not literal meaning here)
[2] wings: Again, the author is using this in the figurative sense.
[3] Great Roles: projected experiences for oneself, those future times that are aspired to
[4] social graces: a sense of what is correct in social situations

---

felt bad at the time. We met every Sunday for five weeks and found many marvelous things. We walked until our despairs resolved themselves and then we parted. We gave London to each other.

4   For almost four years I have had a remarkable friend whose imagination illumines mine. We write long letters in which we often discover our strangest selves. Each of us appears, sometimes prophetically, sometimes comically, in the other's dreams. She and I agree that, at certain times, we seem to be parts of the same mind. In my most sacred and interesting moments, I often think: "Yes, I must tell _____." We have never met.

5   It is such exceptional (in a sense divine) companions I wish to **salute**. I have seen the glories of the world reflected briefly through our encounters. One bright hour with **their kind** is worth more to me than a lifetime guarantee of the services of a Job's[5] comforter whose "helpful" lamentations will only clutter the healing silence necessary to those darkest moments in which I would rather be my own best friend.

commend, congratulate
them

Discussion Points

1. What are "skin-deep" friends?
2. What kind of friend does the author prefer?
3. What occupied the time of Godwin and her eighth-grade friend while their classmates were learning social graces?
4. Interpret "We gave London to each other" (paragraph 3) relative to the author's London friendship.
5. Describe Godwin's four-year friendship-via-letters.
6. What sign of friendship does the writer reveal to us in paragraph 4?
7. During her own "darkest moments," what kind of friend does Godwin prefer?

[5] Job: main character in the Hebrew and Christian scripture called The Book of Job; known for enduring hardship with courage and faith

Composition Topics

From the following three themes, select one on which to base a two-page composition:

1. Recall a best friend from your childhood years. Are you still friends? If so, depict the special characteristics of this person, and try to explain why this relationship has endured.
2. Have you ever had a friendship that was only "skin-deep"? Try to remember what incident proved that person to be a superficial friend only. Describe your emotional reaction to making this discovery.

3. Given Godwin's definition of friendship, consider which of your present circle of friends might be a "noble companion." Explain your choice and provide an anecdote or two of your shared experiences.

Research Ideas

In order to gain a fuller appreciation of Godwin's essay, prepare a two-page background report on the psychology of friendship.